PRESENTED TO

_____

Name

_____

Date / Occasion

Personal Note

_____

_____

_____

_____

_____

_____

A YEAR
WITH THE
ANGELS

A YEAR
WITH THE
ANGELS

DAILY MEDITATIONS
WITH THE
MESSENGERS OF GOD

MIKE AQUILINA

SAINT
BENEDICT
PRESS

CHARLOTTE, NORTH CAROLINA

DEDICATION

Dedicated to Terry Fenwick,
whose devotion to the angels inspires me.

Quotations from Scripture are from the Revised Standard Version
(Catholic Edition), unless the writer's argument depends on a
significantly different translation, such as the Septuagint.

SAINT
BENEDICT
PRESS

ISBN: 978-1-61890-417-1

Book design by A.R.T. Services
Christopher J. Pelicano and Abby M. Pelicano

Printed and Bound in the United States of America.

Saint Benedict Press
Charlotte, North Carolina
2012

Introduction

Christians believe in angels. That goes without saying. From the first pages of the Old Testament to the last pages of the New, God speaks of these mysterious beings. They appear as mighty creatures, pure spirits, guarding the gates of paradise, offering purest worship, guiding and protecting God's people. When God delivers the law, he does so through the ministry of angels. When he delivers his people in battle, it is through the intervention of an angelic host.

The Scriptures speak also of fallen angels, who use their phenomenal power to tempt human beings and thwart our salvation.

Angels appear at every moment in the story line of human history. St. Paul explains that in the Old Testament, they act as glorified babysitters— "guardians and trustees" (Gal. 4:1-3)—trying their best to keep an unruly people in line. When they appear to the human senses, their form is terrifying. When people see an angel, their immediate response is to fall on the ground in fear and awe (Num. 22:31).

In the New Testament, however, the relationship changes. In the opening chapters of the Gospels of Matthew and Luke, we find angels attending a human birth. We even see an archangel paying homage to a peasant woman of Nazareth, hailing her as "full of grace."

Angels appear often in the New Testament, but now as the servants of Jesus Christ, who is true God and true man. Moreover, they appear as servants of those who are in Christ, those who have been "changed into his likeness" (2 Cor. 3:18) and have come to share in his riches (2 Cor. 8:9). As children of God, we are now heirs of God and "fellow heirs with Christ" (Rom. 8:17). In every Christian, angels serve the divinized humanity of Jesus Christ.

The first generation lived with an intense awareness of the presence

MIKE AQUILINA

of the angels. In the Acts of the Apostles, Rhoda's companions would have been far less surprised by the apparition of an angel than they were by the sudden appearance of St. Peter (Acts 12:11).

This does not mean that the angels are any less powerful in relation to us. Nor does it mean they are any less awe-inspiring. In the Book of Revelation, when St. John encounters an angel, his instinct is to fall down and worship (Rev. 22:8f). But the angel lifts him up to stand as his fellow.

This is what Christ has accomplished: the holy communion of heaven and earth, all united in him, all united in worship. Thus, when we go to Mass, we are constantly invoking the angels, because they are present with us, and we sing their songs with them. The "Gloria" is the song they raised at the birth of Jesus (Luke 2:14). The "Sanctus" is what they sing at heaven's throne (Rev. 4:8).

We should not cease to marvel that the angels are now our "fellows." We should not let this truth grow old or grow cold for us.

Consider the fact that you have a guardian angel. Jesus assured us that each of us has one, from our earliest days (Matt. 18:10).

Consider that God has made this person exclusively for your care. Your guardian angel is smarter than a thousand Einsteins, and stronger than any army on earth. And God created him to serve you!

What difference does that make in your life? What difference should it make?

If a human relative or benefactor gave you a sports car, or a half-million dollars, or your dream home, you would find frequent and creative ways to express your gratitude. How often do you thank God for the extraordinary gift of your guardian angel?

And how often do we thank our angels for their care? Remember: angels are persons. To ignore them, after all they do for us, is at least rude, but also daft. Why would we choose not to enter into a close friendship and "working relationship" with these creatures who are dear to God and far closer to us than our nearest kin?

What sets too many Christians today apart from their ancestors in the faith is our neglect of devotion to the angels. For the early Christians, this was a lively devotion. Thus, for this book I have selected three hundred and sixty-five meditations from the writings of the early Fathers of the Church. Some of it is admittedly speculative—and the Fathers were the first to acknowledge that there were some things about the angels that they couldn't know. But most of it is plain truth, learned from Scripture and taught by the Church. And it's all classic Christianity. As such, it demands our attention and cries out for our imitation.

I believe the angels are the great neglected intermediaries in human relationships. How much stronger our families would be—our neighborhoods would be—our friendships would be—our workplace would be—our society would be—if only we, habitually and silently, called upon the help of the guardian angels of the people who are with us in the course of a day.

In the coming year, let's draw closer to our angels, through prayer and study, as we meet them in the following pages, and as we meet them wherever we go.

MIKE AQUILINA

How to Use this Book

I recommend that you set aside a time each day when you can read one of the meditations prayerfully.

Begin with prayer. The traditional prayers to the Holy Spirit are ideal for this purpose. The simple aspiration "Come, Holy Spirit" will do.

Then read the brief meditation slowly and make the considerations suggested (or think up your own). Try to refer everything to Our Lord; be aware of his presence. When you need help doing this, try calling upon the help of those Fathers who are canonized as saints.

You may close each day's reading with the prayer provided. Most of these prayers are adapted from the Church's ancient liturgies.

A Note on the Texts

The meditations are taken from classic translations of the Fathers. I've modernized the language to make it more readable, referring back to the original languages when necessary. Because rhetorical styles have changed radically over the centuries, sometimes I've reduced very long complex sentences to two or more simple sentences. (In the case of Dionysius the Areopagite, I have had to do more extensive condensation and elucidation. His works are difficult. I have taken pains, however, to preserve the original sense of his passages.) Since the page-a-day format places strict demands on space, in some instances I've abridged passages for length.

I do encourage you to visit the original texts—and not just for Dionysius, but for all the ancient authors—whenever you can. Most of the books are in print; and you can find almost all of them online. The best places to begin are tertullian.org/fathers and newadvent.org/fathers.

MIKE AQUILINA

A YEAR WITH THE ANGELS

The Daily Readings

We're not the only intelligent life

We tend to place humanity rather proudly at the top of all creation. The Fathers had a more modest and more realistic view. Yes, man is intelligent, but we're not the only intelligence. There are beings above us as well as beings below us. Only God is unique.

The Son, therefore, is the only and true God, for this also is assigned to the Son as his sole right.

It cannot accurately be said of any created being that he is alone. How can anyone or anything that has fellowship in creation be separated from the rest, as though it were alone?

Thus we see that man is a rational being among all earthly creatures; yet he is not the only rational being. For we know that the heavenly works of God also are rational; we confess that angels and archangels are rational beings. So if the angels are rational, we cannot say that man is the only rational being.

–St. Ambrose, *Exposition of the Christian Faith*, 5.2

IN GOD'S PRESENCE, CONSIDER . . .

Do I recognize that I am not alone in the universe? Real extraterrestrials, the guardian angels, are here to help me.

CLOSING PRAYER

My Guardian Angel, help me be obedient to your inspirations, and protect and guide me until you have brought me safe to Heaven.

All things have being through God

St. Augustine presents a hierarchy of living beings, from plants through angels, and shows us how all those things, no matter how noble or complex, can only have their being through God. In doing so he incidentally gives us a good description of how angels compare with other living beings.

Whatever we're thinking of—whether it's the whole world, its shape, qualities, and orderly movement, and all the objects in it; or whether it's all life, either the kind that only nourishes and maintains, as trees do; or what, besides this, has also sensation, as the animals have; or what adds intelligence to all these things, as human beings do; or what does not need the support of food, but only maintains, feels, and understands, as the angels do—all these things can only *be* through God, who absolutely *is*.

For God it is not one thing to be, and another to live, as though he could *be* but not be living. Nor is it one thing for him to live, and another thing to understand, as though he could live, but not understand. Nor is it one thing for him to understand, and another thing to be blessed, as though he could understand and not be blessed. But for him, to live, to understand, to be blessed, are to *be*.

–St. Augustine, *City of God*, 8.6

IN GOD'S PRESENCE, CONSIDER . . .

God gives me the same constant care he gives the glorious angels—all the things I need to keep me alive from moment to moment. Am I careful to give thanks for those things at every opportunity?

CLOSING PRAYER

Heavenly Father, in every place may I show respect to your Angel. May I be grateful for his benefits. May I honor his greatness.

We exist because God knows us

God has angel messengers, says St. Augustine, but they do not bring him information he does not already know. Instead, they learn the truth about their own lives from God. All of us—humans and angels—exist only because God knows us.

Doubtless God has messengers, namely the angels—but not to bring him news of things he does not know about, since there is nothing he does not know. But their good lies in looking into the truth about their own works.

This is what it means when it is said that they bring him word of some things. It is not that he learns from them, but they learn from him, by his word, without bodily sound. They also bring him word of what he wills, since they are sent by him to whomever he wills, and they hear everything by his word—that is to say, they find in his truth what they are themselves meant to do, what word they are to bring, to whom they are to bring it, and when.

And we also pray to God, but we do not inform him of what our needs are: "for your Father knows what you need before you ask him," says his Word (Matt. 6:8). He did not become aware of them at some particular time. He knew beforehand, without any beginning, everything that would happen in time. And among those things he knew what we would ask of him, and when we would ask it. And he knew to whom he would listen or not listen, and on what subjects.

As for all his creatures—both spiritual and bodily—he does not know them because they exist. Rather, they exist because he knows them.

—St. Augustine, *On the Trinity*, 15.13

IN GOD'S PRESENCE, CONSIDER . . .

The angels know God by looking into the truth. Do I search enough in God's Word to find out the truth about what I'm meant to do?

CLOSING PRAYER

Lord, I do not have the glorious power of your angels. But you can overcome my weak nature and make me worthy to be delighted with the sweetness of your divine Scriptures.

The three kinds of intelligence

St. Gregory of Nyssa remembers the opinions of his sister, St. Macrina, whom he always calls "the Teacher," on a famous passage in Philippians. She interprets St. Paul as referring to the three kinds of intelligent beings, all of which will eventually praise Christ.

Therefore God has highly exalted him and bestowed on him the name which is above every name, that at the name of Jesus every knee should bow, in Heaven and on Earth and under the Earth (Phil. 2:9-10).

I do not think (she replied) that the divine Apostle divided the intellectual world into places when he named part as in Heaven, part as on Earth, and part as under the Earth.

There are three states in which reasoning creatures can be: one from the very first received an immaterial life, and we call it the angelic; another is in union with the flesh, and we call it the human; a third is released by death from fleshly entanglements, and is to be found in souls pure and simple.

Now I think that this was what the divine Apostle, in his deep wisdom, was thinking of when he revealed the future concord of all these reasoning beings in the work of goodness; and that he puts the bodiless angel-world in Heaven, and the world still involved with a body on earth, and the world released from a body under the earth.

–St. Gregory of Nyssa, *On the Soul and the Resurrection*

IN GOD'S PRESENCE, CONSIDER . . .

Since we are human, we are composed of body and soul. When our flesh is subordinated to our spirit, as God intended, we can live with the happiness enjoyed by the heavenly spirits, the angels, even now.

CLOSING PRAYER

Guardian Angel, help me to be purified from all pollution of flesh and spirit, and from every shameful and foolish thought.

We're part stone, part angel

A human being, says St. Gregory the Great, is in a way a representation of the whole universe. We have something in common with everything God created, from rocks to angels.

Everything that exists falls into one of these classes:

1. It exists, but does not live.
2. It exists and lives, but does not feel.
3. It exists and lives and feels, but does not understand or choose.
4. It exists and lives and feels and understands and chooses.

Stones exist, but they do not live.

Trees both exist and live, but do not feel: we call the greenery the "life" of plants and trees, as Paul declares: "You foolish man! What you sow does not come to life unless it dies" (1 Cor. 15:36).

Animals exist and live and feel, but they do not understand.

Angels exist and live and feel, and they have knowledge by understanding.

But we have it in common with stones to exist, with trees to live, with animals to feel, with angels to understand. So a human being is rightly called a "universe," because in a way the whole universe is contained within us.

–St. Gregory the Great, *Moralia in Job*, 6.20

IN GOD'S PRESENCE, CONSIDER . . .

If I have something in common with everything in the world around me—even the angels—doesn't that give me the responsibility to take care of that world? How well am I taking care of my own little corner of it—my family and friends, for example?

CLOSING PRAYER

Guardian angels of all people and nations, you are ceaselessly vigilant, ever watching. Teach me to be diligent for the good of whatever in creation is under my protection.

Some truths about angels remain a mystery

St. Augustine addresses the question of whether angels appear to humans by taking on material bodies, or by manipulating their own spiritual essences. But he addresses it only to dismiss it. Some things cannot be known with certainty, and the speculation might distract us from something more important.

But I admit that it would be beyond my purpose here to ask these questions. It may be that the angels, working in secret by the spiritual quality still in their bodies, take on something from the lower and more bodily elements, and fit them to themselves, so that they can change it like clothes into whatever bodily shape they like. In that case, those appearances would be real, in the same way that real water was changed into real wine by our Lord. On the other hand, it may be that they transform their own bodies into whatever they like, to fit themselves to their particular work. But it does not matter in this case which one is true.

As a man, I cannot understand these things by actual experience in the same way that the angels do when they do them. They know these things better than I do. I do know how my own body changes by the working of my will, both by my own experience and by the experiences I have gathered from others. But there is no need to decide which of the alternatives I should believe on the authority of Holy Scripture. I do not wish to be forced to prove it, and make a long digression from our current question.

–St. Augustine, On the Trinity, 3.2

IN GOD'S PRESENCE, CONSIDER . . .

Do I tend to get bogged down in details when I try to learn about angels or other Christian truth? How do I decide what's really important?

CLOSING PRAYER

Guardian Angel, I know that I do not perfectly understand your nature; but always remind me to put love of God first, before my own curiosity.

The creation of angels

Genesis doesn't tell us explicitly when the angels were created, says St. Augustine, but we know that they were created from other passages in Scripture.

Where Scripture speaks of the world's creation, it doesn't tell us plainly whether or when the angels were created. If it does mention them, it mentions them implicitly under the name of "Heaven," when it is said, "In the beginning God created the heavens and the earth." But I can't believe they were completely left out, because it is written that on the seventh day God rested from all his works that he made; and this very book itself begins, "In the beginning God created the heavens and the earth," so that before heaven and earth God seems to have made nothing.

Still, though the fact that the angels are the work of God is not left out here, it's true that it's not explicitly mentioned. But elsewhere Holy Scripture asserts it in the clearest way. For in the Hymn of the Three Children in the Furnace it was said, "Bless the Lord, all works of the Lord" (Dan. 3:57); and among these works mentioned afterwards in detail, the angels are named (Dan. 3:58). And in the psalm it is said, "Praise the Lord from the heavens, / praise him in the heights! / Praise him, all his angels, / praise him, all his host! / Praise him, sun and moon, / praise him, all you shining stars! / Praise him, you highest heavens, / and you waters above the heavens! / Let them praise the name of the Lord! / For he commanded and they were created."

Here the angels are very explicitly—and by divine authority—said to have been made by God. It says about them, among the other heavenly things, "he commanded and they were created."

—St. Augustine, *City of God*, 11.9

IN GOD'S PRESENCE, CONSIDER . . .

Psalm 148 invites everything created, animate and inanimate, to praise the Lord. If inanimate creation spontaneously praises God, how much more lavish should I be in raising my voice with the choir?

CLOSING PRAYER

Pure spirits, who are high glories of God's creation, help us to restore all things in Christ, so that all the world may tell his glories and praise the Father.

Heavenly beings as well were made by the Word

Interpreting Psalm 45, St. Augustine imagines all the things that have been created by the Word: not just the stars, the earth, the sea, but also the angels and all the heavenly beings.

"My heart hath uttered a good word" (Ps. 45:1).

Who is the speaker? The Father, or the prophet? Some take it to be the Person of the Father, who says, "My heart hath uttered a good word," hinting at a certain unspeakable generation. In case you should happen to think that something had been taken into him, out of which God should beget the Son (just as man takes something to himself out of which he begets children, namely, a union of marriage, without which man cannot beget offspring)—in case you should think that God needed some sort of nuptial union to beget the Son, he says, "My heart hath uttered a good word."

You have a thought today, and you don't need a wife to beget it. With that thought, born from your heart, you build something or other, and before that building exists, the design exists; and what you are about to produce exists already in the thought by which you are going to produce it. You praise the structure that as yet does not exist in the visible form of a building, but only drawn up in a design; nor does anyone else praise your design, unless either you show it to him, or he sees what you have done. If then by the Word all things were made (John 1:3), and the Word is from God, think of the structure built by the Word, and learn from that building to admire his counsels!

What kind of Word is that by which Heaven and Earth were made (Heb.11:3) and all the splendor of the heavens; all the fertility of the earth; the expanse of the sea; the air spread wide; the brightness of the constellations; the light of sun and moon? These are visible things—but rise above these, too, and think of the Angels, Principalities, Thrones, Dominions, and Powers. All were made by him.

—St. Augustine, *Exposition on Psalm 45*, 4

IN GOD'S PRESENCE, CONSIDER . . .

Do I give myself time to consider the wonders we know through astronomy and science, and the wonders we cannot know yet in Heaven? Have I praised God for his creation?

CLOSING PRAYER

My God, give me the gift of wonder at your creation. You are Creator of all things, seen and unseen, earthly and angelic. By your grace, may I come to praise the gifts I cannot see, the gift of your holy angels.

Descriptions of angels are figurative

The writer we call Dionysius the Areopagite, beginning a work on the celestial hierarchy, takes care to remind us that the descriptions of angels in Scripture are figurative. The Bible uses these pictures to describe the angels' attributes and abilities in a way our human understanding can grasp.

I think the first thing we need to do is to set forth what we think is the purpose of every hierarchy, and what benefit each one confers upon its followers; and next to celebrate the heavenly hierarchies according to their revelation in Scripture; then following that Scripture, to say in what sacred forms the holy writings of the Scriptures depict the celestial orders, and to what sort of simplicity we must be carried through the representations.

We begin this way so that we may not, like the uneducated, irreverently think that the heavenly and Godlike minds are certain many-footed and many-faced creatures, or shaped in the animal form of oxen, or the savage form of lions, and fashioned like the hooked beaks of eagles, or the feathery down of birds—or imagine that there are certain wheels of fire above the heaven, or material thrones upon which the Godhead may recline, or certain many-colored horses, and spearbearing leaders of the host, and whatever else was transmitted by the Oracles to us under multifarious symbols of sacred imagery.

No, the Word of God artlessly makes use of poetic representations of sacred things when speaking of the shapeless minds, out of regard to our intelligence, so to speak, using a mode of education proper and natural to it, and molding the inspired writings for it.

–Dionysius the Areopagite, *The Celestial Hierarchy*, 2.1

IN GOD'S PRESENCE, CONSIDER . . .

When I find parts of the Bible that are difficult to understand—like the strange and wonderful appearances of the heavenly creatures—where do I go for help? Where *should* I go?

CLOSING PRAYER

Lord, send your angels to enlighten me whenever I hear your holy oracles.

How the Bible describes angels

Scripture, says Dionysius the Areopagite, uses symbolic imagery (in Ezekiel 1, for example) to describe the lives of the heavenly beings. They don't have actual wheels, but the symbolic image fits their actual behavior and existence.

But why does it talk about *rivers*? And why are *wheels* and *chariots* attached to the heavenly beings?

The rivers of fire represent the ceaselessly flowing streams from God that nourish the productive powers of life. The chariots represent the communion of those who are joined together in the same rank. The wheels, which are winged and move without turning or deviation, represent the power of the heavenly beings to go forward in a straight and direct path.

But why does it say that the heavenly orders "rejoice"? For they are completely incapable of our impassioned pleasure.

They are said to rejoice with God when what was lost is found. This fits their divine good nature, their Godlike and ungrudging rejoicing over the care and salvation of those who are turned to God. It is like that joy beyond description that holy men often share while the deifying enlightenment from God is upon them.

–Dionysius the Areopagite, *The Celestial Hierarchy*, 15.9

IN GOD'S PRESENCE, CONSIDER . . .

Am I ungrudgingly joyous, like the good angels, when someone else gains some great benefit? Or am I more inclined to envy?

CLOSING PRAYER

Search my conscience, Lord, and purify me from envy and every other impure thought, and make me worthy of the company of your heavenly host.

The orders of angels

St. John of Damascus summarizes the teaching of Dionysius the Areopagite, who wrote a treatise in very difficult neo-Platonic language on the angelic powers. Here we have the traditional names of the orders of angels, as gathered from the brief mentions of heavenly powers in different places in Scripture.

Dionysius the Areopagite—that most holy, sacred, and gifted theologian—says that all theology (meaning Holy Scripture) has nine different names for the heavenly beings. That divine teacher of the sacred divides these nine kinds into three groups of three each:

1. The first group is made up of those who are in God's presence, and are said to be with him directly and immediately:
   * the *Seraphim*, with their six wings;
   * the many-eyed *Cherubim*;
   * and those who sit in the holiest *Thrones*.
2. The second group contains
   * the *Dominions*,
   * the *Powers*,
   * and the *Authorities*.
3. The third and last group contains
   * the *Rulers*,
   * the *Archangels*,
   * and the *Angels*.

–St. John of Damascus, *Exposition of the Orthodox Faith*, 2.3

IN GOD'S PRESENCE, CONSIDER . . .

The angels themselves are ranked because God establishes an order for all creation. What is my place right now in God's ordered plan? How would I find my place? What should I be doing to live that vocation?

CLOSING PRAYER

Father, you have established a perfect society for the sake of love. Help us gain perfection by living the life of your Church, with the angels and saints.

How many kinds of angels are there?

We commonly mention nine kinds of angels, but Origen, the first great systematic theologian of Christianity, speculates that there might be more orders we don't know about. There may well be angels whose roles we can't understand until we reach Heaven.

In Holy Scripture, we find numerous names of certain orders and offices, not only of holy beings, but also of those of the opposite type. There are certain holy angels of God whom Paul calls ministering spirits, sent forth to minister for them who shall be heirs of salvation. In the writings of St. Paul we find him designating them, from some unknown source, as Thrones, and Dominions, and Principalities, and Powers.

And after this list, as if he knew that there were still other rational offices and orders besides the ones he had named, he says of the Savior that he is "far above all Rule and Authority and Power and Dominion, and above every name that is named, not only in this age but also in that which is to come" (Eph. 1:21). Thus he shows that there were certain beings besides those which he had mentioned, which may be named indeed in this world, but were not listed by him now, and perhaps were not known by anyone else; and that there were others which may not be named in this world, but will be named in the world to come.

–Origen, *De Principiis*, 1.5.1

IN GOD'S PRESENCE, CONSIDER . . .

Do I marvel at the variety of God's creation? Have I stopped to think that life in Heaven is infinitely richer even than life here on Earth?

CLOSING PRAYER

Angels of God, win me the grace of a holy awe before God's creation.

Myriads of myriads

The number of angels is simply unimaginable, says the speculative philosopher Dionysius the Areopagite. Only the angels themselves—and God, of course—can understand how many angels there are.

I believe this is also worth thinking about: the tradition of Scripture tells us that there are thousands of thousands of angels, and myriads of myriads. They multiply up to the very limits of our numbers—and beyond.

This shows clearly that we could never count the ranks of the heavenly beings. The minds above are many hosts, surpassing the weak and restricted measurement of our material numbers. Only their own heavenly knowledge above can actually count them—the knowledge given to them by the supremely divine, all-knowing Framer of Wisdom, the Cause of being, the connecting Force, and the encompassing Term of all created things.

—Dionysius the Areopagite, *The Celestial Hierarchy*, 14

IN GOD'S PRESENCE, CONSIDER . . .

How willing have I been to accept that there are things I can never understand about the nature of angels and all God's plan of creation?

CLOSING PRAYER

Bless the Lord, O you his angels, you mighty ones who do his word, hearkening to the voice of his word. Bless the Lord all his hosts, his ministers that do his will. —Psalm 103:20-21

The angels earned their roles in the hierarchy

Origen, speculating about the different orders of angels, believes that each angel earned its place in the order, rather than being assigned it from the beginning. Like us, he says, the angels were assigned their work in the world according to their particular virtues.

We must not suppose that it is just an accident that a particular office is assigned to a particular angel—as curing and healing are to Raphael, for example, or the conduct of wars to Gabriel; or attending to the prayers and supplications of mortals to Michael. We should not imagine that they obtained these offices in any other way than by their own merits, and by the zeal and excellent qualities each one of them displayed before this world was formed; so that afterwards in the order of archangels, this or that office was assigned to each one, while others deserved to be enrolled in the order of angels, and to act under this or that archangel, or that leader or head of an order.

All these things were disposed, as I have said, not indiscriminately and haphazardly, but by a very appropriate and fair decision of God, who arranged them according to merits, in accordance with his own approval and judgment. In this way the church of the Ephesians was to be entrusted to one angel; the church of the Smyrnæans to another; one angel was to be Peter's, another Paul's; and so on through every one of the little ones that are in the Church—for of the angels that daily behold the face of God, this or that one must be assigned to each one of them; and there must also be some angel that encamps round about them that fear God.

We must assuredly believe that all these things do not happen by accident or chance, or because the angels were created that way. If we thought so, the Creator might be accused of partiality. But we must believe that they were conferred by God, the just and impartial Ruler of all things, according to the merits, good qualities, and mental strength of each individual spirit.

–Origen, *De Principiis*, 1.8.1

IN GOD'S PRESENCE, CONSIDER . . .

By their roles, the angels teach me the importance of service. Do I serve according to my role in the Church?

CLOSING PRAYER

Lord, I wish to do your will, according to the sacred order you have established for me as for the angels, in the Church as in Heaven.

Angels are holy because of the Spirit

Though Scripture does not explicitly mention the creation of angels, we know from our own case (says St. Basil) that their holiness comes from the Holy Spirit, not from their own nature.

The pure, intelligent powers that live above this world are called holy because they get their holiness from the grace given by the Holy Spirit. Thus there is no mention of the creation of the heavenly powers, because the historian of creation has revealed to us only the creation of things our senses can perceive.

But you have the power to form an analogy of things you cannot see from the things you can see. Glorify the Maker who made all things, visible and invisible—Principalities, Powers, Authorities, Thrones, and Dominions, and all other rational beings we cannot name.

And when you think of creation, I beg you to think first of the original cause of all things that are made, the Father; of the creative cause, the Son; and of the perfecting cause, the Spirit. The ministering spirits exist by the will of the Father, are brought into being by the work of the Son, and are perfected by the presence of the Spirit.

—St. Basil the Great, *On the Holy Spirit*, 38

IN GOD'S PRESENCE, CONSIDER . . .

Even angels are holy only because of the Spirit. Do I make enough use of the sacraments Christ gave me to make me holy?

CLOSING PRAYER

Come, Holy Spirit. Fill the hearts of your faithful as you fill the being of the angels in Heaven.

A hierarchy of merit—or demerit

The hierarchy of angels, Origen says, must be arranged according to the merit of each angel. Likewise, the hierarchy of demons must be arranged according to the wickedness of each demon.

All we need to know to demonstrate the impartiality and righteousness of God is this: that, as the Apostle Paul declares, "there is no partiality with him" (Eph. 6:9), but instead he disposes everything according to the deserts and moral progress of each individual.

So, then, the angelic office does not exist except because of their desert; nor do Powers exercise power except by virtue of their moral progress; nor do those which are called Thrones (that is, the powers of judging and ruling) administer their powers unless by merit; nor do Dominions rule undeservedly—for that great and distinguished order of rational creatures among celestial beings is arranged in a glorious variety of offices.

And we can say the same of those opposing influences that have given themselves up to such places and offices, that they derive the property by which they are made Principalities, or Powers, or rulers of the darkness of the world, or spirits of wickedness, or malignant spirits, or unclean demons, not from their essential nature, or from having been created that way; but that they have obtained these degrees in evil in proportion to their conduct, and the progress they made in wickedness.

—Origen, *De Principiis*, 1.8,4

IN GOD'S PRESENCE, CONSIDER . . .

Am I striving to make progress in the spiritual life, corresponding to God's grace, so that I may occupy a place close to the angels?

CLOSING PRAYER

Angels of God, teach me to imitate your progress. Help me to go with God's grace, from glory to glory.

Angels are unchangeable because they love God

The nature of angels is changeable, says St. Gregory the Great. But the good angels are unchangeably good, because they are bound by love to their unchangeable Creator.

"Even in his servants he puts no trust, and his angels he charges with error; how much more those who dwell in houses of clay, whose foundation is in the dust, who are crushed before the moth" (Job 4:18-19).

Although the angelic nature remains unchangeable in its own state, because it stands fast in the contemplation of its Creator, yet in that it is a created being it does have the possibility of change in itself.

To be changed is to go from being one thing to being another; a thing that changes does not have stability in itself. Every being is becoming some other thing, by as many steps as there are changes it goes through. Only the incomprehensible Nature cannot be moved from its fixed state: it is always the same, and cannot be changed.

Since the essence of angels was created good by its Maker, if it had not been changeable, that nature in the corrupt spirits would never have fallen from the pinnacle of its blessed condition. But in a wonderful way God created the nature of the highest spiritual beings good; yet he made them at the same time capable of change, so that those who refused to remain would come to ruin, and those who continued as they were created might be confirmed in that state even more worthily because it was their own choice, and become all the more meritorious in the sight of God because they had resisted the motions of change by the staying power of the will.

So the angelic nature itself is also changeable, but it has overcome that changeability by being bound by chains of love to God, who is always the same.

—St. Gregory the Great, *Moralia in Job*, 5.68

IN GOD'S PRESENCE, CONSIDER . . .

Every human being is changing—but are my changes leading me closer to the unchangeable angelic nature that is bound by chains of love to God?

CLOSING PRAYER

Save me from the difficulties of this world, Lord, and lead my will in conformity with yours, so that at the end I may be counted worthy to dwell with all your angels in eternal bliss.

Angels derive their honor from worshiping God

An angel is a glorious being, says St. Ambrose—but the angel's glory is re-flected, so to speak: it comes from being a servant of the God who is glorious by nature.

Let our adversaries now admit that it is proved beyond doubt: the majesty of the Father and of the Son is one—especially since the Lord himself has said, "For whoever is ashamed of me and of my words, of him will the Son of Man be ashamed when he comes in his glory and the glory of the Father and of the holy angels" (Luke 9:26). What is the meaning of the words "and of the holy angels," but that the servants derive their honor from the worship of their Lord?

The Son, therefore, ascribed his majesty to his Father as well as to himself—not, of course, in such a way that the angels should share in that majesty on equal terms with the Father and the Son, but that they should behold the surpassing glory of God. For truly not even angels possess a majesty of their own, after the manner in which Scripture speaks of the Son, "then he will sit on his glorious throne" (Matt. 25:31); but they stand in the presence, so that they may see the glory of the Father and the Son, in such degrees of vision as they are either worthy of or able to bear.

–St. Ambrose, *Exposition of the Christian Faith*, 3.12

IN GOD'S PRESENCE, CONSIDER . . .

Do I remember, like the good angels, that everything good in me comes from God? Or do I tend to be proud of my accomplishments as if they were really my own?

CLOSING PRAYER

Guardian Angel, lead me to place all my glory and pride, as you do, in God alone.

The angels serve for their own benefit

St. Irenaeus indulges in some speculation about the nature of Heaven, and probably most theologians today would dismiss his ideas as metaphorical at best. But there's an important theological truth in this passage. The angels serve God, not because God needs help, but because it's good for them to serve.

This world is surrounded by seven heavens, in which live angels and archangels serving God, the Almighty, Maker of all things—not because he needs help, but so that they may not be idle, useless, and unproductive.

For the same reason the Spirit of God also dwells in us in many ways. Isaiah counts him as resting on the Son of God (that is, the Word), when he comes as a man in seven forms of service: "And the Spirit of the Lord shall rest upon him, the spirit of wisdom and understanding, the spirit of counsel and might, the spirit of knowledge and godliness. And his delight shall be in the fear of the Lord" (Isa. 11:2-3).

These are the heavens, in order from above, so that the first encompasses the rest:

- Wisdom
- Understanding
- Counsel
- Might
- Knowledge
- Godliness
- Fear of the Lord

The seventh is this firmament of ours, which is full of the fear of that Spirit which gives light to the heavens. As a pattern of this, Moses was given that seven-branched candlestick that glowed continually in the holy place; for, according to what the Word spoke to him, he received that service as a pattern of the heavens: "And see that you make them after the pattern for them, which is being shown you on the mountain" (Ex. 25:40).

—St. Irenaeus, *Demonstration of the Apostolic Preaching*, 9-10

IN GOD'S PRESENCE, CONSIDER . . .

How does it change my idea of my "duties" to know that even the angels serve, not because God needs help, but because they *need* to serve?

CLOSING PRAYER

Lord, teach me to serve you, as your holy angels serve you, in everything I do.

Angels never lose the vision of God

Angels are limited in place: they cannot be everywhere at once. So when they are sent to us, how do they still behold the face of the Father? St. Gregory the Great answers that they keep the vision of God before them in contemplation.

Well, now we're adding one question to another. When we try to untangle the loop, we're only tying a knot. How can the angels either always be in the presence of the Father, or always behold his face, if they are sent on their missions for our salvation?

But we will find this easier to believe if we remember how subtle the angelic nature is. They never go so far away from the vision of God that they are deprived of the joys of inner contemplation. If they did lose the vision of the Creator when they went out, they could never have raised up the fallen or announced the truth to those who were ignorant of it. They could not give the blind that fountain of light if they were deprived of it by leaving it behind.

This is how the nature of angels is different from our nature in its present state: we are limited by space and hemmed in by the blindness of ignorance, but the spirits of angels—though they are indeed bound by space—have a knowledge that extends incomparably far beyond ours.

So they do always behold the face of the Father, yet at the same time they come to us. As a spiritual presence, they go out to us; but they always keep themselves there in the place from which they left, by their inner contemplation.

–St. Gregory the Great, *Moralia in Job*, 2.3

IN GOD'S PRESENCE, CONSIDER . . .

Even though I do not have the subtle nature of the angels, do I try to keep the vision of God before me as much as I'm able?

CLOSING PRAYER

Fill my intellectual vision with the light the angels see, gracious God, and make me worthy to serve you in the world.

The armies of God

The angels are God's armies, says St. Gregory the Great, because they are at war with the fallen angels. And those of us who free ourselves from earthly concerns join that heavenly army and share the victory with the angels.

"Is there any number to his armies? Upon whom does his light not arise?" (Job 25:3).

We rightly call the angelic spirits the armies of God, because we are aware that they are at war against the powers of the air. They carry on these conflicts, however, not by labor but by authority. Whatever they wish when they act against impure spirits, they can accomplish it by the aid of God, who rules all things.

Of this army it is written that, when our King was born, "suddenly there was with the angel a multitude of the heavenly host" (Luke 2:13). And the number of the elect from humanity is joined to this heavenly host, when by the lofty aspirations of the mind they are set free from the bondage of an earthly connection. About this Paul said, "No soldier on service gets entangled in civilian pursuits" (2 Tim. 2:4).

Though they are shown as few in number, in the invisible country they reign innumerably, because—although they are few compared to the evil-minded—when they are assembled together they cannot be measured in any way.

But because the goodness of those soldiers is made firm, not by their own powers, but by the inspiration of grace from above, it is rightly added, "Upon whom does his light not arise?"

—St. Gregory the Great, *Moralia in Job*, 17.19

IN GOD'S PRESENCE, CONSIDER . . .

What earthly things are tying me down and keeping me from joining the victorious army of Heaven?

CLOSING PRAYER

Lord, with all the spirits of the just and of prophets; souls of martyrs and of apostles; Angels, Archangels, Thrones, Dominions, Principalities, and Authorities, and dread Powers; and the many-eyed Cherubim, and the six-winged Seraphim, let me sing the victorious hymn of your majestic glory.

What angels do

St. John of Damascus admits that there are many things we can't know about angels. But Scripture and reason tell us quite a bit. Angels are beings above us, but they are not naturally perfect. Only God is perfect. The good angels can no longer be moved to evil—but that is by God's grace, not by their own nature.

Angels are powerful, and quick to do God's will. Their nature is so speedy that, as soon as the divine glance orders them to go somewhere, immediately they are there. They are the guardians of the divisions of the earth: they are placed over countries and areas that the Creator assigns to them. They govern all our affairs and bring us aid. And certainly the reason is that they are placed over us by God's will and command, and they are always near him.

It is hard for them to be moved to evil. But they are not naturally immovable. They are completely immovable now, but that is because of God's grace and their nearness to the Only Good, not because of their nature.

They see God as far as they are able to see him, and that is their food.

Because they are bodiless, they are above us, and they are free of all bodily passion. But they are not passionless, since only God is passionless.

They take different forms as God, their Master, commands them, and thus reveal themselves to human beings and unveil the divine mysteries to them.

They live in Heaven, and their one duty is to sing God's praise and to carry out his will.

–St. John of Damascus, *Exposition of the Orthodox Faith*, 2.3

IN GOD'S PRESENCE, CONSIDER . . .

Angels' only duties, says St. John of Damascus, are to praise God and do his will. How would my life be different if I took those as my marching orders as well?

CLOSING PRAYER

Holy angels, who are carried through the universe faster than light in your zeal for the will of God, keep his will present to my soul, and give me your aid in my own efforts.

Angels know and do God's will immediately

God spoke the law to humans in a way we could understand—word by word, syllable by syllable, each sound taking up the time necessary for us to hear it. But the angels, St. Augustine says, receive God's instructions directly in their minds, and they instantly accomplish what God wills them to do.

And so it has pleased Divine Providence, as I have said, and as we read in the Acts of the Apostles (7:53) that the law demanding the worship of one God should be given by the disposition of angels.

But among them the person of God Himself visibly appeared—not, of course, in his proper substance, which is always invisible to mortal eyes, but by the infallible signs given by creation in obedience to its Creator. He also used the words of human speech, speaking them syllable by syllable one after the other, though in his own nature he speaks not in a bodily but in a spiritual way—not to sense, but to the mind—not in words that occupy time, but, so to speak, eternally, neither beginning to speak nor coming to an end.

And what He says is accurately heard, not by the bodily but by the mental ears of his ministers and messengers, who are immortally blessed in the enjoyment of his unchangeable truth. Whatever directions they receive in some unspoken way, they execute them without delay or difficulty in the sensible and visible world.

–St. Augustine, *City of God,* 10.15

IN GOD'S PRESENCE, CONSIDER . . .

For angels, understanding and obedience are instantaneous. My human abilities are more limited, but could I at least start to do God's will as soon as I understand what it is?

CLOSING PRAYER

Holy angels, who worship beside me in adoration of the one True God, the Blessed Trinity: Help me to be as prompt and unhesitating as you are in my obedience to the law and the directives of the Lord and his Church.

Like the angels, but different

St. Gregory Nazianzen says that we were created as a sort of second world, both earthly and heavenly. Like the angels we have a spiritual nature fit for praising God, but we also have a material nature that learns through suffering.

The Creator, the Word took a body from matter that already existed, and placed his own breath in it. And the Word knew that this was an intelligent soul, and the image of God.

Thus he made man as a sort of second world. He placed him, great in his littleness, on the earth—a new angel, a mixed worshiper, fully initiated into the visible creation, but only partially into the intellectual creation. He is earthly and heavenly, temporal yet immortal, visible yet intellectual, halfway between greatness and lowliness, combining spirit and flesh in one person—spirit because of the favor bestowed on him, flesh because of the height to which he has been raised—spirit so that he might continue to live and praise his Benefactor, flesh so that he might suffer, and by suffering remember and be corrected if he became proud of his greatness.

He is a living creature trained here and moved elsewhere—and, to complete the mystery, deified by his inclination to God.

–St. Gregory Nazianzen, Oration 38.11

Do I appreciate the life I share in common with the angels? Do I understand the ways I differ from them? Do I glory in that difference?

Holy Angel, help me to see that I am fearfully and wonderfully made, as are you and all my neighbors in Heaven and on Earth.

Angels are spiritual, but still limited

An angel, says St. John of Damascus, is not limited by a physical body the way we are. But angels are still limited; they exist, mentally, in a particular place and at a particular time. Only God is everywhere at all times.

The angel, although not contained in place with a particular shape, as a body is, is still said to be in a place because he has a mental presence and energizes in accordance with his nature; when he energizes somewhere, he is not somewhere else, but has his mental limitations there. For it is impossible to energize at the same time in different places.

God alone can energize everywhere at the same time. The angel energizes in different places by the quickness of his nature and the promptness and speed with which he can change his place: but the Deity, who is everywhere and above all, energizes at the same time in different ways with one simple energy.

But the angel is circumscribed alike in time (for his being had a beginning) and in place (but *mental* space, as we said above) and in understanding. For they know somehow the nature of each other and have their bounds perfectly defined by the Creator. Bodies, in short, are circumscribed both in beginning and end, and bodily place and apprehension.

—St. John of Damascus, *Exposition of the Orthodox Faith*, 1.13

IN GOD'S PRESENCE, CONSIDER . . .

Like the angels, I have limitations imposed by my nature, which was given to me by God. Do I strive for clear self-knowledge, like that of the angels, so that I may serve God as he made me to serve him?

CLOSING PRAYER

Glorious angels, you see me as I am. Help me to see myself as clearly, so that I may serve God perfectly.

Angels are limited; the Spirit is not

Against those who would relegate the Holy Spirit to inferior status, St. Basil the Great points out that Scripture consistently treats the angels as limited beings: here but not there, in one place and not another. But the Spirit, as God, is everywhere at once.

Of the rest of the powers of Heaven, each is believed to be in a limited place. The angel who stood by Cornelius (Acts 10:3) was not with Philip at exactly the same time (Acts 8:26); the angel who spoke with Zechariah from the altar (Luke 1:11) was not simultaneously up in Heaven at his post.

But the Spirit is believed to have been working in Habakkuk and Daniel at the same time in Babylon, and to have been at the prison with Jeremiah, and with Ezekiel by the Chebar.

For "the Spirit of the Lord has filled the world" (Wis. 1:7). "Whither shall I go from your Spirit? Or whither shall I flee from your presence?" (Ps. 139:7).

–St. Basil the Great, *On the Holy Spirit*, 23

IN GOD'S PRESENCE, CONSIDER . . .

A powerful guardian angel is with me all the time, and the power of the Spirit is infinite. Am I mindful of their presence every day?

CLOSING PRAYER

Have mercy on me according to your great compassion, Lord. Send your angels to protect me, and send forth on me your all-holy Spirit.

Angels have knowledge through the Creator

Like us, says St. Augustine, angels know things in themselves—that is, by experience of them. But they have a much deeper knowledge in the Word of God, which is always present to their souls and gives them a bright and clear knowledge of all things.

The holy angels come to the knowledge of God not by words that they hear, but by the presence in their souls of immutable truth—that is, of the only-begotten Word of God. And they know this Word himself, and the Father, and their Holy Spirit, and that this Trinity is indivisible, and that the three persons of it are one substance, and that there are not three Gods but one God—and they know all this in such a way that they understand it better than we understand ourselves.

In the same way, they know the creature too, not in itself, but by this better way, in the wisdom of God, as if in the art by which it was created; and, consequently, they know themselves better in God than in themselves. In Him, therefore, they have a noonday knowledge; in themselves, a twilight knowledge.

So is it with all other things—the firmament between the water above and below, which was called the heaven; the gathering of the waters beneath, and the laying bare of the dry land, and the production of plants and trees; the creation of sun, moon, and stars; and of the animals out of the waters, fowls, and fish, and monsters of the deep; and of everything that walks or creeps on the earth, and of man himself, who excels all that is on the earth—all these things are known in one way by the angels in the Word of God, in which they see the unchanging causes and reasons for which they were made, and in another way in themselves: in the former, with a clearer knowledge; in the latter, with a knowledge dimmer, and rather of the bare works than of the design. Yet, when these works are referred to the praise and adoration of the Creator Himself, it is as if morning dawned in the minds of those who contemplate them.

–St. Augustine, City of God, 11.29

IN GOD'S PRESENCE, CONSIDER . . .

What things do I know fairly well—my special areas of expertise? How would that knowledge be illuminated if I tried to see it in the light of the Word of God—according to God's eternal plan?

CLOSING PRAYER

Holy angels, you see God and all things with unclouded eyes. Help us to see with such clarity; unselfishly, and with a pure desire.

Angels are immortal by grace, not by nature

Attempting to define what an angel is, St. John of Damascus comes to some interesting conclusions. Since angels are created, they're not naturally eternal. Like us, they have eternal life ahead of them only by the grace of God.

An angel is an intelligent being, always in motion, with free will, bodiless, ministering to God, with an immortal nature obtained by grace.

Its will is changeable or inconstant: for everything that is created is changeable, and only what is uncreated is unchangeable. And everything rational is endowed with free will. Since it is rational and intelligent, it is endowed with free will. And since it is created, it is changeable, able either to persist in goodness or to turn to evil.

It cannot repent, because it is bodiless. The weakness of the body is the reason mankind has repentance.

It is immortal—not by nature, but by grace. Everything that had a beginning also comes to its natural end; God alone is eternal—or rather, above the eternal, since he who created time is not under the power of time but above time.

Angels are secondary intelligent lights derived from that first Light which is without beginning. They have the power of illumination: they need no speech or hearing, but communicate their thoughts and ideas to one another without speaking.

Thus through the Word all angels were created, and through the sanctification of the Holy Spirit they were brought to perfection, each one sharing in brightness and grace according to its worth and rank.

–St. John of Damascus, *Exposition of the Orthodox Faith,* 2.3

IN GOD'S PRESENCE, CONSIDER . . .

Life is a gift, and immortality extends that gift endlessly. Do I appreciate the fact that I can know the companionship of my angel forever, since God has made us both to be immortal?

CLOSING PRAYER

Holy Angel, my constant friend, may I grow closer to you every day of this life, that I may recognize you with joy and without hesitation in Heaven.

The angels' immortality depends upon God's will

The angels are immortal, says St. Ambrose, but they don't have the same kind of immortality that God has. God is immortal by nature; angels are immortal because God gives them immortality.

The immortality of God's nature is one thing, and the immortality of ours is another. Perishable things cannot be compared to divine things. The Godhead is the only Substance that death cannot touch, and therefore it is that the Apostle, though knowing that both our soul and the angels are immortal, declared that God only had immortality (1 Tim. 6:16). In truth, even the soul may die: "The soul that sins shall die" (Ezek. 18:20). And an angel is not absolutely immortal, because his immortality depends on the will of the Creator.

Do not hastily reject this, because Gabriel does not die, or Raphael, or Uriel. Every creature has within it the possibility of corruption and death, even if it is not dying or committing sin right now. And if it does not hand itself over to sin in anything, this blessing does not come from its immortal nature, but from discipline or grace. Immortality, then, that comes as a gift is one thing; immortality without the possibility of change is another.

–St. Ambrose, *Exposition of the Christian Faith*, 3.3

IN GOD'S PRESENCE, CONSIDER . . .

God wills my soul to be immortal like the good angels. Am I cooperating with God's will, as Gabriel and Raphael do?

CLOSING PRAYER

Guardian Angel, lead me to hear the life-giving commandments of the Lord, so that I may be found worthy to spend eternity in your company.

Immortally mortal and mortally immortal

Both human beings and angels are mortal in a certain sense, says St. Gregory the Great. They can cease to be what they are now. But neither one can cease to be altogether.

Now either a human soul or an angelic spirit is immortal in such a way that it is capable of dying. And it is mortal in such a way that it can never die.

It is deprived of living *happily* either by sin or by punishment. But it never loses its essential property of living, either by sin or by punishment. It stops living in a particular way, but not even dying can bring an end to every mode of its being.

In a word, I might say that it is both immortally mortal and mortally immortal.

–St. Gregory the Great, *Moralia in Job,* 4.6

IN GOD'S PRESENCE, CONSIDER . . .

If death is to be deprived of living happily, what am I doing to avoid the death of the fallen angels?

CLOSING PRAYER

Lord, give me life from death, and bring me home at the end of this life to praise you forever in joy with your holy angels.

Angels are kept alive by God

A particularly poetic passage from Dionysius the Areopagite tells us that the angels, and all other living beings, are alive only because they share in the self-existing Life of God. When we say that angels are immortal, we don't mean that they are immortal by nature; we mean that God keeps them alive forever.

Now let us sing the eternal life, from which comes the self-existing Life, and every life; and from which, to every single thing that shares in life, is distributed the power to live appropriately to each.

Certainly the life and the immortality of the immortal angels, and the very indestructibility of the angelic perpetual motion, exist because of the eternal life, and is sustained from it and because of it. For that reason they are also called everliving and immortal—not immortal because they have immortality and eternal life by their own nature, but because they have it from the life-giving Cause that forms and sustains all life. As I said before, God only is self-existing Being; and again I say here that the divine life, which is above life, is life-giving and sustaining even to the self-existing Life. Every life and life-giving movement comes from that Life that is above every life and every source of life.

From God even the souls have their indestructible nature. All living creatures, and plants in their most remote echo of life, have their power to live from God. And, as Scripture says, when that Life above all life is taken away, all life fails. But even things that have failed through their inability to share in that life, if they return, become living creatures again.

–Dionysius the Areopagite, *The Divine Names*, 6.1

IN GOD'S PRESENCE, CONSIDER . . .

Have I thanked God today for his gift of life—not only to me, but to everything from angels down to the bacteria I couldn't live without?

CLOSING PRAYER

Lord, I thank you continually. I adore and glorify you, O Lord of all, without whom I would not exist, and not even the angels would have life.

There is an order in Heaven

Arguing against the heretic Jovianus, St. Jerome explains that there are ranks even of angels; we shouldn't be surprised, therefore, to hear that there will be ranks among the saints.

Christ tells us that in Heaven there are many different mansions, prepared for many different virtues, and they will be awarded, not to persons, but to persons' works.

But if there are not many mansions, then how does the Old Testament teach, like the New, that the chief priest has one rank, the priests another, the Levites another, the doorkeepers another, the sacristans another? How is it that in the book of Ezekiel, which gives a description of the future Church and of the heavenly Jerusalem, the priests who have sinned are degraded to the rank of sacristans and doorkeepers (Ez. 44:10-14), and although they are in the temple of God, that is on the right hand, they are not among the rams, but among the poorest of the sheep? How again is it that in the river which flows from the temple, and replenishes the salt sea, and gives new life to everything, we read there are many kinds of fish? Why do we read that in the kingdom of Heaven there are Archangels, Angels, Thrones, Dominions, Powers, Cherubim, and Seraphim, and every name that is named, not only in this present world, but also that which is to come?

A difference of name is meaningless where there is not a difference of rank. An Archangel is of course an Archangel to other inferior angels, and Powers, and Dominions have other spheres over which they exercise authority. This is what we find in Heaven and in the administration of God.

−St. Jerome, *Against Jovianus*, 2.28

IN GOD'S PRESENCE, CONSIDER . . .

If there are ranks in Heaven, am I striving to earn the highest rank? Or am I just scraping by?

CLOSING PRAYER

Guardian Angel, help me to know my particular gifts clearly, that I may work to perfect them for God's use on Earth, and through them give praise to him forever in Heaven.

Why a hierarchy?

Dionysius the Areopagite uses neo-Platonist language to explain the purpose of hierarchy. The hierarchy in Heaven, and its mirror in the Church, both exist to make our lives into images of the life of God, and to reflect the divinity of God to others.

The purpose of hierarchy is to bring all its members together, as far as attainable, with God, making him the Leader of all religious science and operation, by looking unflinchingly on his divine beauty, and copying it as far as possible.

Hierarchy perfects its own followers as divine images, luminous and flawless mirrors, which receive the original light and the supremely divine ray and are devoutly filled with radiance entrusted to them, and then spread this radiance generously to those after them, in accordance with God's own regulations.

For it is not lawful for the mystic rites of sacred things, or for things religiously done, to do anything whatsoever beyond the sacred regulations of their own function. They must not even attempt otherwise if they desire to attain its deifying splendor, and look to it religiously, and are molded after the example of each of the holy minds.

Whoever says "hierarchy," then, means a certain completely holy order, an image of the supremely divine freshness, ministering the mysteries of its own illumination in hierarchical ranks and sciences, and assimilated to its own proper Head as far as it is lawful.

—Dionysius the Areopagite, *The Celestial Hierarchy*, 3.1-2

IN GOD'S PRESENCE, CONSIDER . . .

Whatever my place is in the Church, do I fill it as the angels do, as if I were one part of the great mind of God? Or do I do it grudgingly?

CLOSING PRAYER

Lord, grant your Spirit to all your bishops, priests, deacons, readers, and singers, and the entire body of your holy Catholic and Apostolic Church. May your Church on earth be a perfect image of your Church in Heaven.

The hierarchy imitates God

Dionysius the Areopagite explains that each member of a hierarchy—among the angels or in the Church—finds his own perfection in his own particular role in the greater organization.

Each of those who have been called into the hierarchy finds perfection in imitating God in his own way—and, what is more divine than all, in becoming a fellow-worker with God, as the Scriptures say, and in showing the divine energy in himself manifested as far as possible.

One of the rules of hierarchy is that some are purified and that others purify; that some are enlightened and others enlighten; that some are perfected and others perfect. The imitation of God will fit each one in this fashion.

The blessedness of God, to speak in human terms, is in fact unstained by any dissimilarity, and is full of invisible light—perfect, and needing no perfection; cleansing, illuminating, and perfecting. Indeed, we might say it is a holy purification, illumination, and perfection—above purification, above light, preeminently perfect. It is the source and cause of every hierarchy, perfect in itself, and raised far above every holy thing.

–Dionysius the Areopagite, *The Celestial Hierarchy*, 3.1-2

IN GOD'S PRESENCE, CONSIDER . . .

Do I recognize that even now God is purifying me through the ministry of angels? Do I submit willingly to purification, no matter how demanding it may seem?

CLOSING PRAYER

Send your angels to purify my soul, O Lord, and cleanse my heart from all wickedness, that I may make my life a sweet offering to you.

The orders of angels teach one another

The hierarchy of Heaven, like the hierarchy on Earth, keeps to a definite order of teaching, according to Dionysius the Areopagite. The higher levels teach the subordinate levels. Like some other Fathers, our writer imagines the beginning of Isaiah 63 as a description of the scene in Heaven when Christ ascended.

Theologians show that the superior orders of heavenly beings teach the subordinate orders the knowledge of becoming like God. The highest orders of all receive their illumination directly from God, as far as possible for them, in revelations of the divine mysteries. Some (the theologians say) were instructed by those of higher rank that he who ascended into Heaven as a man is Lord of the heavenly powers, and King of glory; others asked Jesus himself, because they wished to be taught about his divine work on our behalf, and Jesus taught them directly, showing them what he had done out of love for humanity. "It is I," Jesus said, "announcing vindication, mighty to save" (Isa. 63:1).

Personally, I am amazed that even the foremost of the heavenly beings, so far above all the rest, should reverently look for the divine teachings as intermediate beings. They do not ask directly, "Why is your apparel red?" (Isa. 63:2). But first they raise the question among themselves. This shows that they desire to learn, and crave the knowledge of being like God, and do not demand the knowledge of what God has done before it is time for them to know.

—Dionysius the Areopagite, *The Celestial Hierarchy*, 7.3

IN GOD'S PRESENCE, CONSIDER . . .

Do I reverently accept the teaching authority of those to whom the Church has given it—both angels and bishops?

CLOSING PRAYER

Lord, you chose the lamp of the twelve apostles with its twelve lights, and sent them forth to proclaim throughout the whole world and teach the gospel of your kingdom; send your angels to keep their successors safe from all error.

Each order interprets the order above

Dionysius the Areopagite tells us that the angels on any level of the hierarchy interpret what they learn from the rank above for the sake of the rank below. The Seraphim, at the top of the hierarchy, learn from God himself. And even within the same rank of the hierarchy, there are different positions.

All angels are interpreters of those above them. The most reverend angels interpret God, who moves them, directly. The rest are interpreters, in their own positions, of the ones who have been moved by God.

In the harmony of all things, each of the rational and intellectual beings has its own place and its own work. We also see that each hierarchy is placed in a sacred order, and every one of the three hierarchies is itself divided into first, middle, and last powers.

But, to speak correctly, God has given each division itself the same kind of divine organization. This is why the theologians say that the Seraphim cry one to another. I think this shows distinctly that the first give their knowledge of the divine to the second.

–Dionysius the Areopagite, *The Celestial Hierarchy*, 10

IN GOD'S PRESENCE, CONSIDER . . .

All earthly authority is dependent on light from Heaven. From whom do I usually learn about things that have to do with faith?

CLOSING PRAYER

Lord of all light, send your angels to enlighten the bishops, elders, deacons, readers, singers, and laity, with the entire body of the Holy Catholic and Apostolic Church.

The hierarchy in your mind

Dionysius the Areopagite tells us that hierarchy is not just a way of organizing either individual angels or humans. There is a similar hierarchy in every mind. Your own mind is organized in such a way as to lead you toward participation in the perfection of God.

It would be appropriate to add here that each mind, either heavenly or human, has within itself its own special first, and middle, and last ranks, and powers, which work separately in our own minds, just as we said the different ranks of the hierarchy work in passing down mystical enlightenment.

In this way each mind participates in the most spotless purification, the most abundant light, and the greatest degree of perfection possible and ordained for that individual. For there is nothing really perfect in itself, or completely without need of being perfected, except God, who is self-perfect and preeminently perfect.

–Dionysius the Areopagite, *The Celestial Hierarchy*, 10

IN GOD'S PRESENCE, CONSIDER . . .

Do I allow the higher parts of my mind to lead the lower parts, the way the higher beings in Heaven lead the lower? Or do the lower parts of my mind take the lead?

CLOSING PRAYER

Lord, repel the dark assaults of sin from my understanding, and gladden my mind with the divine radiance of your angels.

The body as a map of the angels' minds

In a flight of philosophical fancy, Dionysius the Areopagite uses the human body as a symbol of the intellectual powers of the heavenly beings, and our own similar intellectual powers as well.

I think we can find fitting images of the heavenly powers in the parts of our own body.

Vision symbolizes the clear elevation toward the light of God, and the reception of enlightenment from God. The power of distinguishing smells symbolizes being able to receive, as far as possible, the sweet-smelling grace of God, and the ability to distinguish what is not God's grace and to reject it. Hearing symbolizes consciously receiving and participating in God's inspiration.

Taste symbolizes the intellectual nourishment that comes in plentiful streams from God. Touch symbolizes the skill of deciding what is good or harmful.

Eyelids and eyebrows symbolize guarding the conceptions that see God.

Manhood and youth symbolize the perpetual bloom and vigor of life.

Teeth symbolize dividing the nourishing perfection given to us—for each intellectual being has the ability given by God to divide and multiply the unified idea given to it by the beings above, so that it in turn can elevate the beings below.

The shoulders, elbows, and hands symbolize the power of making, doing, and accomplishing.

The heart symbolizes the Godlike life, sending its own life-giving power out to the objects of its concern, as is fitting for the good. The chest, which is placed above the heart, symbolizes the invincible protection of this life-giving distribution.

The back holds together all the productive powers of life.

The feet symbolize the swift and skillful perpetual movement toward the divine.

–Dionysius the Areopagite, *The Celestial Hierarchy*, 15.3

IN GOD'S PRESENCE, CONSIDER . . .

Is my own body a fitting symbol of the angelic life? Is every part ordered toward accomplishing God's will?

CLOSING PRAYER

Lord, let me fulfill in my own place, as a member of your spiritual body, your holy and blessed will.

Everything is under God's control

When all the forces of nature and even the angels themselves seem to be arrayed against us, says St. Gregory the Great, we must remember that it is not the things acting of themselves, but God arranging everything for the true good.

All things continue to exist in God, by whom they were created. Things that live do not owe their life to themselves, and things that move but do not live are not set in motion by their own whim. God moves all things: he gives some of them life, and preserves some that are not alive, arranging everything down to the last and lowest being in a wonderful way. All things were made out of nothing, and they would go back to being nothing if the Author of all things did not hold them by the hand of governance.

By themselves, all the things that have been created cannot either continue to exist or be moved. They exist only so far as it is given to them that they should be, and they move only so far as they are influenced by a secret impulse.

Here is a sinner ordained to be scourged by human accidents. The earth is parched in his toil—the sea is tossed to shipwreck him—the air is on fire to make him sweat—the heavens are darkened to flood on him—his fellow creatures burn with fire to oppress him—the angelic powers are stirred up against him.

Are all the inanimate things, and all the living beings, that I have mentioned here put into action by their own instincts? No, they are put into action by impulses from God.

Whatever is arrayed against us outwardly, we must see in it that Being who ordains it inwardly.

—St. Gregory the Great, *Moralia in Job*, 16.45

IN GOD'S PRESENCE, CONSIDER . . .

When even the angels themselves seem to be going against me, do I still have Job's courage not to curse God?

CLOSING PRAYER

Together with all the heavenly host, O Lord, I praise you and say, Blessed are you, O God, and glory becomes you, the Father, Son, and Holy Spirit, now and forever.

"Lord of all" includes the angels

When Peter says that Christ is "Lord of all," he means Lord of every-thing, says St. Cyril of Jerusalem. That includes angels and all the heavenly beings.

"He is Lord of all" (Acts 10:36). But when he says "of all," do not leave out anything from his lordship. Angels, Archangels, Principalities, Powers, or any other created thing named by the Apostles—they are all under the lordship of the Son.

He is the Lord of angels, as you have read in the Gospels: "Then the devil left him, and behold, angels came and ministered to him" (Matt. 4:11). The Scripture does not say, "they helped him," but "they ministered to him"—that is, like servants.

When he was about to be born of a virgin, Gabriel was his servant, having received his service as a particular dignity. When he was about to go into Egypt, so that he might overthrow the gods of Egypt made with hands, again an angel appeared to Joseph in a dream (Matt. 2:13). After he had been crucified and had risen again, an angel brought the good news, and as a trustworthy servant said to the women, "Then go quickly and tell his disciples that he has risen from the dead, and behold, he is going before you to Galilee; there you will see him. Lo, I have told you" (Matt. 28:7)—almost as if to say, "I have not neglected my command: I declare that I have told you, and if you disregard it the blame will not be on me, but on those who disregard it."

This, then, is the one Lord Jesus Christ, of whom the lesson we just read speaks: "For although there may be so-called gods in Heaven or on Earth—as indeed there are many 'gods' and many 'lords'—yet for us there is one God, the Father, from whom are all things and for whom we exist, and one Lord, Jesus Christ, through whom are all things and through whom we exist" (1 Cor. 8:5-6).

–St. Cyril of Jerusalem, *Catechetical Lecture 10*, 10

IN GOD'S PRESENCE, CONSIDER . . .

Do I recognize that I occupy a creation that includes creatures much more intel-ligent and stronger than I am? Do I strive to praise God with these creatures, the holy angels?

CLOSING PRAYER

Merciful God, teach me to be humble. Give me the light to see myself as I am, to see the angels as they are, and to praise you for your creation.

All creation gives thanks to God

*All God's works give thanks to him, the psalm says. How? St. Augustine asks.
Not because stones and trees can speak, but because the perfectly ordered beauty
of creation makes God's intelligent creatures praise him.*

"All your works shall give thanks to you, O Lord, and all thy saints shall
bless thee!" (Ps. 145:10).

"All your works shall give thanks to you." How will they give thanks? Isn't the
earth his work? Aren't the trees his work? Cattle, animals, fish, birds—aren't they
his works? Of course they are. So how will they give thanks to him?

Certainly I can see how the angels give thanks to him. The angels are his
works, and we are his works. When we give thanks to him, his works give thanks to
him. But do trees and stones have a voice to give thanks? Yes, they certainly have:
"*All* your works shall give thanks to you."

Now, no one should think that speechless stones or animals have an intelligence that can comprehend God. Anyone who thinks this strays far from the truth.
God has arranged everything and made everything: he has given sense and understanding and immortality to some, such as the angels; to others he has given sense
and understanding with mortality; and to some he has given neither sense, understanding, nor immortality, such as plants, trees, and stones. But even these cannot
be lacking in their kind, and by degrees he has ordered his creation, from Earth up
to Heaven, from visible to invisible, from mortal to immortal. This framework of
creation—this most perfectly ordered beauty—ascending from lowest to highest,
descending from highest to lowest, never broken, but compounded of dissimilar
things—all of it praises God.

Why does it all praise God? Because when you think about it, and see its
beauty, in it you praise God.

–St. Augustine, *Exposition on Ps. 145*, 13

IN GOD'S PRESENCE, CONSIDER . . .

Have I taken time lately to enjoy the wonders of God's creation—by a walk in the
park, for example, or a look at the stars, or reading and thinking about the angels—and
to praise God for it?

CLOSING PRAYER

*Lord, I praise you for your creation, from the most glorious angels to the humblest and
tiniest stones.*

Degrees of knowledge

Each creature, says St. Ephrem the Syrian, has a degree of knowledge proper to it. The different ranks of angels never ask questions beyond what they know to be their ability. Yet some human philosophers think they can vault over all the ranks of angels and figure out the most hidden secrets of God's own nature!

The knowledge of angels searches in measure; human knowledge roams without measure. Your mercy put inns and milestones in your way, so that the unsettled disputers might come into order. Blessed is he who has measured his wonder with his knowledge so as to reach the inns.

Human knowledge is like a feeble twilight compared to the angels' knowledge; and even the angels' knowledge is like a little twinkling compared to the Spirit's knowledge. The Spirit says of the Son, "who shall declare his generation?" (Isa. 53:8). It is pure rashness to run on beyond this boundary when the Spirit came up to it and stopped.

When the angels searched to learn the generation of the Son, they directed their questions to those who were higher than they were; and those great ones learn at the suggestion of the Spirit. As are the ranks of angels, so are the questions of angels. There is none among them that dares to reach beyond what belongs to him. Nature witnesses to this by its own subordination: rank leads to rank, up to that which is the crown. Yet human beings, who are of low rank, trespass over the ranks of angels to search into the First-Born!

–St. Ephrem the Syrian, *Rhythm 5*

IN GOD'S PRESENCE, CONSIDER . . .

The angels know how far each rank can reach, and do not pretend to reach any further. Am I sometimes tempted to declare my opinions on things I can't possibly know?

CLOSING PRAYER

Lord, grant me the wisdom to understand your mysteries as far as I am capable; but when I cannot understand, grant me the humility to serve you in my proper place, the way each rank of your angels serves you.

Sharing the knowledge of the angels

Dionysius the Areopagite tells us that the angels see the marvelous unity of God because they get their conceptions directly from God. We are too divided and scatterbrained to see that way under normal circumstances; but when we are gathered together in unity, we can have something of this same experience.

From the self-existing Life of God, the contemplated and contemplating powers of the angelic minds have their simple and blessed conceptions; collecting their divine knowledge, not in portions, or from portions, or sensible perceptions, or detailed reasonings, or arguing from something common to these things, but purified from everything that is material and separate, they contemplate the conceptions of divine things intuitively, immaterially and uniformly. They have their intellectual power and energy resplendent with the unmixed and undefiled purity, and see at a glance the divine conceptions indivisibly and immaterially. By the godlike One they are molded, as attainable by reason of the divine wisdom, to the divine and super-wise mind and reason.

And souls have their reasoning power, investigating the truth of things by going through them step by step. Through their divided and manifold variety they fall short of the single minds. But when the many are gathered together towards the One, they are deemed worthy even of conceptions equal to the angels, so far as is proper and attainable to souls.

–Dionysius the Areopagite, *The Divine Names*, 7.2

IN GOD'S PRESENCE, CONSIDER . . .

When I look for the truth, does it help to remember that Christ promised we would share the knowledge of the angels in the Church—that is, gathered together like the angels above, rather than apart?

CLOSING PRAYER

Father, with the Cherubim and Seraphim let me glorify you without ceasing in your Church, crowned and filled with every aid and blessing, because you are Lord and Father, Creator of all.

Angels bring us the vision of God

The speculative philosopher Dionysius the Areopagite says that the heavenly beings deserve their title of "angel" (which means "messenger") because they bring us the light of God, which they experience at first hand.

The holy orders of the heavenly beings share in the supremely divine participation in a higher degree than things that merely exist, or that lead an irrational life, or that are rational like ourselves. By imitating God, they shape themselves, keeping the image of God before them in a way we cannot do. Since they shape their intellectual appearance on the model of God, they naturally have a more complete communication with God than we have. The unwavering love of God is so intense that it raises them ever upwards, as far as is lawful for them. They receive the light of God without any earthly shadow, and they align themselves with that light, and live a purely intellectual life.

These are the ones who participate in God at first hand, under many forms, and make known what is hidden in God. For that reason, these are most worthy, beyond all others, of the name "angel" or "messenger," because the light of God comes to them at first hand, and they pass it on to us.

Thus the Law, as the Word of God tells us, was given to us through angels. Before and after the Law, angels led our illustrious ancestors toward God—either by leading them to what was to be done, and away from error and an unholy life toward the straight way of truth; or by revealing sacred laws to them, or hidden visions, or heavenly mysteries, or certain divine predictions through the prophets.

–Dionysius the Areopagite, *The Celestial Hierarchy*, 4.2

IN GOD'S PRESENCE, CONSIDER . . .

When was the last time I looked into the light of God, as revealed in Scripture, through the ministry of angels?

CLOSING PRAYER

Lord, in your mercy, you have given us the angels as the ministers of your light. I praise you for your wisdom; I thank you for all you have revealed through your messengers. Give me the grace to see how they serve me in my mind and heart.

Angels as counselors

In the hierarchy of angels, says St. Gregory the Great, the lower receive from the higher the knowledge they need to transmit to us. Angels are our counselors, because they want us to be with them in the kingdom of Heaven.

From things that have no sense, we can learn how to understand beings with sense and intelligence.

Now, the air makes the earth fertile, and the quality of the heaven governs the air. Likewise, human beings are placed over animals, and angels over human beings, and archangels over angels.

If the superior powers did not direct the inferior powers in the service of the holy spirits, one angel would never have learned from another's lips what he should say to a person.

The Creator of the universe upholds everything by himself, but—so as to make up an order of the universe characterized by beauty—he rules one part through the administration of another part. The angels are also rightly called counselors, because they counsel for the spiritual commonwealth, while they unite us to the kingdom as heirs along with them. From their lips we hear the will of the Creator; in them, certainly, we find the counsel to escape from the misery that surrounds us.

–St. Gregory the Great, *Moralia in Job*, 4.55

IN GOD'S PRESENCE, CONSIDER . . .

Do I listen to what my angel counselors are trying to tell me?

CLOSING PRAYER

Guardian Angel, lead me safely through the dangers of this life to the bosom of God, as Tobias was led back to his father.

Spiritual bodies

St. Augustine speculates that angels have a kind of spiritual body that adapts itself to various forms. But he's always careful to distinguish what he himself believes from what everyone is required to believe.

Do angels have bodies adapted to their duties and their swift motions from place to place, or are they only spirits?

If we say that they have bodies, we are met by the passage, "Who makest thy angels spirits" (Ps. 104:4). But if we say that they have no bodies, we are met by the still greater difficulty in explaining how, if they have no bodily form, it is written that they appeared to human senses, allowed their feet to be washed, and ate and drank what was provided for them. It seems to involve us in less difficulty if we say that angels are called "spirits" in the same way that human beings are called "souls"—as when it says (in Genesis) that a certain number of "souls" went down with Jacob into Egypt, not mentioning that they had bodies as well—than if we suppose that angels did all these things when they had no bodily form.

But whether angels have bodies or not, and whether or not anyone can show how they could do all these things without bodies, still it is certain that, in the city of the holy in which those of the human race who have been redeemed are united forever to thousands of angels, voices that come from organs of speech will give expression to thoughts of minds in which nothing is hidden. For in that divine fellowship it will not be possible for any thought in one being to remain concealed from another, but there will be complete harmony and oneness of heart in the praise of God. And this will be spoken not just from the spirit but through the spiritual body as its instrument. At least this is what I believe.

—St. Augustine, *Letter 95*

IN GOD'S PRESENCE, CONSIDER . . .

In Heaven there will be "complete harmony and oneness of heart" among both people and angels. But how can I work toward that goal while I'm still here on earth?

CLOSING PRAYER

Father, purify me from all deceit and hypocrisy, and unite me with your holy angels and all my brothers and sisters by the bond of peace and love.

We can't understand all the mysteries of Heaven

On his way to martyrdom, St. Ignatius writes to the Trallians that he could tell them more about Heaven's mysteries—but he's afraid to burden them with too many things they couldn't understand.

Don't you think I could write to you about things that are even more mysterious? But I'm afraid to do so. I don't want to injure you, who are still only babes. Please excuse me here: I'm afraid that you would not be able to understand their weighty meaning, and you would be strangled by them.

I'm bound for Heaven, and can understand heavenly things—the orders of angels, and the different sorts of angels and hosts, the distinctions between Powers and Dominions, and the differences between Thrones and Authorities, the mightiness of the eons, and the preeminence of the Cherubim and Seraphim, the sublimity of the Spirit, the kingdom of the Lord, and above all, the incomparable majesty of Almighty God. But though I'm acquainted with these things, that doesn't mean I'm anything like perfect. I'm not the disciple that Peter or Paul was. Many things are still lacking in me, not to fall short of God.

—St. Ignatius, *Trallians* 5

IN GOD'S PRESENCE, CONSIDER . . .

When there are things in the faith that I can't understand—like the orders of angels or the difference between a Power and a Dominion—do I have the faith to wait for understanding?

CLOSING PRAYER

Angels of God, though I know I cannot yet fully understand you, I rely on your help in always leading me toward the incomparable majesty of Almighty God.

Keep speculation in bounds

There are many things we can try to know about angels, says St. Augustine, but we can never know for sure. It can be good to speculate, but we have to admit it frankly when we just don't know the answer.

How is life arranged there in that blessed heavenly fellowship? What differences are there in rank among the angels? They're all called by the generic name "angels," as we read in the letter to the Hebrews: "But to what angel has he ever said, 'Sit at my right hand'?" This phrase shows clearly that they're all "angels," with no exceptions. But there are archangels, too. Should we call these archangels "powers," so that the line, "Praise him, all his angels; praise him, all his powers" (Ps. 148:2) means the same as, "Praise him, all his angels; praise him, all his archangels"? What differences does it imply when the Apostle seems to take in the entire heavenly city with four names: "whether Thrones or Dominions or Principalities or Authorities" (Col. 1:16)?

If anyone can answer those questions, go ahead. As far as I'm concerned, I confess that I don't know anything about it. I'm not even sure of the answer to another question: whether the sun, the moon, and all the stars belong to that same heavenly fellowship, though they do seem to be nothing more than glowing bodies that don't feel or understand.

And aside from all that, who can explain what kind of bodies the angels had when they appeared to people, so that they could be not only seen but also touched? And also, how do they bring certain visions—not by physical stimulation but by spiritual force—to the eyes of the mind—not the physical eyes, but the spiritual eyes? How do they speak something, not to the ears, as if they were outside us, but from right inside the human soul—since they are present there as well?

To ask questions like these, and to guess the answers as well as we can, is not just useless speculation—as long as we keep the argument moderate, and we avoid the mistake of thinking we know what we don't know.

–St. Augustine, *Enchiridion*, chapter 15

IN GOD'S PRESENCE, CONSIDER . . .

Do I indulge my curiosity for the sake of my vanity? Do I ask for the help of the angels in becoming a more sincere seeker of truth?

CLOSING PRAYER

Holy Guardian Angel, help me to know God and to know his creation, not for the sake of pride or domination, but for love. In this way may my knowledge be like you.

Remember your weakness

St. Augustine probably ventured deeper into the uncharted territories of theology than any of the other Fathers. Yet he was always careful to remember what his own limits were, and he was always ready to confess them candidly to his readers.

It certainly is a useful caution to myself that I should remember what my own powers are, and warn my brethren to remember what theirs are as well. We must not let our human weakness pass beyond safe limits.

I do not know how the angels do these things—or, rather, how God does these things by his angels, and how far he wills them to be done even by the evil angels, and whether he permits, or commands, or compels them from the hidden seat of his own supreme power. I cannot know it: I cannot penetrate it with the sight of the eyes, or clear it up by the certainty of reason, or reach out to understand it with my intelligence.

So I cannot answer every question someone might ask about these things; I cannot speak as certainly as if I were an angel, a prophet, or an Apostle.

–St. Augustine, *On the Trinity*, 2.10

IN GOD'S PRESENCE, CONSIDER . . .

Where I don't understand something about Christian teaching—something about the angels for example—do I allow the Apostles and their successors to enlighten me?

CLOSING PRAYER

Guardian Angel, you know my ignorance better than I know it myself; but keep it always before my mind, so that I may not sin through pride of knowledge.

The face of God is the angels' Scripture

We read God's Word in the Bible. But the angels, says St. Augustine, read the will of God directly, without sounding out syllables, and this eternal Scripture is always before them.

Let us look, Lord, "at your heavens, the work of your fingers." Clear from our eyes the mist with which you have covered them.

Let them praise your name, those people above the heavens, your angels, who have no need to look up at this firmament, or to gain knowledge of your Word by reading. Let them praise you. They always see your face, and read in it without any syllables in time what your eternal will wills. They read, they choose, they love. They are always reading, and what they read never passes away. For, by choosing and loving, they read the very unchangeableness of your counsel. Their book is not closed, nor is the scroll folded up, because you yourself are their book, and indeed you are so eternally.

–St. Augustine, *Confessions*, 13.15

IN GOD'S PRESENCE, CONSIDER . . .

Could I imitate the angels' unceasing reading a little better by giving a little more time to Scripture each day?

CLOSING PRAYER

Father, who sent your Word to live among us, teach me to love your life-giving oracles, and let me read your will as readily as the angels do.

The Seraphim declare the Trinity

Arguing against the Arians, who insisted that the Son was not equal to the Father, St. Athanasius—the great defender of orthodoxy—says that the angelic hymn "Holy, holy, holy" proves the equality of the Persons of the Trinity. It is a hymn we offer with the angels whenever we go to Mass.

How can these ungodly men dare to speak such foolishness, when—since they're only men—they can't even figure out how things on earth work? But why do I even say "things on earth"? Let them explain their own nature. Can they figure out how to investigate their own nature?

They certainly are rash and willful if they don't tremble to look into things even the angels long to look into (1 Pet. 1:12)—the angels who are so far above them, both in nature and in rank. What's nearer to God than the Cherubim or the Seraphim? Yet even they don't see God or stand on their feet; they don't dare offer their praises with bare faces, but veil them, while with untiring lips they glorify the divine and indescribable nature with the "Holy, holy, holy."

And nowhere has any one of the prophets who spoke for God—men who were specially selected for that vision—told us that the first "Holy" is spoken in a loud voice, the second in a lower voice, and the third very quietly. They don't tell us that the first denotes lordship, the second subordination, and the third a lower status still.

No, forget the foolishness of these senseless God-haters. The Trinity, praised, revered, and adored, is one and indivisible without different ranks. It is united without confusion, just as the Unity of God is distinguished without separation. The fact that these venerable living creatures (Isa. 6, Rev. 4) offer their praises three times—"Holy, holy, holy"—proves that the three Persons are perfect, just as in saying "Lord" they declare that the Essence is one.

—St. Athanasius, *On Luke 10:22 and Matthew 11:27*

IN GOD'S PRESENCE, CONSIDER . . .

Do I imitate the angels in their approach to the reality—their reverence and respect for the mystery?

CLOSING PRAYER

We should always give thanks to you, Father almighty, who with your only begotten Son and the Holy Spirit are one God, one Lord. In confessing the true and everlasting Godhead — distinct in persons, one in being, and equal in majesty — we join the Angels and Archangels, Cherubim and Seraphim as they praise you with one voice: Holy, Holy, Holy!

The Trinity in the hymn of the Seraphim

"Holy, holy, holy is the Lord of hosts," we sing with the Seraphim (Isa. 6:3).
St. Ambrose sees a proclamation of the Trinity in that heavenly hymn.

The Father is holy. The Son is holy. The Spirit is holy. But they are not three holies. There is only one Holy God, one Lord. The true holiness is one, as the true Godhead is one. The true holiness of the divine nature is one.

Everything we call holy proclaims that one Holiness. Cherubim and Seraphim praise him with unwearied voices, saying, "Holy, holy, holy is the Lord of hosts." They do not say it once, which might make us think there was only one, and not twice, which might exclude the Spirit. They do not say "holies are," which might make us think there was a plurality. But they repeat the same word three times, so that even in a hymn you can understand the distinction of the Persons in the Trinity, and the oneness of the Godhead. And while they say this they proclaim God.

—St. Ambrose, *On the Holy Spirit*, 3.16

IN GOD'S PRESENCE, CONSIDER . . .

St. Ambrose seems to think that doctrine matters. It is important even to the Seraphim. Do I make an effort to understand what the Church teaches about the nature of God?

CLOSING PRAYER

Glory be to you, O Lord Almighty. The innumerable hosts of Angels, Archangels, Thrones, Dominions, Principalities, Authorities, and Powers adore you. The Cherubim and the six-winged Seraphim, with two covering their feet, two covering their heads, and with two flying, say, "Holy, holy, holy, Lord of hosts, Heaven and Earth are full of your glory."

The Seraphim surround Christ in the flesh

Jesus was born in humble circumstances, but the eye of faith, says St. Methodius of Olympus, can see the tiny child surrounded by the glorious Seraphim even in the manger.

Look! As a throne, lifted up on high by the glory of God who made it, the virgin mother is made ready, clearly for the King, the Lord of hosts.

Think of the Lord coming to you now in sinful flesh! On this virginal throne, I say, worship him, who now comes to you in this new and praiseworthy way.

Look around you with the eye of faith, and you will find the royal and priestly company of the Seraphim around him, as their duty demands. As his bodyguard, they always attend the King wherever he is.

Thus in this place we say not only that they hymn with their praises the divine substance of the divine unity, but also the glory, to be worshiped by all, of the sacred Trinity—which now has come to earth, because God has appeared in the flesh. "The whole earth is full of his glory," they say. For we believe that, along with the Son, who was made man for our sake, according to his will, the Father was also present, who is inseparable from him in his divine nature, and also the Spirit, who is of one and the same being.

–St. Methodius of Olympus, *Oration on Simeon and Anna*, 2

IN GOD'S PRESENCE, CONSIDER . . .

When I go to Mass, how will I see my parish church differently if I remember that Christ on our altar is surrounded by the glorious Seraphim?

CLOSING PRAYER

Holy Seraphim, who dwell in the eternal home of love, light in my heart that holy fire that consumes you.

Thrice holy, one Lord

Making an argument we hear more than once from the Fathers, St. Ambrose tells us that the "Holy, holy, holy" sung by the Seraphim (Isa. 6:3) indicates the Trinity: thrice holy, one Lord. If that is the way the powers of Heaven worship, he says, then that is the way he will worship.

The Seraphim say "Holy, holy, holy."

What does it mean, speaking the same name "Holy" three times? And if it's repeated three times, why is it only one act of praise? If it's one act of praise, why repeat it three times?

Why repeat it three times, unless because the Father, the Son, and the Holy Spirit are one in holiness?

The Seraph did not speak the name once, because that might exclude the Son. He did not speak it twice, because that might leave out the Holy Spirit. He did not speak it four times, because that might add in some created beings.

Then to show that the Godhead of the Trinity is *one*, he added "the Lord"—singular—"of hosts" (Isa. 6:3).

Holy is the Father; holy is the Son; and likewise holy is the Spirit of God. Therefore the Trinity is worshiped, but does not worship—is praised, but does not praise.

As for me, I prefer to believe as the Seraphim do, and worship the way all the Principalities and Powers of Heaven worship.

–St. Ambrose, *Exposition of the Christian Faith*, 2.12

IN GOD'S PRESENCE, CONSIDER . . .

What does it mean to worship as the angels and heavenly powers worship? Is it just saying the words, or is it being—as an angel is—a minister and messenger of God?

CLOSING PRAYER

Thousands of thousands of heavenly spirits, and ten thousand myriads of holy angels, hosts of spirits, ministers of fire and spirit, bless and adore your majesty, O Lord. Let me, with the holy Cherubim and the spiritual Seraphim, sanctify and celebrate your name, crying and praising without ceasing, "Holy, holy, holy is the Lord of hosts."

Praise and be silent

The Seraphim and the Cherubim will not even look on God, says St. Ephrem the Syrian, though they stand by his throne and carry his chariot. We should learn from their example to praise God unceasingly, and not to second-guess what we have learned about God.

The Seraph that flies with wings is too weak to search You out. His wing is weak compared to You; it cannot be compared with your majesty. The Seraph whose voice proclaims You holy maintains his reverential silence and keeps from searching into You.

Woe to the bold, when the Seraph covers his face with his wings before You!

The hosts of Cherubim bow down in fear beneath your chariot. They veil themselves and fear to look inside. They carry You, but are not able to find You.

Blessed are those who have learned from them the honor due to You, and have praised and been silent in fear!

—St. Ephrem the Syrian, *Rhythm 4*

IN GOD'S PRESENCE, CONSIDER . . .

Even the glorious Seraphim are not too glorious to be humble before God. How much of my prayer life is devoted to simple praise like theirs?

CLOSING PRAYER

Holy angels who are so much more glorious than I am, teach me your love of humble praise.

The vocal silence of God

St. Ephrem the Syrian meditates on the mysteriously intimate communication between the Father and the Son. If we could understand the language of the angels, he says, we still would not comprehend the silence in which the Father speaks to the Son.

The human ear cannot hear the mighty crash, nor can it hear the still silence. Then how will it hear the voice of the Son, or the silence of the Father—when the silence too is vocal?

The heavens declare the glory of God. Behold: a silence, of which the whole whispers in all languages to all languages. This firmament declares the glory of its Maker every day.

We are too small to be able to hear all languages. But if we were big enough to hear the language of the angels, which are spirits, then we might lift ourselves up to hear the silence that speaks between the Father and the Son.

Our language is incomprehensible to the beasts. The language of angels is incomprehensible to all the other languages. And that silence with which the Father speaks to his Well-Beloved is incomprehensible to the angels.

–St. Ephrem the Syrian, *Rhythm 11*

IN GOD'S PRESENCE, CONSIDER . . .

Though the language of angels is incomprehensible, do I join their praise in the liturgy at every opportunity?

CLOSING PRAYER

Lord, who are above all, your silence is incomprehensible even to the angels, and I am not worthy to venture into speculation on your nature. Yet I know that your mercy also puts me to shame, and on your mercy I rely.

Angels hide their faces from the Triune mystery

If Christ, the only-begotten Son, has existed from eternity, how was he begotten? Even the angels, says St. Ambrose, hide their faces from that mystery, and we should follow their example.

Do you ask me how he is a Son, if he does not have a Father existing before him? Then I ask you: when or how do you think the Son was begotten? For me the knowledge of the mystery of his generation is more than I can reach. The mind fails, the voice is dumb—yes, and not mine alone, but the angels' too. It is above Powers, above Angels, above Cherubim, Seraphim, and all that has feeling and thought. For it is written, "the peace of God, which passes all understanding" (Phil. 4:7). If the peace of Christ passes all understanding, how can such a marvelous generation not be above all understanding?

So cover your face with your hands, like the angels. For it is not your business to look into surpassing mysteries! We are allowed to know that the Son is begotten, not to argue about how he was begotten. I cannot deny the one; the other I fear to search into. If Paul says that the words he heard when caught up into the third Heaven might not be uttered (2 Cor. 12:2-5), how can we explain the secret of this generation from and of the Father, which we can neither hear nor reach with our understanding?

—St. Ambrose, *Exposition of the Christian Faith*, 1.10

IN GOD'S PRESENCE, CONSIDER . . .

When it comes to the deepest mysteries of the Faith, am I willing to show the intellectual modesty of the angels, who cover their faces with their wings rather than gaze deeply at the mysteries they can't understand?

CLOSING PRAYER

My Guardian Angel, you know so much more than I, and I know so much less than I think I know. Increase my self-knowledge, that I may be humble and grow in the knowledge of God.

Angels know the Father through the Son

Only the Son truly knows the Father, says St. Ephrem the Syrian. No matter how far superior the angels are to us, they—like us—cannot know the Father except through the Son.

No mind can reach the mighty height of its Maker. To go above this height, or below it, is merely to pry like the over-curious. They harry themselves to come up with some likeness of him who is only like himself. They all go astray when they try to know him, because the Only-Begotten is the only one who knows him.

He is not of the family of created things, so they cannot look into him as if he were their equal. He is not one of the things framed, so that we could describe him. He is not like the angels, so that they could pry into him as if he were their relative. He is not an equal of the Cherubim, who carry him as Lord. He does not fly among the Seraphim, since his glory is at the right hand. He is not with the ministering spirits, since with his Father he is ministered to. All the hosts of Heaven are entrusted to his command. They cannot see the Father without the First-Born, their Commander, because without him they were not framed when they were made.

The eye is enough for the light, and with it the whole body is lightened. The ear understands the voice, and the limbs hear by it. The mouth tastes food, and the whole body tastes by it and with it.

In the same way, by the Son who is from his bosom do the angels see the Father; by him they hear his voice as well; by him they receive his gift.

–St. Ephrem the Syrian, *Rhythm 1 on the Faith*

IN GOD'S PRESENCE, CONSIDER . . .

If even angels can know the Father only through the Son, am I taking every opportunity to cultivate the acquaintance of the Son?

CLOSING PRAYER

My Guardian Angel, you were sent by god to be my faithful guide. Always lead me to the Son, through whom alone I can know the Father.

The Son has the unceasing praise of angels

Christ didn't perform miracles because he wanted to show off, says St. Hilary of Poitiers. After all, he has all the hosts of heaven praising him without ceasing. No, his miracles were performed so that we might believe and be saved.

There is no deception in these miracles of God, no subtle pretense to please or to deceive. These works of the Son of God were not done from any desire to show off. He whom countless angels serve never deluded us. What did we have that he could need, when everything we have was created through him? Did he need to have praise from us who are first heavy with sleep, and then sated with lust, and then loaded with the guilt of riot and bloodshed, and then drunk from reveling—he whom Archangels, and Dominions, and Principalities, and Powers, without sleeping or stopping or sinning, praise in Heaven with everlasting and unwearied voice?

They praise him because he, the Image of the Invisible God, created all their host in himself, made the worlds, established the heavens, appointed the stars, fixed the earth, laid the foundations of the deep; because in a later time he was born, he conquered death, broke the gates of hell, won for himself a people to be his fellow-heirs, lifted flesh from corruption up to the glory of eternity.

There was nothing, then, that he might gain from us that could induce him to take on the splendor of these mysterious and inexplicable works, as though he needed our praise. But God foresaw how human sin and folly would be misled, and knew that disbelief would dare to pass its judgment even on the things of God, and therefore he vanquished presumption by tokens of his power that must give pause to our boldest.

−St. Hilary of Poitiers, *On the Holy Trinity*, 3.7

IN GOD'S PRESENCE, CONSIDER . . .

Christ does not need the prayers of human beings or angels, yet he calls us together to praise him. Do I take delight in the liturgical worship I share with the Church on Earth and the angels in Heaven?

CLOSING PRAYER

In the company of angels, I praise the Lord. I give thanks to the Lord with my whole heart in a congregation that is both earthly and heavenly.

To Christ through Christ

The truth is the way, says St. Augustine. The only way to Christ is through Christ. We eat the bread of angels because "the Word became flesh and dwelt among us."

If you are looking for truth, stick to the Way—for the truth *is* the Way. The truth is the destination to which you are going, and it is the Way by which you go. You are not going by one thing as your way to something else as your destination; you are not coming to Christ by something that is other than Christ. You are coming to Christ *through* Christ.

What does that mean, to Christ through Christ?

Through Christ the Man to Christ the God. Through the Word made flesh, to the Word that in the beginning was with God, and was God (John 1:1). From what human beings used to eat to the bread that angels eat every day. For this is what is written: he "gave them the grain of Heaven. Man ate of the bread of the angels" (Ps. 78:24-25).

In what sense did man eat of the bread of the angels? "And the Word became flesh and dwelt among us" (John 1:13).

St. Augustine, *Homily 13 on the Gospel of John*, 4

IN GOD'S PRESENCE, CONSIDER . . .

Do I always move from ordinary bread toward the bread of angels Do I start from faith as my point of departure?

CLOSING PRAYER

Lord Jesus Christ, feed me with the bread of angels, so that I may send up praise to you now and forever.

Even angels can't really see God

St. Augustine, quoting St. Jerome, tells us that we will never really know everything about God, because that is impossible for any creature. We'll be made equal to the angels, but even angels can't really see God's true nature.

St. Jerome says, "The human eye cannot see God as he is in his own nature. And this is not true only of human beings. Neither angels, nor Thrones, nor Powers, nor Principalities, nor anything we can name can see God, for no creature can see its Creator."

By these words this very learned man clearly shows what his opinion was on this subject in regard not only to the present life, but also to the life to come. However much the eyes of our body may be changed for the better, they will only be made equal to the eyes of the angels. Here, however, Jerome has told us that the nature of the Creator is invisible even to the angels, and to every creature without exception in Heaven.

But if a question should arise on this point, and someone should wonder whether we might not be superior to the angels, the mind of the Lord himself is plain from the words he uses in speaking of those who will rise again to the kingdom: "they are equal to angels" (Luke 20:36).

—St. Augustine, *Letter 148*

IN GOD'S PRESENCE, CONSIDER . . .

If the angels can never see God in his true nature, certainly we can't. But where would I look to get a good idea of what God looks like? How about at a homeless shelter? Or a nursing home?

CLOSING PRAYER

Remember, Lord, the poor, the widows, the orphans, and the needy who bear your image. Send your angels to guide them and minister to them in their troubles.

Angels confess their ignorance

Angels see the majesty of God, says St. Gregory the Great, but they cannot understand it. Like Job, we should be ready to admit that we can't debate on equal terms with God.

"God, whose wrath no man can resist, and under whom they stoop that bear up the world" (Job 9:13).

When it says "under whom they stoop that bear up the world," we may also understand the angelic powers. They "bear up the world" in that they perform the duties of governing the universe—as Paul tells us when he says, "Are they not all ministering spirits sent forth to serve, for the sake of those who are to obtain salvation?" (Heb. 1:14).

So when he says "God, whose wrath no man can resist, and under whom they stoop that bear up the world," it's as if he were seeing the humiliation of every created being, and said in fear and trembling, "Who among weak mortals resists your nod, before whose might even the angelic powers stoop?"

Or certainly, since we see nothing of things above us when we stoop, those subtlest spirits must have stood straight if they completely reached the power of God's majesty. But although, when they are lifted up, they do see the loftiness of the divine nature, yet not even the angelic powers manage to comprehend it; therefore "they stoop that bear up the world."

And since the righteous man, from his weakness, cannot understand the divine nature, he remembers who he is with careful humility, and makes himself small in his own eyes compared with the omnipotence of the Supreme Majesty, saying, "How then can I answer him, choosing my words with him?" (Job 9:14).

–St. Gregory the Great, *Moralia in Job*, 9.26

IN GOD'S PRESENCE, CONSIDER . . .

When things seem to go badly for me, am I tempted to second-guess God? Does it help to remember that even the righteous Job—even the angels themselves—could never really understand the divine nature?

CLOSING PRAYER

Guardian Angel, teach me to remember my ignorance, and ask forgiveness for the sins I do not know.

Even angels don't see the essence of God

Angels are spiritual beings that live in the presence of God. Yet even they never saw God until Christ was manifested in the flesh, says St. John Chrysostom. Created beings simply aren't capable of gazing on the Uncreated, but God loved us so much that he came to us in a way we could see and understand.

Since his Son was about to appear in the flesh, God had been preparing the prophets for a long time to see the substance of God, as far as it was possible for them to see it.

But not only have the prophets not seen what God really is, but not even angels or archangels. If you ask them, you won't hear them answer anything about his essence, but only singing, "Glory to God in the highest, and on earth peace among men with whom he is pleased" (Luke 2:14). If you want to learn something from the Cherubim or Seraphim, you'll hear the mystic song of his holiness, and that "Heaven and Earth are full of his glory" (Isa. 6:3). If you ask the higher powers, you'll find out that their only task is to praise God. "Praise him, all his angels, praise him, all his host!" says David (Ps. 148:2).

Only the Son and the Holy Ghost see him. How can any created nature even see the Uncreated? We can't even see any incorporeal spirit at all, even the created ones, as we've often proved with the angels. Then how could we discern the incorporeal and uncreated Essence?

This is why Paul says, "whom no man has ever seen or can see" (1 Tim. 6:16).

Furthermore, Paul shows that he is invisible not just to us, but also to the powers above: after he says, "He was manifested in the flesh," he adds that he was "seen by angels." So he became visible even to the angels when he put on the flesh, but before that time, they didn't see him that way, because even to them his essence was invisible.

—St. John Chrysostom, *Homily 15 on the Gospel of John*

IN GOD'S PRESENCE, CONSIDER . . .

Do I love the Lord's incarnation all the more because it is a gift to angels as well as to human beings?

CLOSING PRAYER

Holy Guardian Angel, let us look together on the glories of redemption. Let us praise God together. Let us thank god together. May we do this together through all eternity.

"Not even the angels in Heaven"

As Scripture tells us, not even the angels in Heaven know when Christ will come to Earth again. St. Augustine sees Psalm 10 as a description of the world ready for the return of Christ as King.

Now, after the hidden things of the Son, of which many things have been said in this Psalm, the end of the same Psalm will say a little about the *apparent* things of the Son. But the title is given from the hidden things, which take up the larger part of the Psalm.

Indeed, the very day of the Lord's coming may be rightly counted among the hidden things of the Son, although the very presence of the Lord itself will be apparent. For of that day it is said, "no one knows, not even the angels in Heaven, nor the Son" (Mark 13:32) What can be more hidden than what is said to be hidden even to the Judge himself—not as regards knowledge, but disclosure?

But concerning the hidden things of the Son, even if you prefer to take it not as the Son of God, but as David himself, to whose name the whole Psalter is attributed (for the Psalms, as we know, are called the Psalms of David), then listen to those words in which it is said to the Lord, "Have mercy on us, Son of David" (Matt. 20:30), and so even in this way understand the same Lord Christ, concerning whose hidden things is the inscription of this Psalm. For so likewise is it said by the angel: "the Lord God will give to him the throne of his father David" (Luke 1:32).

–St. Augustine, *Exposition on Psalm 10*, 15

IN GOD'S PRESENCE, CONSIDER . . .

Since not even the angels know the time, am I ready for the coming of Christ right now? What would it take to make me ready?

CLOSING PRAYER

Lord Jesus Christ, send me your angels to keep my soul pure, so that I may be ready for your glorious coming, when you will judge the living and the dead according to their works.

Angels speak to God in admiration

How do angels "speak" to God? Their love and admiration are clear speech, says St. Gregory the Great. When they contemplate God, they feel in themselves the emotions that Revelation expresses in words: "Worthy is the Lamb who was slain."

But the angels speak to God in a different way. For example, in the Revelation of John they say, "Worthy is the Lamb who was slain, to receive power and wealth and wisdom" (Rev. 5:12). The voice of the angels praising God is itself simply the admiration of inner contemplation.

To be speechless at the wonders of divine goodness is to speak with a voice. The emotion of the heart moved with a feeling of awe is a powerful voice when it speaks to the ears of a Spirit that has no limits. This voice seems to unfold itself in distinct words, while it shapes itself in the countless different ways of admiration.

So God speaks to angels when they perceive his inner will as it is revealed to them. But angels speak to the Lord when, by contemplating what is above them, they rise up to emotions of admiration.

–St. Gregory the Great, *Moralia in Job*, 2.8-9

IN GOD'S PRESENCE, CONSIDER . . .

When I contemplate the divine, what do my emotions speak in the ear of the Spirit? Is my speech a clear hymn of praise like the angels' or is it all mixed up with the cares of the day?

CLOSING PRAYER

Holy angels, who never cease praising, teach me to bring to the Lord a pure sacrifice of thanksgiving.

God speaks to angels in their contemplation

God doesn't really give verbal commands to the angels, says St. Gregory the Great. Instead, by contemplating God, which is their greatest delight, the angels understand what God wills them to do.

But, again, we need to understand that, even when an incorporeal nature is said to "speak," it does not always "speak" in the same way. There is one way in which God speaks to the angels, and another in which the angels speak to God. God speaks to the souls of the saints in one way, and the souls of the saints speak to God in another way. And God speaks to the devil in one way, and the devil speaks to God in another way.

Since there is no barrier in the way of a spiritual being, God speaks to the holy angels just by revealing his mysterious secrets to their hearts, so that, just by contemplating the truth, they read what they are supposed to do. The delights of contemplation are like a kind of vocal command to them. What is inspired in them when they contemplate is as if it were spoken to them, and they heard it.

–St. Gregory the Great, *Moralia in Job*, 2.8-9

Do I set aside some time just for contemplation, trying to hear God the way the angels hear him? Does it help me understand God's will for me?

Father, let me praise you, sing of you, bless you, worship you, glorify you, and give you thanks together with the many-eyed Cherubim and the six-winged Seraphim who surround your throne.

The inner speech of spiritual beings

When Scripture says that the Lord "speaks" to an angel, says St. Gregory the Great, we need to remember that angels don't have lungs and throats and all the organs of speech. These things belong to human beings, who are mixtures of mind and body.

We need to give this careful consideration: what it means to say that the Lord speaks to Satan, or Satan answers the Lord. We need to figure out what it means by "speaking."

Neither the Lord (who is the supreme and boundless Spirit) nor Satan (who does not have a fleshly nature) breathes in air with the lungs, like human beings, so that it should be forced back out through the throat in vocal sounds. When the incomprehensible Nature "speaks" to an invisible nature, our imagination needs to rise above the properties of our own bodily speech and be lifted up to the sublime and unknown ways of inner speech.

When we need to express something that we know inwardly, we do so through the vocal cords, by the sounds of the voice, because, as far as others can see, we stand in the secret dwelling place of the mind behind the body as if it were a sort of curtain. When we want to make ourselves known, we go out through the door of the tongue, so to speak, to show what kind of people we are inside.

But that is not true of a spiritual nature, which is not a binary mixture of mind and body.

–St. Gregory the Great, *Moralia in Job*, 2.8

IN GOD'S PRESENCE, CONSIDER . . .

When I speak, what kind of person do I reveal standing behind the curtain? Do the people who hear me see an angel or a devil?

CLOSING PRAYER

Guardian Angel, be with me whenever I speak, so that I may call on the Lord with a pure heart and with sanctified lips.

When did God make angels?

St. Augustine notes that Bible scholars don't agree on what it meant when God said, "Let there be light." The sun, moon, and stars were made later. Was this first "light" the spirits of the angels? We can't know with certainty. But we can know that it was created, and God was the Creator.

So, when darkness was over the deep, he who was Light said, "Let there be light."

From what Light this light came is clear; for the words are, "God said." But it is not so clear exactly what light was made. There has been a friendly discussion among students of the sacred Scriptures about whether this was when God made the light in the minds of the angels—or, in other words, these rational spirits themselves—or whether it was some material light that exists in the higher regions of the universe beyond our knowledge. It was on the fourth day that he made the visible luminaries of heaven. And it is also a question whether these bodies were made at the same time as their light, or were somehow kindled from the light made already.

But whoever reads the sacred writings in the pious spirit that is required to understand them must be convinced that, whatever the light was that was made when, at the time when darkness was over the deep, God said, "Let there be light," it was *created* light, and the creating Light was the maker of it.

–St. Augustine, *Reply to Faustus the Manichean*, 10

IN GOD'S PRESENCE, CONSIDER . . .

When I read Scripture, is it in a pious spirit? Do I have the faith to accept that there will always be some things—like the creation of angels—that I can't completely understand?

CLOSING PRAYER

Guardian Angel, be with me as I contemplate the Scriptures, and lead me away from the temptation to judge what I cannot understand.

The mystery of the Seraphim

St. Ephrem the Syrian poetically describes the mysteries of divine things. Even the six wings of the Seraphim is an idea too high and too deep for us to search out.

In the beginning God created all things, and his Thought was with him without any beginning. He did not think as a human thinks; he was not moved in any new way, as a child of flesh is moved. His movement was not new, nor was his thought fresh. But his knowledge comes before times and transcends beginnings.

The natures of the Seraphim are concealed from us, so that we must ask how an angel has six wings, and what its wings are, and where they are, and how a spirit needs to fly by means of wings.

Is this a parable, or is it plain truth? If it is truth, it is a very hidden one. If it is a metaphor, it is a very perplexing one.

That infinite hidden Being, then, is withdrawn from us, and searching into him is too deep for feeble men, and seeking after him too high for mortals. Who shall fly up to his height, or search out his depths?

—St. Ephrem the Syrian, *Rhythm 26*

When Scripture is too deep or hard for me to understand, where do I look for guidance? Have I asked the angels themselves for their help in understanding them?

CLOSING PRAYER

Guardian Angel, be my guide as I contemplate the mysteries of Scripture, and help me have patience when I cannot understand everything at once.

The saints will take the place of the fallen angels

When Satan and his followers were cast out of Heaven, it reduced the number of angels. The saints, says St. Augustine, will replace the angels who were lost, so that Heaven will have its full number of citizens, and maybe—in God's generosity—even more.

Some of the angels, in their wicked pride, deserted God, and were thrown out of the brightness of their heavenly home into the lowest darkness. But the remaining angels stayed in eternal bliss and holiness with God.

These faithful angels were not all descended from one single angel, fallen and condemned. The original evil thus did not bind them all in the shackles of inherited guilt, and it did not turn the whole group over to just punishment, the way it happened with humans. Instead, when the one who became the devil first rebelled with his wicked company and was then defeated, the rest of the angels stayed obedient to the Lord. So they received what the others had not had: a certain knowledge of their everlasting security in God's unfailing steadfastness.

Since not all the angels had perished in this desertion of God, it pleased God that those who had perished would remain lost forever, but those who had stayed loyal in the revolt would go on rejoicing in the certain knowledge that they would have eternal bliss.

The other part of the rational creation, mankind, had completely perished through its own sins, both original and personal, and the punishments for them. But God decided that a part of mankind would be restored, and would make up the loss that the disaster of the devil had made in the society of the angels. For this is the promise to the saints: at the resurrection, they will be equal to the angels of God (Wis. 11:20).

Thus the heavenly Jerusalem, our mother and the commonwealth of God, will not be cheated of her full number of citizens. Instead, she may end up ruling over an even larger number.

—St. Augustine, *Enchiridion*, 28-29

IN GOD'S PRESENCE, CONSIDER . . .

Right now, am I making myself ready to take my place among the angels? Will I be fit for citizenship in the heavenly Jerusalem?

CLOSING PRAYER

Lord, make me ready to praise you in the new Jerusalem, with the heavenly assembly and the church of the first-born that are written in Heaven; spirits of the just and of prophets; souls of martyrs and of apostles; Angels, Archangels, Thrones, Dominions, Principalities, Authorities, and dread Powers.

Light and darkness

Genesis 1:4 says that "God separated the light from the darkness"; St. Augustine suggests that it refers to the separation of the good angels from the evil angels. But even if that's not what the original author intended, he says, describing the one group as "light" and the other as "darkness" is still accurate.

"God opposes the proud, but gives grace to the humble" (James 4:6). One group lives in the Heaven of heavens; the other is thrown out of there, and rages through the lower regions of the air. One is tranquil in the brightness of piety, the other tempest-tossed with desires that cloud the way. One, at God's pleasure, tenderly helps and justly avenges; the other, attacked by its own pride, boils with the lust of conquering and hurting. One is the minister of God's goodness to the utmost of their good pleasure; the other is kept back by God's power from doing the harm it wants to do. The first laughs at the second when it does good unwillingly by its persecutions; the second envies the first when it gathers in its pilgrims.

These two angelic communities, then, are different from and contrary to one another, the one both by nature good and by will upright, the other also good by nature but by will depraved. We see them thus in other and more explicit passages of holy writ, but I think they are spoken of in this book of Genesis under the names of *light* and *darkness*.

And even if the author might have had a different meaning, yet our discussion has not been wasted time; for, though we have not been able to discover his meaning, yet we have stuck to the rule of faith, which the faithful gather well enough from other passages of equal authority. For, though it is the material works of God that are spoken of here, they have certainly a resemblance to the spiritual, so that Paul can say, "For you are all sons of light and sons of the day; we are not of the night or of darkness" (1 Thess. 5:5).

–St. Augustine, *City of God*, 11.33

IN GOD'S PRESENCE, CONSIDER . . .

In St. Augustine's description, which most resembles my own inner life: the life of the fallen angels, or the life of the holy angels?

CLOSING PRAYER

Holy angels, humble angels, may I desire what you desire—to serve—that I may be found in the city of God at the fulfillment of history.

The right and left hands of God

The heavenly host stands at the right and left hands of God. One side is the good angels, says St. Gregory the Great, and one side is the evil angels. Both serve God, though the evil ones are working for their own evil purposes.

"I saw the Lord sitting on his throne, and all the host of Heaven standing beside him on his right hand and on his left" (1 Kings 22:19).

What is the "throne" of the Lord, unless we understand it as the angelic powers? He is enthroned on high in their minds, and thus he controls everything below.

What is "the host of Heaven," unless it means the many ministering angels?

Then why does it say that the host of Heaven stands "on his right hand and on his left"? Since God exists in everything, and is also outside everything, he is not limited by right and left hands.

But the right hand of God is the elect part of the angels, and the left hand of God means the fallen part of the angels. Not just the good serve God by the help they give us, but the wicked also serve him by the trials they inflict on us—not just the ones who lift up anyone who turns back from sin, but also the wicked who push down anyone who refuses to turn back.

So the angelic host stands on the right hand and on the left hand of God: the will of the elect spirits harmonizes with the divine mercy, and the minds of the fallen ones, when they serve their own evil ends, obey the judgment of God's stern decrees.

–St. Gregory the Great, *Moralia in Job*, 2.38

IN GOD'S PRESENCE, CONSIDER . . .

Do I work in harmony with the Divine Mercy, as the holy angels do? Or does God have to work his will in spite of me, as he does with the fallen angels?

CLOSING PRAYER

Holy angels, teach me to serve God in everything with my own will, as you do, so that at last I may join you in praising God eternally in Heaven.

Day and night

St. Gregory the Great sees an image of Satan in the "day" and "night" that Job curses. Satan is a false day, promising us the light but actually leading us into the darkness of death.

"Let the day perish wherein I was born, and the night which said, 'A man-child is conceived'" (Job 3:3).

Satan presents himself as the "day," in that he seduces us with prosperity. And his end is in the darkness of the "night," because he leads us to adversity. Thus he showed us day when he said, "in what day soever you shall eat thereof, your eyes shall be opened: and you shall be as Gods" (Gen. 3:5). And he brought on the night when he led us to the darkness of mortality.

The day, then, is the promise he gives us of better things, but the night is the experience of evils that actually presents itself. The old enemy is the day, because he was created good by nature; but he is the night, because he is sunk deep down into darkness by his own fault. He is day when he disguises himself as an angel of light in our eyes by promising good things—as Paul confirms, saying, "for even Satan disguises himself as an angel of light" (2 Cor. 11:14). But he is night when he clouds the minds of those who allow him with the darkness of error.

—St. Gregory the Great, *Moralia in Job*, 4.6

IN GOD'S PRESENCE, CONSIDER . . .

How easily am I led astray by Satan's promises of prosperity? Do I let the lure of easy money tempt me into doing things my conscience doesn't like?

CLOSING PRAYER

Father, your angels praise you by day and night without ceasing. Teach me to do the same, with voice, lips, and heart.

God was in charge of creation

Some heretics have believed that the devil and his angels created the world against the wishes of the good God. St. Irenaeus says they're suggesting that God is less competent than a good foreman at a construction site.

Now, some say that the world was formed by angels, or by some other maker of it, against the will of the supreme Father. But they're wrong, first of all, in this main point: when they say that angels formed such a great and mighty creation, against the will of God Most High.

That would imply that the angels were more powerful than God—or, if not, then that God was careless, or inferior, or paid no attention to those things that were happening in his own possessions. It implies that he didn't care whether they turned out well or badly, so that he could prevent them from turning out badly, and praise and rejoice over their turning out well.

We wouldn't even expect a man who was at all competent to act that way. We certainly couldn't expect it from God!

–St. Irenaeus, *Against Heresies*, 2.2

IN GOD'S PRESENCE, CONSIDER . . .

If God made creation the way he wanted it, how does what I do with my own free will correspond to God's plan for the world? Do I remember to ask for angelic help in knowing and following God's will?

CLOSING PRAYER

O Lord, together with the Seraphim and Cherubim and all the hosts of Heaven, I praise you for the glories of creation.

Reason tells us God is our Ruler

Against heretics who claimed that angels or a sub-divine creator made the universe without knowing about the Supreme God, St. Irenaeus says that no intelligent being can be so ignorant. All beings with reason know that there is a God, and that he is our Ruler.

And how could either the angels or the supposed creator of the world have been ignorant of the Supreme God? They were his property, and his creatures, and were contained by him.

It's true that he might have been invisible to them because of his superiority, but because of his providence he certainly could not have been unknown to them. Even though it is true, as they say, that their inferiority kept them very far separated from him, yet it was fitting for them to know their Ruler, since his dominion extended over them. And they especially had to be aware of this: that he who created them is Lord of all. Since his invisible essence is mighty, it gives every creature a profound mental intuition and perception of his powerful—in fact omnipotent—greatness.

Therefore, although "no one knows the Son except the Father, and no one knows the Father except the Son and any one to whom the Son chooses to reveal him" (Matt. 11:27), still all beings do know at least this one fact, because reason has been implanted in their minds, and it moves them and reveals to them that there is one God, the Lord of all.

—St. Irenaeus, *Against Heresies*, 2.2

IN GOD'S PRESENCE, CONSIDER . . .

Like the angels, I have the gift of reason that tells me there is a God. Do I use my reason as they do, to understand God's will and to serve him?

CLOSING PRAYER

Holy angels, you were never ignorant of the Supreme God, and you chose to serve. Strengthen me in my resolve, so that I may serve God eternally with you.

Why didn't God prevent evil?

Couldn't God have made creation so that evil never happened? Yes, he could have, says St. Justin Martyr. But God knew that creation would be better if both we and the angels had free will.

Couldn't God have cut off the serpent in the beginning, so that he never existed, rather than saying, "I will put enmity between you and the woman, and between your seed and her seed" (Gen. 3:15)? Couldn't he have created a multitude of people all at once?

But since God knew that it would be good, he created both angels and human beings free to do what is righteous, and he set periods of time during which he knew it would be good for them to be able to exercise their free will. And because he also knew it would be good, he made general and particular judgments. But each one's freedom of will was limited.

Thus Scripture says this when the tower was destroyed and the languages were divided and altered: "Behold, they are one people, and they have all one language; and this is only the beginning of what they will do; and nothing that they propose to do will now be impossible for them" (Gen. 11:6).

—St. Justin Martyr, *Dialogue with Trypho*, 102

IN GOD'S PRESENCE, CONSIDER . . .

Do I tend to second-guess God, asking why he allowed Satan to fall and Adam and Eve to sin? Wouldn't it help if I remembered that these things are a consequence of the divine gift of free will that God gave not only to the angels but to me as well?

CLOSING PRAYER

Guardian Angel, God made us both with free will. Help me always to choose the right path, as you do, so that in the end we may both adore our Creator in Heaven.

The devil has free will—and so have we

God made Satan good, says St. John of Damascus. He fell into evil by his own free choice, not because of the nature God gave him. And we also have free will. The devil can attack us with temptations, but he never has the power to overwhelm us unless we give it to him.

Out of those angelic powers, the one who was set over the earthly realm to guard the earth was not made wicked by nature. He was made good, and for good purposes, and his Creator put no trace of evil in him. But he did not keep up the brightness and honor the Creator had given him, and—by his free choice—was changed from being in harmony with his own nature to going against it. Thus he became angry with God and decided to rebel against him. He was the first to leave the good and become evil...but along with him went an innumerable host of angels under him, who followed him and shared his fall. They were of the same nature as the angels, but they became wicked, turning away from good to evil by their own free choice.

Thus they have no power or strength against anyone except when God, as part of his plan, allows it—as he did against Job (Job 1:12) and the pigs mentioned in the Gospels (Mark 5:13). When God allows it, they have their way, and they can change into any form they like.

So all wickedness and all impure passions are their work. But while they have been given the liberty to attack us, they do not have the strength to overcome anyone. We have it in our power to receive the attack or not. That is why unquenchable fire and everlasting punishment have been prepared for the devil and his demons and all who follow them.

We should also remember that the fall is to the angels what death is to us: there is no possibility of repentance for them after the fall, just as there is no repentance for us after death.

—St. John of Damascus, *Exposition of the Orthodox Faith*, 2.4

IN GOD'S PRESENCE, CONSIDER . . .

If the devil and his demons are constantly attacking me, am I choosing to resist or to succumb? What choices have I made just today that were victories for the demonic powers?

CLOSING PRAYER

Lord, deliver me from every temptation of the devil, and send your Spirit to guide my will.

God gave us and the angels free will

St. Justin Martyr says that God gave us and the angels free will so that we could choose righteousness. God, who is omniscient, knows ahead of time that some of his creatures will choose evil, but that does not mean he created them for evil. Their own wills have acted freely in choosing it.

God wanted human beings and angels to follow his will. So he resolved to create them free to do what was righteous. He gave them reason, so that they could know by whom they were created, and through whom they exist, when they did not exist before. He gave them a law that they would be judged by him if they did anything contrary to right reason. And by ourselves we—both human beings and angels—will be convicted of having acted sinfully unless we repent beforehand.

But if the word of God foretells that some angels and human beings will certainly be punished, it does so because it knew beforehand that they would not change their wickedness. But that isn't because God created them that way.

–St. Justin Martyr, *Dialogue with Trypho*, 141

In the decisions I've made today, have I followed the loyal angels in choosing God's way? Where did I fail in my loyalty, and how can I repair the damage?

Father, you created me with the same free will you gave to the angels, and you have shown me the way to salvation: send your Spirit to me so that I may be worthy of your service.

When angels speak, God speaks

When one of God's messengers speaks, says St. Augustine, the words come from God himself. Angels do not announce anything but what God wills them to announce.

When the clerk proclaims the words of the judge, it is not usually written in the record, "The clerk said this and this," but "The judge said this and this." When Abraham's son was ordered to be sacrificed, this is what we read: "After these things God tested Abraham, and said to him, 'Abraham!' And he said, 'Here am I.'

He said, 'Take your son, your only son Isaac, whom you love, and go to the land of Mori'ah, and offer him there as a burnt offering upon one of the mountains of which I shall tell you.' " Certainly it mentions God here, not an angel. But a little while later the Scripture has it this way:

"Then Abraham put forth his hand, and took the knife to slay his son.

But the angel of the Lord called to him from Heaven, and said, 'Abraham, Abraham!'

And he said, 'Here am I.'

He said, 'Do not lay your hand on the lad or do anything to him.' " (Gen. 22:1-12) What can anyone answer to this? Will they say that God commanded that Isaac should be killed, but an angel prohibited it? Will they even say that the father himself, against the decree of God, who had commanded that his son should be killed, obeyed the angel who said to spare him? We must reject such an interpretation as absurd. And low and unsophisticated as it is, Scripture does not leave any room for it: it immediately adds, "for now I know that you fear God, seeing you have not withheld your son, your only son, from me." And what does "from me" mean, except from God who commanded Isaac to be killed?

—St. Augustine, *On the Trinity*, 3.2

IN GOD'S PRESENCE, CONSIDER . . .

Do I listen obediently to God when he speaks through his messengers—Scripture and the Church?

CLOSING PRAYER

Father, teach me to obey your word the way the angels obey.

Imitate Abraham's hospitality

St. John Chrysostom tells his flock to look actively for opportunities to help strangers or foreigners in need—not only for the benefit of the strangers, but even more for their own benefit. By seeking out strangers, Abraham entertained angels.

The patriarch didn't know that he was entertaining angels, but he entertained them. We should be ashamed of ourselves! There he was sitting at midday in a foreign land, where he had no property, not so much as to set his foot on. He was a stranger. And as a stranger, he entertained strangers—for he was a citizen of Heaven. For that reason he wasn't really a stranger to God, even when he was on earth. We're more strangers than he was if we don't welcome strangers. He had no home, but his tent was a place of hospitality. Look how generous he is: he killed a calf, and kneaded fine flour. Look how quick-minded he is—both he and his wife. See his unassuming manner: he shows them respect and pleads with them. Anyone who entertains strangers should have these qualities: readiness, cheerfulness, generosity. For the soul of the stranger is embarrassed, and feels ashamed. Unless his host shows excessive joy, he feels slighted and goes away. That's worse than not having welcomed him at all!

"But we're not in a foreign land," you say. But we can still imitate him if we want to. How many Christians are strangers? There is a common apartment, the Church, which is the house of strangers. Be inquisitive. Sit in front of the doors, and welcome those who come yourselves. If you don't want to take them into your houses, at least give them what they need.

"Doesn't the Church have what it takes to do that?" you ask. Yes—but what good does that do you? Can it benefit you if strangers are fed from the Church's funds? If someone else prays, does that mean you don't have to pray? Why don't you just go ahead and say, "Don't the priests pray? Then why should I pray?"

–St. John Chrysostom, *Homily 45 on Acts*

IN GOD'S PRESENCE, CONSIDER . . .

What opportunities have I missed lately to help strangers or visitors in need? How would I have changed my behavior if I had remembered the story of Abraham and the strangers?

CLOSING PRAYER

Lord, I beseech the protection of your angels for all the strangers in our midst.

Entertaining angels

"Some have entertained angels unawares": the only way to do that, says St. John Chrysostom, is to show hospitality to the poor and insignificant. In entertaining them, we may entertain angels, and we certainly entertain Christ himself.

It is worthwhile to ask this here: Why did the rich man see Lazarus, not in company with any other of the just, but in the bosom of Abraham?

Abraham was hospitable; the rich man saw Lazarus there as a rebuke to his own inhospitality. Abraham used to lie in wait for those who passed by, and constrain them to come into his dwelling; but this rich man neglected even one that lay within his very porch. He had such a treasure—such an opportunity of salvation—but he overlooked it each day, and didn't show kindness to the poor man. He wouldn't even give him the necessaries of life.

But the patriarch was not like this. He was the very opposite. Sitting at the tent door he captured, so to speak, all those that passed by. A fisherman casting his net into the sea draws up fish, and perhaps also sometimes draws up gold or pearls. In the same way he, a fisher of men, once entertained even angels—and there was this wonderful circumstance, that he did so without knowing it.

St. Paul, with much admiration, insists on the very same thing: "Do not neglect to show hospitality to strangers, for thereby some have entertained angels unawares" (Heb. 13:2). And well does he say "unawares." For if they had knowingly received them with such goodwill, they would have done no great or wonderful thing: all the praise depends on the fact that, not knowing who they were that passed by, and supposing them to be simply wayfaring men, they invited them to enter so quickly.

Christ, too, speaking of those who acted this way, said, "as you did it to one of the least of these my brethren, you did it to me" (Matt. 25:40).

–St. John Chrysostom, *Four Discourses, Chiefly on the Parable of the Rich Man and Lazarus*, Discourse 2, chapter 5

IN GOD'S PRESENCE, CONSIDER . . .

How could I be more hospitable to the poor, the way Abraham was hospitable to the angels? Do I listen when the angels point out someone in need?

CLOSING PRAYER

Guardian Angel, help me to notice and remember all the poor among God's creatures.

Make your house Christ's hotel

Abraham, says St. John Chrysostom, didn't know he was receiving Christ and the angels—he just welcomed three strangers. But we do know that every time we welcome strangers, we're welcoming Christ. What's our excuse for not welcoming them?

Abraham welcomed the strangers into his own home. His wife acted as a servant—and treated the guests as the masters.

He didn't know he was receiving Christ. He didn't know he was receiving angels. If he had known, he would have lavished everything he had on them. But we *know* that we're receiving Christ—and yet we don't even show as much zeal as he did when he thought he was receiving ordinary men!

"But many of them are ungrateful fakes," you say. Well, so much the greater is your reward when you welcome them for the sake of Christ's name! If you really do know that they're fakes, then don't welcome them into your house. But if you don't know for sure, how can you accuse them so lightly?

"That's why I tell them to go to the shelter," you say. But what kind of excuse do we have when we don't even receive the ones we know, but slam the door in everyone's face?

Our house should be Christ's general guest-house. For our reward we should ask, not money, but that they make our house a welcoming place for Christ. We should run all over the place and drag them in! We should seize our prizes! The benefits we receive are greater than what we give.

–St. John Chrysostom, Homily 45 on Acts

IN GOD'S PRESENCE, CONSIDER . . .

If I wanted to go out and find an angel in disguise to welcome, where would I go?

CLOSING PRAYER

Let your angels protect everyone who travels, Lord and grant them all a safe journey and a peaceful return.

How to treat your guests

St. Cyril of Alexandria has some advice for those who might entertain wandering monks, or any other stranger who comes by. Don't try to impress them with a magnificent feast: be grateful to them for coming, and give them just as much as they need to take care of their hunger.

But if you do open your house to them, meet them cheerfully, and quickly, and as their equals—and not so much as if you were giving something to them, but as if you were receiving something from them—as if you were gaining and not spending. And the more so because you profit doubly. In the first place, you enjoy the instruction of those whom you hospitably entertain. Secondly, you also win the reward of hospitality. Either way, you profit.

But when you receive the brethren into your house, do not be distracted with much service. Do not seek anything beyond your means, or more than enough. For everywhere and in everything excess is harmful. Often it produces hesitation in those who otherwise would be glad to receive strangers, and causes but few houses to be found fit for the purpose—while it proves a cause of annoyance to those who are entertained.

But when holy men are assembled at the house of one who fears God, let the table be plain and temperate, the food simple and free from superfluities. In everything, a small supply of such necessaries as will take care of the bodily appetite with simple fare.

This is how to receive strangers. In this way, Abraham by the oak at Mamre received those three men, and won as the reward of his carefulness the promise of his beloved son Isaac. In the same way Lot in Sodom honored the angels, and for doing so was not destroyed by fire with the rest, and did not become the prey of the inextinguishable flame.

—St. Cyril of Alexandria, *Commentary on Luke*, Sermon 59

IN GOD'S PRESENCE, CONSIDER . . .

Am I more concerned to impress *people* than I am to impress the angels? Do my efforts really impress people anyway?

CLOSING PRAYER

Guardian Angel, make me attentive to others, so that I may never fail in the duty of hospitality.

The strange case of Sodom

The unnatural lust of the Sodomites, says St. Ephrem the Syrian, was only possible because they thought the angels were human. What can we say about someone who knows that God is God, yet treats God as if he were a creature?

With brightness, glorious though borrowed, the angels entered into Sodom. They saw the brightness that was fairer than all, and they were frantic, old men and young. The fire of the Most High came down to aid the sons of the Most High—not so that it might deliver the holy, but so that it might burn up the proud ones.

The high ones changed their appearance, and that is why those below were bold. If the spiritual beings had shown their light, the fleshly beings would have been prostrated. They thought the angels, a spiritual nature, were of their own nature, and that is why they lusted, though they did not change their nature. Lust lusted after those of its own race in a way that was contrary to nature; it would not have lusted after the high ones, who were foreign to its nature. Lust lusted after the high ones, because they had taken the form of those below. It was against nature, and yet it was in nature, because lust lusted for what was its own.

Whoever pries into God is mad beyond all nature. You confess his Essence, but you pry into him as if he were a creature? If you call him God, there is no room for prying. Faith is the medium that must go between you and God.

−St. Ephrem the Syrian, *Rhythm 3 on the Faith*

IN GOD'S PRESENCE, CONSIDER . . .

Even the angels are beyond my understanding without faith. Is faith always the medium in my relationship with God?

CLOSING PRAYER

Guardian Angel, always be with me to check my pride, and to remind me that humble faith is always the proper approach to God.

Anointing the stone

When Jacob had his vision of the angels on the ladder, he anointed the stone at his head. Why? Because, says St. Augustine, the stone is a figurative representation of Christ, which means "anointed."

So the Lord goes on to say, "Because I said to you, I saw you under the fig tree, do you believe? You shall see greater things than these." What greater things does he mean? "And he said to him, 'Truly, truly, I say to you, you will see Heaven opened, and the angels of God ascending and descending upon the Son of man'" (John 1:50-51).

Brethren, there is something greater in what I have just said than just in those words, "I saw you under the fig tree." It is more important that the Lord justified us when we were called than that he saw us lying under the shadow of death. Would we have been any better off if we had remained where he saw us? Wouldn't we still by lying there?

What greater thing is this? When have we seen angels ascending and descending upon the Son of Man?

In a dream, Jacob saw a ladder, and on the ladder angels ascending and descending. He *anointed* the stone he had placed at his head (Gen. 28:12-18).

Now, you know that *Messiah* and *Christ* mean the same thing, and *Christ* and *Anointed* mean the same thing. Jacob did not place the stone he had anointed so that he could come and adore it—that would have been idolatry, not a figurative representation of Christ. But what he did *was* a figurative representation—as far as it was appropriate to make such a representation. And the thing represented was Christ. The stone was anointed, but not as an idol.

Why was it anointed, then? Because it was *Christ*, from *Chrisma*, which means *anointing.*

–St. Augustine, *Homily 7 on John*, 22-23

IN GOD'S PRESENCE, CONSIDER . . .

St. Augustine sees a connection between Jacob's vision of the angels and what Christ said to Nathanael. When I read the Old Testament Scriptures, am I careful to look for the ways in which the New Testament lies hidden there?

CLOSING PRAYER

Angels who constantly ascend and descend, always point my way to Christ, the Son of God.

Sleep with your head on a stone

Jacob lay with his head on a stone, says St. Gregory the Great—and he saw angels (Gen. 28:11-22). The stone is Christ, and if we keep Christ in our thoughts, we will know wonderful truths even in our sleep.

We certainly should observe here that someone who lays his head on a stone is someone who sees angels in his sleep. Surely it is because whoever tries to imitate our Redeemer with all his mind—which is our ruling principle—penetrates inner truths by resting from outer works. To lay your head on a stone is to stick to Christ in your mind.

On the other hand, some may withdraw from the business of this world, but have no love to carry them upward. They may sleep, but they never can see the angels, because they scorn to keep their heads on a stone. There are some who run away from the business of this world, but never exercise any of the virtues. These people sleep because they're groggy, but not from any serious intention. They never see those inner truths, because they lay their heads on the earth, not on a stone. And it often happens to them that, the more they rest from outward actions, the more they gather from their idleness a plentiful cacophony of impure thoughts.

–St. Gregory the Great, *Moralia in Job*, 5.55

IN GOD'S PRESENCE, CONSIDER . . .

What is the last thing in my thoughts before I drift off to sleep? Is my mind fit for visions of angels?

CLOSING PRAYER

Guardian Angel, be with me all through the night, and guide my inmost thoughts, so that the Lord may grant me rest and peace all the days of this life.

Christ at Jacob's head

When Jacob saw his vision of angels on a ladder to Heaven, he was resting his head on a stone. That stone, says St. Augustine, is symbolically Christ.

The patriarch Jacob had placed a stone at his head: sleeping with that stone at his head, he saw Heaven opened, and a ladder from Heaven to Earth, and angels ascending and descending; after this vision he awoke, anointed the stone, and departed (Gen. 28:11-18).

In that stone he understood Christ; for that reason he anointed it. Notice how Christ is preached here. What is the meaning of that anointing of a stone, especially in the case of the patriarchs who worshiped only one God? It was done as a figurative act—and then he departed. He did not anoint the stone, and come to worship there constantly, and to perform sacrifice there. It was the expression of a mystery; not the beginning of sacrilege.

And notice the meaning of the stone. "The stone which the builders rejected has become the head of the corner" (Ps. 118:22; see Matt. 21:42). Notice here a great mystery. The stone is Christ. Peter calls him "that living stone, rejected by men but in God's sight chosen and precious" (1 Pet. 2:4). And the stone is set at the head, because Christ is the Head of the man (1 Cor. 11:3). And the stone was anointed, because Christ was called "Christ" from his being anointed.

—St. Augustine, *Exposition on Ps. 45*, 18

IN GOD'S PRESENCE, CONSIDER . . .

Do I always place Christ at my head when I rest? What visions come to me when I go to bed? Are they visions of angels, or are they supplied by the competition?

CLOSING PRAYER

Lord, let me rest my head on you, and may my visions always be of the angels of Heaven.

Angels ascending and descending

In Jacob's ladder, with angels ascending and descending, St. Augustine sees an image of the good preacher, who goes up to learn the most exalted truths, and comes down to bring them to the simplest followers of Christ.

What did Jacob see on the ladder? Angels ascending and descending.

This, brethren, is what the Church is like. The angels of God are good preachers, preaching Christ. This is what it means when it says they ascend and descend upon the Son of Man (John 1:51).

How do they ascend and descend? We have an example in one of them. Hear the Apostle Paul, and when we find it in him, let us also believe it of the other preachers of the truth.

Here is Paul ascending: "I know a man in Christ who fourteen years ago was caught up to the third heaven—whether in the body or out of the body I do not know, God knows. And I know that this man was caught up into Paradise—whether in the body or out of the body I do not know, God knows—and he heard things that cannot be told, which man may not utter" (2 Cor. 12:2-4).

You have heard him ascending. Now hear him descending: "But I, brethren, could not address you as spiritual men, but as men of the flesh, as babes in Christ. I fed you with milk, not solid food" (1 Cor. 3:1-2).

You see? He ascended, and now he descends. Where did he ascend? To the third heaven! Where did he descend? To giving milk to babes!

–St. Augustine, *Homily 7 on John*, 23

IN GOD'S PRESENCE, CONSIDER . . .

Do I give the homily my full attention at Mass, so that the one who preaches—God's "angel" or messenger—has a chance to lead me up toward Heaven?

CLOSING PRAYER

Guardian angels of all priests and teachers, keep them always mindful of their mission to descend to our understanding and ascend with us to heavenly things.

Christ above and below

Christ, says St. Augustine, is both above in Heaven and below in us. If our eyes were opened, we could see the angels constantly ascending and descending.

He who could do such great things was hungry and thirsty, was wearied, slept, was apprehended, beaten, crucified, slain.

This is the way: walk in humility, that you may come to eternity. Christ as God is the country we want to go to; Christ the man is the Way by which we go. To him we go, by him we go; why should we worry about losing the way? He did not leave the Father; and came to us. He sucked the breasts, and he contained the world. He lay in the manger, and he fed the angels.

Therefore, from now on, having now suffered in this humiliation, died, and been buried, he has now risen again, and ascended into Heaven. There he is, sitting at the right hand of the Father; and here he is needy in his poor.

Yesterday too I brought this up in the context of what he said to Nathanael, "You shall see greater things than these. Truly, truly, I say to you, you will see Heaven opened, and the angels of God ascending and descending upon the Son of man" (John 1:50-51). He would not say, "ascending upon the Son of man," unless he were above; he would not say, "descending upon the Son of man," unless he were also below. He is at once above and below: above in himself, below in those who are his; above with the Father, below in us.

—St. Augustine, *Sermon 73 on the New Testament*, 3-4

IN GOD'S PRESENCE, CONSIDER . . .

Angels, says St. Augustine, are constantly going between the body of Christ on earth and the Head in Heaven. When the angels come to me, what kind of member do they find me? Am I doing my part in the Body?

CLOSING PRAYER

Lord, you were pleased to make my weakness a spiritual member in the great body of your Holy Church. Send your angels down to me to guide me to eternity with your Son.

Sleep humbly and dream of angels

*Jacob had a stone for his pillow when he had his vision of the heavenly ladder,
St. John Chrysostom reminds us. How can we expect to see visions of angels
when we sleep in luxuries, and deny even the necessities of life to the poor?*

Shall I show you another bed? I mean that of Jacob. He lay on the ground, and a stone was under his head. Therefore also, he saw the symbolical stone, and that ladder on which angels were ascending and descending.

We should have that kind of bed, so that we may see such visions. If we lie on silver, we not only gain no pleasure, but also endure trouble. For whenever you remember that in the severest cold in the middle of the night, while you're sleeping on your couch, the poor man lying on chaff in the porticoes of the baths, covered with straw, is trembling, numb with cold, and fainting with hunger, even if you really had a heart of stone, be assured that you'll condemn yourself for being content that, while you luxuriate in excess, he can't even enjoy the necessaries of life.

"No soldier on service gets entangled in civilian pursuits," says the Apostle (2 Tim. 2:4). You're a spiritual soldier. But such a soldier doesn't sleep on an ivory bed, but on the ground. He doesn't use scented oils—that's the habit of sensual and dissolute people, of those who live on the stage, or in indolence. It's not the smell of ointment that you should have, but the smell of virtue. The soul is no purer when the body is scented. In fact, this fragrance of the body and clothes may even be a sign of inward corruption and uncleanness. For when Satan makes his approaches to corrupt the soul and fill it with all indolence, then he also uses ointments to stamp on the body the stains that mark its inner defilement.

For nothing—nothing is worse than luxury.

–St. John Chrysostom, *Four Discourses, Chiefly on the Parable
of the Rich Man and Lazarus*, Discourse 1, chapter 8

IN GOD'S PRESENCE, CONSIDER . . .

What luxuries could I give up so that I might live a more angelic life?

CLOSING PRAYER

*Guardian Angel, always keep the poor, the needy, the widows, the foreigners, and the
orphans before my eyes and in my mind, so that I may serve them, and serve Christ in them.*

Angels come to the virtuous

St. Ambrose recalls the story of Samson's birth in Judges 13 and rejects one writer's interpretation that would make Samson's father merely a jealous husband. Angels would not come to him, says St. Ambrose, if he were full of sinful thoughts.

By this time the spirit of the Hebrews had been so subdued by long oppression that no one dared to rouse them to liberty with a manly spirit. But then Samson, foreordained by the divine oracle, was raised up for them.

His father was of the tribe of Dan, a man fearing God, born of no mean rank, and eminent above others. His mother was barren of body, but certainly not in virtues of the mind—seeing that in the sanctuary of her soul she was counted worthy to receive the visit of an angel, and that she obeyed his command and fulfilled his prophecy. But because she could not stand to know the secrets even of God apart from her husband, she mentioned to him that she had seen a man of God, of beautiful form, bringing her the divine promise of future offspring, and that she, confiding in this promise, was led to share with her husband her faith in the heavenly promises. But he, informed of this, devoutly offered his prayers to God, that the grace of this vision might be conferred on him also, saying, "Lord, let your angel come to me."

I am of the opinion that he did not act this way out of jealousy of his wife, but rather that he was filled with desire of the divine grace, and sought to participate in the benefit of the heavenly vision. For one whose mind was depraved could not have found such favor with the Lord that an angel should return to his house, who, having given those warnings that the divine announcement required, was suddenly carried away in the form of a smoking flame. This sight, which terrified the man, the woman interpreted more auspiciously, saying that to see God is a sign of good not evil. In that way she made him stop worrying.

—St. Ambrose, *Letter 19*, 10-12

IN GOD'S PRESENCE, CONSIDER . . .

What thoughts in my mind are keeping the angels away?

CLOSING PRAYER

Guardian Angel, keep me free of every base desire, every evil imagination, and every unbecoming thought.

The modesty of Daniel

Daniel, says St. Ephrem the Syrian, was afraid even to approach the angel he saw. How can some philosophers pretend that they've figured out everything about the Son of God?

Daniel saw wondrous living creatures. He also saw that the Ancient of Days was sitting in glory (Dan. 7:9). He approached the living creatures, because he wanted to ask and learn. But he did not approach to search into the glory of the Most High.

Fools have left searching creation and run off to the Creator to search out who he is. Daniel saw one of the angels and was frightened (Dan. 8:16). He did not approach to search into him. He could not bear the sound of his voice. He was not even able to listen.

Daniel did not look on the minister; who can look on the One to whom he ministered?

The sea that saw the sign of him feared, and fled back, and was moved; it was divided into two heaps (Exod. 14:21-22).

Daniel, when he asked about the words, heard that they were sealed, and that it was not fitting to search out the hidden things of the future. Who will dare to search into the Treasury in whom all knowledge dwells? The First-Born is the Treasury of the Father, in whom is all his counsel. Who is up to the task of searching into him?

—St. Ephrem the Syrian, *Rhythm 8*

IN GOD'S PRESENCE, CONSIDER . . .

Where do I draw the line between what I can know and what I can only speculate on? Do I imitate the modesty of Daniel when he was faced with the angel?

CLOSING PRAYER

Lord, I am not worthy even to look on your angels, but I long for the day when you will be revealed to me.

Jerusalem and Babylon

*The angels are citizens of the spiritual Jerusalem, says St. Augustine, and so
are we. But for the present we on earth are held captive in the spiritual Babylon.
We begin to be freed from our captivity as soon as we confess our sins.*

You've heard, and you know, that there are two cities, for the present
outwardly mixed up together, yet separated in heart, running together through
the course of time until the end. One, whose end is everlasting peace, is called
Jerusalem; the other, whose joy is peace in this world, is called Babylon. You also
remember the meanings of these names: Jerusalem means "Vision of Peace," and
Babylon means "Confusion."

Jerusalem was held captive in Babylon—but not all of it, for the angels too
are its citizens. But those human beings who are predestined to the glory of God,
to become fellow heirs with Christ by adoption, whom he has redeemed from this
very captivity by his own blood—this part of the citizens of Jerusalem are held
captive in Babylon because of sin. But they begin to go out of Babylon by confessing their sins and loving righteousness. Afterwards, at the end of the world, they
will be separated from Babylon in body as well.

–St. Augustine, *Exposition on Ps. 137,* 1

IN GOD'S PRESENCE, CONSIDER . . .

Though I live in Babylon, what about my life distinguishes me as a citizen of the
Jerusalem of the angels?

CLOSING PRAYER

*Lord, let me praise you with angels and archangels and the spiritual Jerusalem, the assembly of
the first-born whose names are written in Heaven.*

They listened to angels; we listen to the Son

St. Augustine tells us that, in Old Testament times, the word of God was given through the angels—and it was heard with earnest obedience. We who have the word directly from the Son should be even more careful to listen.

Whenever God appeared to the patriarchs, presented to them according to his own dispensation suitable to the times, he did so through created beings. We have the authority of the divine Scriptures, and our reason should not stray from them; it should not leave the solid support of God's own word and fall off the cliff of its own speculations in matters where the perceptions of the body cannot settle the question, and the truth does not shine forth by clear reason.

Now, the letter to the Hebrews distinguishes the dispensation of the New Covenant from the dispensation of the Old, according to the fitness of ages and times; and it certainly says that not only were those things we can *see* made through the angels, but also God's speaking was itself done through angels. This is what it says: "But to what angel has he ever said, 'Sit at my right hand, till I make your enemies a stool for your feet'? Are they not all ministering spirits sent forth to serve, for the sake of those who are to obtain salvation?" (Heb. 1:13-14). From which it is plain that all those things were not only done through angels, but done for our sake—that is, for the sake of the people of God, who are promised the inheritance of eternal life. And then, showing that it clearly follows that, as the word was spoken by angels then, it is spoken by the Son now: "Therefore we must pay the closer attention to what we have heard, lest we drift away from it. For if the message declared by angels was valid and every transgression or disobedience received a just retribution, how shall we escape if we neglect such a great salvation?" (Heb. 2:1-3).

–St. Augustine, *On the Trinity,* 3.2

IN GOD'S PRESENCE, CONSIDER . . .

In old times, says St. Augustine, God sent his messages through the angels, but now he speaks to us through the Son himself. Do I listen with reverent attention to the readings at Mass, as though Christ himself were speaking to me?

CLOSING PRAYER

Angels of God who surround me, be with me especially at Mass, and help me to keep my mind from straying when I hear the Word of God.

Christ is the teacher

One generation teaches another, but who taught the first humans? Not other humans, says St. Clement of Alexandria, since there were none. Not angels, because we cannot hear the way angels normally speak. No, our original teacher was the Word himself.

I lead you up to the first generation of human beings; and from that point I begin to investigate: who is their teacher? Not a human, for they had not yet learned. Not any of the angels, for humans do not hear the way angels, as angels, speak. We have ears, but they do not have a tongue to correspond; nor would any one attribute to the angels organs of speech—I mean lips and the parts connected to them, throat, and windpipe, and chest, breath and air to vibrate. And God certainly does not call aloud in his unapproachable sanctity, separated as he is from even the archangels.

And we also have already heard that angels learned the truth, and their rulers over them; for they had a beginning.

It remains, then, for us to keep going up to seek their teacher. And since there is one unoriginated Being, the Omnipotent God; the First-begotten is also one; "all things were made through him, and without him was not anything made that was made" (John 1:3). This is the Teacher of all created beings.

–St. Clement of Alexandria, *Stromata*, 6.7

IN GOD'S PRESENCE, CONSIDER . . .

The angels themselves had to learn what they know from Christ. Is Christ's teaching—in the Sermon on the Mount, for example—the starting point for everything else I know?

CLOSING PRAYER

Your angels, O God, would live in darkness without your Word. Confirm me in your divine knowledge, through your only-begotten Son, our Lord and Savior Jesus Christ.

Everything comes from the Good

Dionysius the Areopagite tells us that the angels have all their perfections because of the one Good, namely God, from whom all perfections flow. But not just the angels: our own souls, and the life of lower animals and plants, and even the existence of inanimate objects—all of it depends on God.

Whatever belongs to the heavenly hierarchy—the purifications appropriate to angels, the heavenly illuminations, and everything that perfects the whole angelic perfection—all of it comes from the Fountain of goodness, from whom they were given the idea of goodness, and the ability to reveal the hidden goodness in themselves. We might say that the angels are heralds of God's silence, and shine a bright light on him who is in secret.

And after these sacred and holy minds, our souls exist, and whatever is good in them exists, because of that Goodness that is more than good. The fact that they have reason, that they have essential life, that they are indestructible, and that they exist in the first place, all comes from God—as does the fact that they can be elevated to the level of the angels, and be led by the angels as their guides to God, the Origin of all things. Then our souls also can share in the illuminations that bubble forth from the Origin, according to each one's capacity, and can participate in that godlike gift as much as we are able.

But if I may also speak of the irrational souls—the creatures that fly through the air, and walk on the ground, and creep on the ground, and swim in the water—all these things have their life of growing and moving because of the Good. Plants also have their growing and moving because of the Good; and even matter without soul or life exists because of the Good, because of which it exists in the first place.

—Dionysius the Areopagite, *The Divine Names*, 4.2

IN GOD'S PRESENCE, CONSIDER . . .

Could I spare a bit of time today to enjoy the beauty of the world God made—and to praise God for it, as the angels do unceasingly?

CLOSING PRAYER

Praise be to your holy name, O Lord Jesus Christ, who gives life to the whole world—from the most glorious angels to the humblest creeping things on the ground.

Satan was created good

If Satan was one of God's creatures, then isn't God to blame for evil? Against the heretic Marcion, who believed that the God of the Old Testament was evil, Tertullian argues that the devil's sin is not God's doing. Like us, Satan was created with free will, and—like us—he alone is to blame for his own sins.

Where did the devil's malice, his lying and deceiving mankind and slandering God, come from?

Certainly not from God. He made the angel good, as he did all his good works. In fact, before he became the devil, he was known as the wisest of all creation, and wisdom is not evil.

As a spirit, he was created with free will—for God certainly would not fail to give that kind of liberty to a being who was meant to be next to God himself.

When God condemned him, God bore witness that the devil had left behind the nature in which he was created, by lusting after the wickedness that had sprung up by itself in him. At the same time, by allowing him some room for his schemes, God acted in accordance with his own good purpose. In that way he made room for a conflict in which mankind might crush his enemy with that same free will that had fallen victim to the enemy (which proves, by the way, that the fault was his own, not God's), and thus worthily gain back his salvation through victory. Likewise the devil's punishment is more bitter, because he is conquered by the one he had formerly injured.

Thus God is shown to be even more good, because he waits for man to come back from his present life to a more glorious paradise, where he will have the right to take the fruit of the tree of life.

—Tertullian, *Against Marcion*, 2.10

IN GOD'S PRESENCE, CONSIDER . . .

Am I using my free will to fight with the holy angels against Satan? Or does the enemy sometimes enlist my will on his side?

CLOSING PRAYER

Lord, you have graciously brought me out of slavery into freedom. Send your angels to guide my will, so that I may not fall into Satan's snares.

Demons are not evil by nature

The demons, says Dionysius the Areopagite, are not made evil. What we call "evil" is a negative quality: it is a failure to preserve themselves in the good.

But how are the demons evil if they are created by God? For the Good brings forth and sustains good things—but, someone might say, we call the demons evil.

But we call them "evil" not because of what they are, for they come from the Good, and were created with a good essence. We call them evil from what they are not, because they did not have the strength, as Scripture tells us, to keep their original condition.

What do we mean when we say that demons become evil, except that they have fallen out of the habit of working for divine things? If the demons were evil by nature, they would always be evil—but evil is unstable, so if they were always in the same condition, they would *not* be evil. To be the same all the time is a characteristic of the Good. But if they are not always evil, they are not evil by nature, but by straying from the good qualities of angels.

Demons do not altogether lack a share in what is good. They exist, and they live, and they think, and they have a sort of movement of aspiration. But we call them "evil" because of their weakness in what they do. The evil is a turning away and stepping out of things appropriate for them; it is missing the mark, imperfection and impotence, a weakness and a departure, and a falling away from the power that preserves their integrity.

—Dionysius the Areopagite, *The Divine Names*, 4.22

IN GOD'S PRESENCE, CONSIDER . . .

How much of what I do every day seems to be "missing the mark," the way the demons do? What would help me stick more consistently to my good nature, the way the angels do in Heaven?

CLOSING PRAYER

Lord, you created me good, and I desire to live in a way consistent with that creation. Send me your angels to help me avoid the temptation to stray from the path on my journey toward Heaven.

Evil exists only in the good

Human beings and angels are good creations, says St. Augustine. Even the evil angels are good creations; they are evil only in relation to the good things that they were. It is not possible for there to be evil without good.

But the logical rule doesn't apply in these two opposites that we call "good" and "evil." The weather can't be both dark and light at the same time. Food or drink can't be sweet and sour at the same time. An object can't be both white and black at the same time and in the same place. It can't be misshapen and shapely at the same time. We see this rule in almost all pairs of opposites: two opposite things cannot coexist in the same thing.

No one says that good and evil aren't opposites. But, nevertheless, not only can they coexist, but evil can't exist at all without good, or in a thing that isn't good. On the other hand, good can exist without evil: a person or an angel could exist and not be wicked, but there cannot be wickedness except in a person or an angel. It's good to be a person, and it's good to be an angel. But it's evil to be wicked.

So these two opposites coexist. If there were no good in what is evil, then the evil just could not exist: it would have no way of existing. There would be no source of corruption, because corruption is only taking away the good.

Evils have their source in what is good, and unless they are parasites on something good they are nothing. There is no other source from which an evil thing can come into existence.

If this is true, then a thing is unquestionably good insofar as it is a being. If it's an incorruptible being, it's a great good. But even if it is corruptible, it still can't exist except as a characteristic of something good. Corruption can only do damage by corrupting something good.

—St. Augustine, *Enchiridion*, chapter 5

IN GOD'S PRESENCE, CONSIDER . . .

When I think of anyone I consider evil, can I see past the evil acts to the good nature? Do I remember that even those who behave wickedly have guardian angels?

CLOSING PRAYER

Father, you have made nothing wicked by nature, not even the angels who deserted you. Let me be a light to guide your erring sheep back into the fold.

Angels have no creative power

> *God makes creation to operate by certain principles, says St. Augustine. If evil angels can make use of those principles to help magicians do apparent miracles, that doesn't mean that anyone but God was the Creator.*

The Apostle Paul distinguishes God's creating and forming on the inside from the acts of the creature that are applied from without. Drawing a metaphor from agriculture, he says, "I planted, Apollos watered, but God gave the growth" (1 Cor. 3:6).

In the spiritual life, no one but God can work righteousness in our minds. But people can preach the gospel as an outward means—the good can do it sincerely, but the evil can also do it in pretense.

In the same way, God works from within in the creation of visible things. What the good or the bad do—what angels or people do—even what animals do—all these things are done by the nature that God has given them, according to his own absolute power. He has given them their appetites for pleasant things, and their abilities to respond to those appetites. His creation is what agriculture is to the soil.

So I cannot call the evil angels, who are invoked by magic, the creators of the frogs or serpents (Exod. 7-8), any more than I can say that evil people were the creators of the grain crop when I see that it has sprung up through their labor.

—St. Augustine, *On the Trinity*, 3.8

IN GOD'S PRESENCE, CONSIDER . . .

Am I planting and watering the seeds God has given me to care for? Do I, like God's good angels, use what God has given me for the good of his creatures?

CLOSING PRAYER

Holy Guardian Angel, you are devoted to my care: teach me to guard and keep God's creation with the same devotion.

Angels know the truth because they love God

Demons often predict the future, says St. Augustine, because they're intelligent, and they can see things we can't. But they often get it wrong. Angels always know the truth even about worldly things, because they love God and make his will their own.

The good angels, therefore, put little value on the knowledge of material and transitory things that the demons are so proud of possessing. It's not that they're ignorant of these things. But the love of God, by which they are sanctified, is very dear to them. Compared to that not merely immaterial but also unchangeable and ineffable beauty that they love with such a fire, they disdain everything beneath it, and everything that isn't it, so that they may enjoy that good, the source of their goodness, with all the good that is in them.

And therefore they have a more certain knowledge even of those worldly and changeable things, because they contemplate their principles and causes in the Word of God, by which the world was made—those causes by which one thing is approved, another rejected, and everything arranged.

But the demons do not see the wisdom of God, so they don't see these eternal and (so to speak) fundamental causes of worldly things, but only foresee a larger part of the future than we do, because they know more about the signs that are hidden from us. Sometimes, they're predicting what they themselves intend to do.

And, finally, the demons are often wrong, but the angels never are. For it is one thing, by the aid of worldly and changeable things, to guess what changes may happen in time, and to change such things by one's own will and power—and this is to a certain extent permitted to the demons. But it is another thing to foresee the changes of times in the eternal and immutable laws of God, which live in his wisdom, and to know the will of God, the most infallible and powerful of all causes, by participating in his spirit. This is granted to the holy angels by God's just choice.

−St. Augustine, *City of God*, 9.22

IN GOD'S PRESENCE, CONSIDER . . .

Do I desire to know the truth? Do I take the steps necessary to grow in my understanding of doctrine? Do I ask the help of my guardian angel as I undertake the prayerful study of Christian doctrine?

CLOSING PRAYER

Guardian Angel, who gaze upon the loveliness of God even as you guide my every step: help me to see what you see and behold the loveliness of God as much as I can even today.

Covetousness made an archangel the devil

St. Asterius of Amasea gives us a good working definition of covetousness, and explains that this sin—wanting more than you deserve—was what made the devil fall from Heaven.

Covetousness, then, is not simply being mad for money and other possessions, wishing to add to what you have that to which you have no right. To speak more broadly, it is the desire to have, in every transaction, more than what's due or belongs to you.

And you know that the devil was the first to have this fault. He was an archangel, and appointed to the most honorable life and station; but the arrogant creature conceived of absolute rule, and rebellion against God, and was cast down from Heaven after that, and, falling into this atmosphere of earth, he became your malicious neighbor.

So he did not get the divinity to which he aspired, and he lost the rank he had enjoyed of being archangel. He was an unfaithful servant, changed by gradually increasing audacity into a robber. He was like the dog of the Greek fable, who was both deprived of his meat and failed to grasp the shadow—for how could he grasp an intangible thing?

—St. Asterius of Amasea, *Sermon 3: Against Covetousness*

IN GOD'S PRESENCE, CONSIDER . . .

We live in a world where covetousness seems like a virtue. Do I long, like Lucifer, for more than I need or deserve? How can I overcome that longing? Will it help to remember that God is ready to give me, not only more than I deserve, but more than I can possibly imagine?

CLOSING PRAYER

Lord, sanctify me through the ministry of your holy angels, and free me from all covetousness, and from every disposition that is not in accordance with your will.

Satan fell, and we followed

The first of all the angels, Tatian tells us, was worshiped as a god by human beings. For his pride, Satan was cut off from all fellowship with the Word, and he and his angelic followers became the demons.

The power of the Word had the ability in itself to foresee future events—not that those events were fated, but rather they came about through the choice of beings who acted freely. From time to time the Word foretold what would happen in times to come. It also began to forbid wickedness by prohibitions, and at the same time to praise those who remained good.

But people attached themselves to one being who was more subtle than the rest, because he was the first-born, and declared that he was God, though he went against the will of God.

Then the power of the Word excluded the originator of this foolishness from all fellowship with the Word. Thus he who was made in the likeness of God becomes mortal, because the more powerful spirit has separated itself from him. But that first-begotten one, through his transgression and ignorance, becomes a demon. Those who imitated him—that is, his illusions—have become a host of demons, and through their own free choice have been given up to their folly.

—Tatian, *Address to the Greeks*, 7

IN GOD'S PRESENCE, CONSIDER . . .

What do I do to make sure that I'm not attaching myself to Satan?

CLOSING PRAYER

King of glory, accept my prayer; cleanse my mind from all influence of the devil, and guard me from everything evil..

Not hurting anyone but himself

The devil, says St. Augustine, did no damage to God in his fall, but only to himself. God knew beforehand what would happen, and how to bring good out of it.

So why shouldn't God make human beings, although he knew beforehand that we would sin, when he might crown us if we stood, and set us right if we fell, and help us if we rose, being always and everywhere glorious in goodness, righteousness, and mercy? Above all, why shouldn't he do so, since he also knew beforehand that from our mortal race would spring saints—people who would not seek their own glory, but give glory to their Creator, and who, gaining deliverance from every corruption by worshiping him, would be counted worthy to live forever, and to live in bliss with the holy angels?

He gave us free will, so that we might worship God not out of slavish necessity, but with candid desire. He also gave free will to the angels. Thus the angel who, along with the other spirits who were his followers, abandoned the obedience of God in his pride to become the devil, did not do any damage to God, but only to himself. God knows what to do about souls that leave him, and how to use their righteous misery to furnish the lower sections of his creatures with appropriate and befitting laws of his wonderful dispensation.

Thus the devil did not harm God in any way, either by falling himself or in seducing humanity to death. Nor did the man in any way hurt the truth, power, or blessedness of his Maker, when, after his partner had been seduced by the devil, of his own deliberate choice he consented with her to do what God had forbidden.

—St. Augustine, *On the Catechizing of the Uninstructed*, 18

IN GOD'S PRESENCE, CONSIDER . . .

Do I worship God out of candid desire? Do I will to serve God as the heavenly angels do?

CLOSING PRAYER

Lord, I desire to offer you much more than I have to give; make up my lack with your grace, and let me serve you forever with your holy angels in Heaven.

Satan is more guilty than we are

Satan, says St. Gregory the Great, left his exalted position by his own wicked-ness, whereas we were persuaded by Satan to sin. Of the two, therefore, Satan is the more guilty, which is why we have the chance to be redeemed and he does not.

"May God above not seek it, nor light shine upon it" (Job 3:4).

There is another way in which it was both appropriate that humanity should be recovered when lost, and impossible for the spirit that elevated himself to be recovered. The angel fell by his own wickedness, but humanity fell by the wicked-ness of another.

We are brought to the light of repentance by the coming of the Redeemer, but the fallen angel is not brought back to the light of a restored position by any hope of pardon; he does not change his ways and convert. Therefore it is very appropriate to say, "May God above not seek it, nor light shine upon it." In other words, "Since he has brought on the darkness himself, let him suffer what he him-self has made eternally. And let him never recover the light of his former state, since he left it without even being persuaded to do so."

–St. Gregory the Great, *Moralia in Job*, 4.8

God condemned Satan right away, but offers me a once-in-a-lifetime chance at redemption. Am I doing everything I can to take him up on his offer?

CLOSING PRAYER

Guardian Angel, guide me to true repentance, so that I may not stray into the way of the fallen angels.

We are forgiven because of the flesh

The angels who sinned cannot be forgiven, says St. Gregory the Great, because—having purely spiritual natures—they don't have the excuse of the flesh. God is merciful to us because he knows that our nature is combined with an element that drags us down.

The spirits of the angels sinned without forgiveness for this reason: because they might have stood stronger, since no mixture of flesh held them captive. But we were given pardon after sin for this reason: because, having a body of flesh, we have a thing that makes us beneath ourselves.

Thus, in the eye of the Judge, this weakness of the flesh is itself grounds for showing pity—as the psalmist says:

"Yet he, being compassionate, forgave their iniquity, and did not destroy them; he restrained his anger often, and did not stir up all his wrath. He remembered that they were but flesh" (Ps. 78:38-39).

—St. Gregory the Great, Moralia in Job, 9.26

IN GOD'S PRESENCE, CONSIDER . . .

God has mercy on us because we are weaker than angels. But what am I doing to build up my spiritual strength?

CLOSING PRAYER

I am weak, Lord, but send me your angels to strengthen me and make me worthy for your service.

We don't deserve God's mercy

The evil angels, says St. Augustine, suffer the just punishment for their betrayal. We might have suffered the same way, but instead God chose to show us completely undeserved mercy.

The whole human race was condemned, ruined. It delighted in evil. It plummeted from one evil to another. It made common cause with the fallen angels, and it was suffering the punishment—which was completely deserved—for its wicked betrayal. For we must say that God's anger is quite rightly turned on the things wicked people do freely, in their blind, uncontrolled lust. Obviously, whatever punishments they have to suffer, in the open or in secret, come from that anger. But the goodness of the Creator never stops sustaining life and vigor, even for the evil angels. If that sustenance were taken away, they would no longer exist.

Humanity comes from a corrupt and condemned line. But we still have the power to conceive offspring, to direct our limbs in their worldly business, and to nourish the body. God decided that it was better to bring good from evil than not to allow any evil to exist.

If God had decided that human beings could never reform—as he did decide with the evil angels—wouldn't that have been just? Humanity deserted God. We used our powers for evil, to stomp down and run afoul of our Creator's laws, though we could easily have kept them. We stubbornly turned away from God's light. We violated the image of the Creator in us. Using our free will for evil, we tore ourselves away from the healthy discipline of God's law. Wouldn't it have been just if God had completely abandoned a creature like that, and sent us to the eternal punishment we deserved?

God would certainly have done that if he were *only* just, and not merciful as well—if he had not decided to manifest his mercy much more dramatically by pardoning some who did not deserve it.

—St. Augustine, *Enchiridion*, chapter 5

IN GOD'S PRESENCE, CONSIDER . . .

How am I repaying God's completely undeserved mercy?

Do I do as the angels do, repaying him with a life of consistent service?

CLOSING PRAYER

Guardian Angel, keep God's mercy in my mind, and teach me to show the same compassion to others.

God showed mercy to our weakness

If fallen humanity deserved mercy, why not the fallen angels? One reason, says St. Gregory the Great, is our very weakness. Satan had the moral strength of a pure spirit, but we constantly struggle with the weakness of the body.

God was able to create good things out of nothing. Likewise, when he willed it, he also restored, by the mystery of his Incarnation, the good things that were lost.

Now, he had made two creations to contemplate him: the angelic and the human. But pride struck down both of them, and dashed them from their upright position of original righteousness. But one was clothed in flesh, and the other had not weakness that comes from the flesh: an angelic being is only spirit, but a human is both spirit and flesh.

Thus, when the Creator had compassion to bring about redemption, it was appropriate that he should bring back to him that creature which, when it sinned, plainly had some weakness. It was also appropriate that the fallen angel should be driven down deeper, since, when he fell from firmness in standing upright, he was not supporting any weakness from the flesh.

Thus the psalmist, speaking of the Redeemer's compassion on humanity, at the same time rightly set forth the very cause of his mercy: "He remembered that they were but flesh." In other words, because he saw their weaknesses, he would not punish their offenses severely.

–St. Gregory the Great, *Moralia in Job*, 4.8

IN GOD'S PRESENCE, CONSIDER . . .

Unlike the angels, we mortals have to deal with the weakness of the flesh and its appetites. Do I try to take into account the weakness of others around me the way God takes my weakness into account?

CLOSING PRAYER

Through your grace, Lord, make my frail nature worthy to sanctify your name with the heavenly beings.

Even angels are darkness without God

The fall of the angels, says St. Augustine, shows us how completely every spiritual being—human or angelic—depends on the illumination that comes from God alone.

The angels fell. The human soul fell. And thus they show us the abyss in that dark deep that would have been ready for the whole spiritual creation, if you had not said from the beginning, "Let there be light," and there had not been light, and every obedient intelligence in your celestial city had not clung to you and rested in your Spirit, which is unchangeably hovering over everything changeable. Otherwise, even the Heaven of heavens itself would have been a dark chasm, whereas now it is light in the Lord.

The spirits who fell away discovered their own darkness when they were stripped of the garments of your light. But even in their wretched restlessness, you clearly show us how noble you have made the rational creature, to which nothing less than you—not even itself—is enough to give a happy rest.

For you, our God, will enlighten our darkness. Our garments of light come from you, and then our darkness will be as noon.

—St. Augustine, *Confessions*, 13.8

When I feel restless or dissatisfied, is my first instinct to turn to God as the angels of Heaven do? Or is it to try to find some way of satisfying myself, as Satan and his angels did?

CLOSING PRAYER

Lord, I depend on your light; let me always be drawn to it, along with the obedient angels, and never seek rest in anything else.

Angels and humans have free will

Tatian tells us that both humans and angels were created through the Word, and that both were created with free will. Therefore it is just that the good are praised and the evil punished, because both good and evil acts come from the free choices of God's creatures.

The heavenly Word, a spirit that comes from the Father, a Word from the power of the word, in imitation of the Father who begot him made human beings an image of immortality, so that, as God is incorruptible, humanity, which shares a part of God, would also have the immortal principle.

The Word also was the Framer of the angels, before the creation of humanity.

Each of these two kinds of creatures was made free to act as it pleased—not that they had the nature of good, which (again) belongs to God alone, but is perfected in creatures through freedom of choice. So those who are bad are justly punished, because they became depraved by their own fault. But the just deserve to be praised for the good things they have done, since, by exercising their free choice, they did not go against the will of God.

This is the way things are both for angels and for human beings.

—Tatian, *Address to the Greeks*, 7

IN GOD'S PRESENCE, CONSIDER . . .

Do the things I've done today deserve more praise or blame? Why did I choose those things, and could I have chosen better? Did I remember to ask my guardian angels for help in making those choices?

CLOSING PRAYER

Lord, I entreat from you a messenger of peace, a faithful guide, and a guardian of my soul and body.

Like the angels, we have free will

Reason, says St. John of Damascus, is very closely linked with free will. With reason, we can decide what's best for ourselves, and with free will we can do it—an ability we share with the angels.

Everyone who deliberates does so believing that the choice of what to do lies in his hands—that he may choose what seems best as the result of his deliberation, and having chosen may act upon it.

And if this is so, free will must necessarily be very closely related to reason. For either man is an irrational being, or, if he is rational, he is master of his acts and endowed with free will. Thus creatures without reason do not enjoy free will: nature leads them, but they do not lead nature. And so they do not oppose the natural appetite, but as soon as their appetite longs for something they rush headlong after it.

But we, being rational, lead nature; nature does not lead us. And so when we want something, we have the power to curb our appetite or to indulge it—whichever we please. Therefore creatures that have no reason are neither praised nor blamed, while man is the subject of both praise and blame.

Note also that the angels, being rational, are endowed with free will, and, since they are created, are liable to change. In fact, this is made plain by the devil, who was made good by the Creator, but of his own free will became the inventor of evil—and by the powers who revolted with him (the demons), and by the other troops of angels who persisted in goodness.

–St. John of Damascus, *Exposition of the Christian Faith*, 2.27

IN GOD'S PRESENCE, CONSIDER . . .

Do I use my freedom faithfully, as the angels do? Do I act with forethought and prayer?

CLOSING PRAYER

Holy Guardian Angel, you are with me in every decision I face. Help me to be attentive to your promptings.

Our freedom is different from the angels'

Like the angels, says St. John of Damascus, we have free will; but it's a little bit different. For the angel, the choice comes instantaneously. For us, limited by our bodies and attacked by the devil, the choice is never instantaneous: we are faced with a situation, and then decide what to do about it.

Freedom of will is used in several senses: one in connection with God, another in connection with angels, and a third in connection with human beings.

Used in reference to God, it is to be understood as transcending ordinary being.

In reference to angels, it is to be taken in the sense that the choice comes at the same time as the state, and no interval of time at all comes between them: for while the angel has free will by nature, he uses it without any hindrance, having neither the body's antipathy to overcome nor anyone to attack him.

Again, used in reference to human beings, it is to be taken in the sense that the state is considered to come before the choice in time. For man is free and has free will by nature, but he has also the assault of the devil and the motion of the body to impede him: and thus through the assault and the weight of the body, the choice comes to be later than the state.

–St. John of Damascus, *Exposition of the Christian Faith*, 3.14

IN GOD'S PRESENCE, CONSIDER . . .

God has given us time to work out our choices. In the time he gives us, we should call upon the help of the angels to help us make the right decision.

CLOSING PRAYER

Lord, send your angels to guide me, so that I may always be found a ready minister of your will.

It's good to be human

Some heretical writers had said that there would be no bodily resurrection, but that we would be pure spirits like the angels. St. Methodius argues that, if God had wanted us to be angels, he wouldn't have made us human.

God didn't make a human being and then—as if he had done it badly, or made a mistake in forming him—decide to make an angel, repenting of his work, as really bad craftsmen do. Nor did he try to make an angel and fail, ending up with a human being instead—that would be a sign of weakness.

Then why did he make human beings and not angels, if he wanted human beings to be angels and not human? Was it because he couldn't make angels? It would be blasphemy to think so! Or was he so busy making the worse that he dilly-dallied about the better? That's silly, too. God doesn't fail in making what is good, and he doesn't put it off, and he's not incapable of it. He has the power to act how and when he pleases, since he himself is Power.

So if he originally made us human, it's because he wanted us to be human.

But if that was what he wanted, then, since God wants the good, to be human is good.

—St. Methodius, *Discourse on the Resurrection*, 1.11

IN GOD'S PRESENCE, CONSIDER . . .

God made me human and not an angel for a reason. Am I close to being the human being God had in mind? Or does my will lead me away from God's original intention for me?

CLOSING PRAYER

Lord, I am weaker than an angel, but you made me weaker because it was good for me to be a human being. Help my weakness through your mercy and the aid of your grace.

Better a prisoner for Christ than an angel

It sounds crazy, says St. John Chrysostom, but a Christian would rather be a prisoner with Paul than be transformed into an angel in Heaven. Suffering for Christ is the greatest privilege a Christian can ever know.

Yes, to everyone else it seems like folly that to suffer dishonor is to be counted worthy, that to suffer dishonor is to rejoice. But to those who understand the love of Christ, this is what counts as the most blessed thing of all!

If anyone offered me the choice of all Heaven or that chain, I'd prefer the chain. If anyone asked whether he should put me up on high with the angels or with Paul in his shackles, I'd choose the prison. If anyone could change me either into one of those powers that are in Heaven all around the throne, or into a prisoner like Paul, I'd choose to be the prisoner.

Nothing is more blessed than that chain. If only I could be in that very spot right now—they say the shackles are still there—to see and admire those men for their love of Christ! If only I could see the chains at which the devils fear and tremble, but which the angels reverence!

Nothing is more noble than to suffer any evil for Christ's sake.

—St. John Chrysostom, *Homily 8 on Ephesians*

IN GOD'S PRESENCE, CONSIDER . . .

What opportunities to suffer for Christ have I passed up recently?

CLOSING PRAYER

Guardian angel, teach me to prefer God's presence to everything, every comfort in creation. Holy Apostle St. Paul, intercede for me, that I may be attentive to the angels, as you were, and that they may lead me to heaven, as they led you.

Satan presents himself before the Lord

Satan still has an angel's nature, says St. Gregory the Great. Although he has fallen, he is still rightly classed with the angels in the Book of Job.

"Now there was a day when the sons of God came to present themselves before the Lord, and Satan also came among them" (Job 1:6).

It is certainly necessary to ask how Satan came to be there among the elect angels, when long before he had been condemned and banished from among them—which is what his pride made necessary.

But he is well said to have been among them. Though he had lost his blessed state, he still had a nature like theirs. Though his demerits sink him down, he is still lifted up by the attributes of his subtle nature.

So it says he came before the Lord among the "sons of God," because the eye of Almighty God looks on everything spiritual and sees that Satan also has a more subtle nature—as Scripture tells us: "The eyes of the Lord are in every place, keeping watch on the evil and the good" (Prov. 15:3).

–St. Gregory the Great, *Moralia in Job*, 2.4

IN GOD'S PRESENCE, CONSIDER . . .

Knowing that "the eyes of God are in every place," are God's eyes on me to protect me, or to protect others from me?

CLOSING PRAYER

Guardian Angel, protect me from temptation, so that I may find mercy and grace with all the saints that have been pleasing to you since the world began.

Whence have you come?

When Satan appears before the Lord, God asks him, "Whence have you come?" That's not because God was ignorant of where Satan had been, says St. Gregory the Great. It's God's way of saying that Satan has not been doing his will.

"The Lord said to Satan, 'Whence have you come?' Satan answered the Lord, 'From going to and fro on the earth, and from walking up and down on it'" (Job 1:7).

Why didn't he ever say to the elect angels, "Whence have you come?"—but he does ask Satan where he comes from? Certainly we never ask unless we don't know.

But for God, "not knowing" means condemning. Thus at the last judgment he will say, "I do not know where you come from; depart from me, all you workers of iniquity!" (Luke 13:27). In the same way, when a truthful man refuses to sin by falsehood, we say he doesn't know how to lie. We don't mean that he is ignorant if he really wanted to lie, but that he refuses to tell a lie because he loves the truth.

So saying "Whence have you come?" to Satan is condemning his ways as if God didn't know them. So while Satan is interrogated about where he came from, the elect angels never have to be questioned about where they came from. God knows what they do, since they do it at his own instigation. While they serve his will alone, they can never be unknown to him.

–St. Gregory the Great, *Moralia in Job*, 2.4-5

IN GOD'S PRESENCE, CONSIDER . . .

Does God know where I'm coming from? What should I be doing to avoid being "unknown" the way Satan is?

CLOSING PRAYER

Lord, you know my frailty; deliver me from the evil one and his works, and all his malice and craftiness.

Satan does not see God

Examining the book of Job, St. Gregory the Great encounters a puzzle very near the beginning. How could Satan come before the Lord when only the pure in heart shall see God? The answer, he says, is that God saw Satan, but Satan did not really see God.

"Now there was a day when the sons of God came to present themselves before the Lord, and Satan also came among them" (Job 1:6).

When it says that Satan came before the presence of God, that raises an important question for us. It is written, "Blessed are the pure in heart, for they shall see God" (Matt. 5:8). But Satan can never be pure in heart. How could he have presented himself to see the Lord?

But we should notice that it says he came before the Lord, but not that he *saw* the Lord. He came to be seen, not to see. He was in the Lord's sight, but the Lord was not in his sight. In the same way a blind man standing in the sun really is bathed in the rays of light, but he himself does not see the light that brightens him at all.

This is how Satan appeared in the Lord's sight among the angels. The power of God penetrates everything with a look. God saw the impure spirit, but the spirit did not see him. Even the things that run away from God's face cannot be hidden. All things are bare in the view of the Most High. Thus Satan, who was absent, came to the Lord, who was present.

—St. Gregory the Great, *Moralia in Job*, 2.4-5

IN GOD'S PRESENCE, CONSIDER . . .

When I come before the Lord, will I be blind like Satan, or will I see what the pure in heart will see?

CLOSING PRAYER

Count me worthy, loving Lord, to call on you with a contrite spirit, with a pure heart, and with sanctified lips, so that I may see you with the pure spirits of Heaven and all the saints.

God's light takes in the darkness

Meditating on the first appearance of Satan in Job, St. Gregory the Great looks at the setting: "there was a day." Why does Scripture specify a certain day? St. Gregory offers one symbolic interpretation.

Or, considering that Satan was there as well, was Holy Scripture intending to point out, by saying that this happened on a certain day, that in the light God saw the darkness?

We cannot take in light and darkness in the same view. When the eye looms on the darkness, the light retreats. When the eye turns to the shining rays of light, the shadows of the darkness vanish.

But to that Power who unchangeably sees all changeable things, Satan was present as in the day. The light of God takes in undimmed the darkness of the fallen angel.

As I said, we cannot look in one view both at the objects that we approve and choose, and at the objects we condemn and reject. Whenever the mind is tuned to one, it turns away from the other, and when it is brought back to the second it turns away from the first.

But God sees everything at the same moment without changing. So Satan is said to come before him on a day, meaning that the light of God's eternity is impervious to any cloud of change.

–St. Gregory the Great, *Moralia in Job*, 2.36-37

IN GOD'S PRESENCE, CONSIDER . . .

Given the choice, do I look more toward the darkness of the fallen angels or toward the light of God?

CLOSING PRAYER

Lord, scatter the darkness of sin within me. Save me from the devil and his temptations, and bring me up from the depths of darkness into light.

Wrath against the devil is mercy on sinners

Why does the Psalmist ask God to "arise in your anger"? St. Augustine suggests that this is actually a prayer of charity. The "anger" of the Lord should punish the devil by taking the souls of sinners away from him and bringing them back to God.

"Arise, O Lord, in your anger" (Ps. 7:6).

We say he is perfect. Then why does he incite God to anger? Shouldn't we ask instead whether he was perfect who, when he was being stoned, said, "Lord, do not hold this sin against them" (Acts 7:60)?

Or is the Psalmist praying, not against human beings, but against the devil and his angels, to whom sinners and the ungodly belong? In that case, he does not pray against him in wrath, but in mercy.

When someone who is ungodly is justified, he is made just instead of ungodly, and he passes out of the possession of the devil and into the temple of God. If you want to rule over something, and the possession of it is taken away from you, that is a punishment. And this punishment—that he should no longer possess those whom he now possesses—is what the Psalmist calls the "anger" of God against the devil.

–St. Augustine, *Exposition on Psalm 7*

IN GOD'S PRESENCE, CONSIDER . . .

How much time have I spent lately praying for the deliverance of sinners who have given themselves over to bondage to the devil?

CLOSING PRAYER

Lord, remember your straying sheep, and all who need the tender care of your holy angels.

The world belongs to Christ, not Satan

Satan tempted Christ by promising to give him all the kingdoms of the world. But those are not his to give, says St. Cyril of Alexandria. All the kingdoms of the world already belong to Christ, and any power Satan has is his only by fraud.

"And the devil took him up, and showed him all the kingdoms of the world in a moment of time" (Luke 4:5). Malignant, wicked, and cursed being! How did you dare show the Lord all the kingdoms of the whole creation, and say, "All these are mine; now therefore if you will fall down and worship me, I will give them to you"? How can you promise what is not yours? Who made you heir of God's kingdom? Who made you lord of all under Heaven? You have seized these things by fraud. Restore them therefore to the incarnate Son, the Lord of all.

Hear what the prophet Isaiah says about you: "For a burning place has long been prepared; yea, for the king it is made ready, its pyre made deep and wide, with fire and wood in abundance; the breath of the Lord, like a stream of brimstone, kindles it" (Isa. 30:33). Then how did you, whose lot is the inextinguishable flame, promise to the King of all what he already owns? Did you think he would worship you—he at whom all things tremble—while the Seraphim and all the angelical powers hymn his glory?

"It is written, 'You shall worship the Lord your God, and him only shall you serve'" (Luke 4:8). It was appropriate for him to mention this commandment, striking as it were his very heart. For before his advent, Satan had deceived all under Heaven, and was himself everywhere worshiped: but the law of God, ejecting him from the dominion he had usurped by fraud, has commanded men to worship only him who by nature and in truth is God, and to offer service to him alone.

–St. Cyril of Alexandria, *Commentary on Luke*, Sermon 12

IN GOD'S PRESENCE, CONSIDER . . .

When I feel tempted to despair over the world, does it help to remember that Satan has no real rule, and that Christ wins in the end?

CLOSING PRAYER

Preserve me, Lord, from all temptations of the evil one, and keep me in your service.

Even Satan's sin accomplished God's will

God's plan is so well thought out that even the sinful free will of Satan and the wicked angels could not go against it. In fact, says St. Augustine, God contrives to use their sin, and ours, to bring about his will.

These are the great "works of the Lord: sought out according to all his wills" (Ps. 111:2). In fact, they are so wisely "sought out" that, when his angelic and human creation sinned—that is, did not do what he willed, but what it willed—he could still accomplish what he himself had willed. And he accomplished it through the same will in his creatures by which the first act against the Creator's will had been done. As the Supreme Good, he made good use of evil deeds, for the condemnation of those whom he had justly predestined to punishment and for the salvation of those whom he had mercifully predestined to grace.

As far as they were concerned, they were doing what God did not will them to do. But as far as God's omnipotence is concerned, they were quite unable to achieve their purpose. By their very act of going against his will, they accomplished his will. This is the meaning of the statement, "Great are the works of the Lord: sought out according to all his wills": that in a strange and indescribable way even what is done *against* his will is not done *without* his will. It would not be done if he did not allow it (and surely his permission is not unwilling but willing), nor would he who is good allow the evil to be done, unless in his omnipotence he could bring good even out of evil.

–St. Augustine, *Enchiridion*, chapter 26

We know that nothing can really be done without God's will. But is God's will being accomplished *through* my own will, as it is with the good angels, or in spite of it, with Satan and his angels?

Lord, make me an instrument of your will, and remove every motion of my spirit that is not in accordance with your will. Make me to serve as your angels serve.

The devil's power to hurt comes from God

The devil wills evil, says St. Augustine, but God's will is always done even through the wickedness of the devil. Nevertheless, Satan will be rightfully punished, because his will was, and is, to hurt us.

Even the power of those who are hurtful is from God alone. For it is not unrighteous that, when the wicked receive the power of being hurtful, both the patience of the good should be tested and the iniquity of the evil punished. Through power given to the devil Job was tested so that he might appear righteous, and Peter was tempted so that he should not be presumptuous, and Paul was buffeted so that he should not be exalted, and Judas was damned so that he should hang himself.

So when, through the power he has given the devil, God himself has done all things righteously, nevertheless punishment will at last be rendered to the devil—not because these things were justly done, but for his unrighteous willing to be hurtful, which was his own will. Then it will be said to the impious who persevered in consenting to his wickedness, "Depart from me into the eternal fire prepared for the devil and his angels" (Matt. 25:41).

–St. Augustine, *On the Nature of Good, Against the Manicheans*, 32

IN GOD'S PRESENCE, CONSIDER . . .

In what ways am I consenting to the devil's wickedness every day?

CLOSING PRAYER

Sovereign almighty, from whom all power comes, cleanse my mind and my thoughts from all influence of the devil.

Even the evil angels are God's instruments

God uses the evil angels as his instruments for correcting us, says St. Augustine. The purpose of these punishments is to bring us back to the right path, so that we won't be condemned forever at the last judgment.

"God is a just judge, strong and patient: is he angry every day?" (Ps. 7:11). What God is judge, but the Lord, who judges the people?

He is just; "he will repay every man for what he has done" (Matt. 16:27).

He is strong, meaning in endurance; though he is all-powerful, for our salvation he even put up with ungodly persecutors.

He is patient; after his resurrection, he did not hurry off right away to punish even those who persecuted him, but put up with them, so that they might at last turn from that ungodliness to salvation. And still he puts up with them, reserving the last penalty for the last judgment, and up to this present time inviting sinners to repentance.

"Is he angry every day?" Perhaps "bringing in anger" would be a better way of putting it than "being angry" (and so we find it in the Greek copies). In other words, the anger with which he punishes is not in him, but in the minds of those ministers who obey the commandments of truth, through whom orders are given right down to the lower ministries, who are called angels of wrath, to punish sin. They delight in the punishment of mortals not for the sake of justice, in which they have no pleasure, but for the sake of malice. God then does not *bring in* anger every day—that is, he does not collect his ministers for vengeance every day. For now the patience of God invites to repentance: but in the last time, when mortals through their hardness and unrepentant hearts have stored up for themselves wrath "on the day of wrath when God's righteous judgment will be revealed" (Rom. 2:5), then he will brandish his sword.

—St. Augustine, *Exposition on Psalm 7*

IN GOD'S PRESENCE, CONSIDER . . .

Do I look upon my misfortunes as occasions of conversion? Do I stand with the good angels in everyday skirmishes of spiritual warfare?

CLOSING PRAYER

Holy angels, win me the fortitude to face adversity, to accept chastisement for my sins, and to grow in virtue through the trials that God permits in my life.

Demons are weapons against the devil

Even when the evil angels turn their strength against us, says St. Augustine, they're actually weapons in our struggle against Satan. If we don't despair when we run into trouble, then Satan loses, and we're made stronger by the struggle.

You have made me the reproach of the foolish. You have so willed it, that I should live among those, and preach the Truth among those, who love vanity; and I can't help being laughingstock to them. For "we have become a spectacle to the world, to angels and to men" (1 Cor. 4:9): to angels who praise us, and to men who censure us. Or rather to angels, some of whom praise, some of whom are censuring us, and to men also, some of whom are praising, and some censuring us.

Both the one and the other are weapons for us. The one is on the right hand, the other on the left, but both of them are weapons. Both of these kinds of weapons, both those on the right hand and those on the left—both those who praise, and those who censure—both those who pay us honor, and those who heap dishonor upon us—with both these kinds, I say, I fight against the devil; with both of these I strike him. I defeat him with prosperity, if I am not corrupted by it; I defeat him by adversity, if I am not broken in spirit by it.

—St. Augustine, *Exposition on Psalm 39*, 15

What's troubling me most right now? How can I use it as a weapon against Satan?

Lord, in my journey, always defend me from the troubles and storms stirred up by the devil.

Even magic comes from God's will

The magicians of Pharaoh, says St. Augustine, were able to duplicate some of the plagues by magic. But their magic had its limits. Nothing can be done, even by magic, without God's will.

Now, a weak judgment might ask why miracles like these can also be done by magic—for the wise men of Pharaoh also made serpents, and did other similar things.

Yet it is still more wonderful that the power of those magicians, though it could make serpents, completely failed when it came to very small flies. Gnats, the third plague that struck the proud people of Egypt, are very short-lived little flies, but the magicians certainly failed to make them, saying, "This is the finger of God" (Exod. 8:19).

This tells us that not even those angels and powers of the air who sinned, who have been thrown down from their homes in the lofty ethereal purity to the lowest darkness as their own special prison, who give the magic arts whatever power they have, can do anything except by power given from above.

–St. Augustine, *On the Trinity*, 3.7

IN GOD'S PRESENCE, CONSIDER . . .

How does it change my view of the world to know that even the wicked angels get their power only from God?

CLOSING PRAYER

Lord, turn me away from dealings with demons and every wicked thing, and let me devote my whole life to you.

The will of God is the cause of everything

St. Augustine argues that the will of God is ultimately the cause of everything that happens in the world. Along the way he gives us a beautiful picture of Heaven, where the angels are "combined in one will by a kind of spiritual fire of love."

Let us turn our thoughts to that heavenly country above, from which we are pilgrims down here. There the will of God, who makes the angels spirits, and his ministers a burning fire (Ps. 104:4), presides among spirits joined in perfect peace and friendship. They are combined in one will by a kind of spiritual fire of love. There God's will, in its own house and temple, sits, so to speak, on a high and holy secret seat. From there it spreads itself through all things by perfectly ordered movements of the creature—first spiritual, and then bodily. It uses everything according to the unchangeable choice of its own will—bodiless or bodily things, rational or irrational spirits, good by his grace or evil by their own will.

But the coarser and lower bodies are governed in due order by the living spirit, and the living spirit without intelligence is governed by the living spirit with intelligence, and the intelligent living spirit that falls and sins is governed by the intelligent living spirit that is pious and just, and that is governed by God himself.

So every creature is governed by its Creator. From, through, and in its Creator it is created and established.

Thus it happens that the will of God is the first and highest cause of every bodily appearance and motion.

–St. Augustine, *On the Trinity*, 3.2

IN GOD'S PRESENCE, CONSIDER . . .

How could I combine my will with the will of the angels?

CLOSING PRAYER

Holy Lord, I am sinful, but accept my praise along with the praise of the holy Cherubim and Seraphim.

Pursued by the angel of the Lord

A terrifying image from Psalm 35 provokes St. Augustine to meditate on how God punishes. When God sends his angel to pursue the wicked, it's not out of anger, but simply the nature of righteousness at work.

"Let them be like chaff before the wind, with the angel of the Lord driving them on! Let their way be dark and slippery, with the angel of the Lord pursuing them!" (Ps. 35:5-6).

A horrible way! Everyone is afraid of darkness alone, and everyone avoids a slippery way alone. How will you go in a dark and slippery way? Where will you find a foothold?

These two evils are the great punishments of humanity. Darkness is ignorance. A slippery way is luxury.

"With the angels of the Lord pursuing them": so that they will not be able to stand. If you were in a dark and slippery way, and you see that you will fall if you move your foot, and there is no light in front of you, you might decide to wait until light came. But here is the angel of the Lord pursuing you!

The Psalmist predicted that these things would happen to them—not as though he wanted them to happen. But even though the prophet says these things in the Spirit of God, in the same way God does, with sure judgment, with a judgment good, righteous, holy, tranquil—not moved with anger, or with bitter jealousy, or with a desire to make enemies, but of punishing wickedness with righteousness—nevertheless, it is a prophecy.

–St. Augustine, *Exposition on Psalm 35*, 6

Am I in danger of falling into the "dark and slippery way," with the angel pursuing me? What am I doing to overcome ignorance and luxury?

CLOSING PRAYER

Lord, send your angels to pursue those who mistreat me, to win them over to your cause, to inspire their conversion, to give them true peace.

Angels are avenging powers

Although the good angels want nothing more than our salvation, sometimes they must be the instruments of God's judgment. St. John Chrysostom points out that, although God came down to earth himself to save us, when it is necessary to punish us that work is usually done by the angels.

Let us not be unduly philosophical. Let us show ourselves pitying, that we may be pitied.

There's nothing like this beautiful trait: to us, nothing so marks the stamp of human nature as showing pity and being kind to our fellow humans. In fact, this is why the laws consign the whole business of punishment to public executioners. They compel the judge to punish so far as to pronounce the sentence, but after that they call on the executioners to perform the act itself.

This is a great truth: though the punishment is just, it is not the part of a generous soul to inflict punishment. It requires another sort of person for this. Even God doesn't punish by his own hand, but by means of the angels.

Then are they executioners, the angels? God forbid! I'm not saying that. But they are avenging powers. When Sodom was destroyed, the whole thing was done by them as the instruments. When the judgments in Egypt were inflicted, it was through them.

–St. John Chrysostom, *Homily 43 on the Acts of the Apostles*

IN GOD'S PRESENCE, CONSIDER . . .

Pity is a virtue woven into our nature by God, and it is a reflection of divine mercy. Do I characteristically show this virtue? Do I reflect God's judgment—as faithfully as the angels do—in my own judgments?

CLOSING PRAYER

Guardian Angel, help me to judge wisely the things of this earth, so that with you I may enjoy the things of Heaven.

Being punished is not an evil

Are the angels evil when they punish sinners? No, says Dionysius the Areopagite: what is evil is not being justly punished when we have earned punishment.

Evil does not exist in the angels. By participation, the angel is in a secondary degree what God, whom he announces, is in the first degree as Cause. If the angel who has the likeness of good proclaims the goodness of God, then the angel is a likeness of Almighty God: a manifestation of the unmanifested Light—an untarnished mirror, as clear as can be, flawless, pure, without spot. He receives, so to speak, the full beauty of the good-stamped likeness of God without stain. Then he pours out, without impurity, the goodness of the Silence who dwells in the innermost shrines.

Evil, then, is not even in angels. But are they evil when they punish sinners? By that rule those who punish criminals would be evil, and so would those priests who shut the profane out of the divine mysteries.

But being punished is not an evil; what is evil is becoming worthy of punishment in the first place. And being deservedly expelled from holy things is not evil; what is evil is becoming accursed by God, and unholy, and unfit for things that are undefiled.

–Dionysius the Areopagite, *The Divine Names*, 4.22

IN GOD'S PRESENCE, CONSIDER . . .

We all sin and become worthy of punishment. But how often do I ask my guardian angel for help in resisting temptation?

CLOSING PRAYER

Guardian Angel, be with me when I confess my sins; remind me of the transgressions I need to confess, and help shield me from the temptation to sin again.

Angels hate chastising us

The angels are sometimes ministers of God's just chastisement. But they don't like it, St. Ambrose tells us. Remember, he says, that the angels in Heaven rejoice over the salvation of even one sinner.

And shouldn't we believe that the angels themselves, who in the toils of this world fulfill various ministries, as we read in the Revelation of St. John, also groan when they're made the ministers of vengeance and destruction? Since their life is blessed, wouldn't they rather spend it in their original state of tranquility than be interrupted by the infliction of vengeance on our sins? If they rejoice in the salvation of one sinner, surely they must groan over the miseries of such grievous sins.

So if the creatures and powers of Heaven suffer the bondage of corruption, but still in hope that hereafter they may rejoice on our behalf and together with us, let us also alleviate the sufferings of this present time by the hope and expectation of future glory.

–St. Ambrose, *Letter 34*, 10-11

IN GOD'S PRESENCE, CONSIDER . . .

When I hear of someone receiving a just punishment, is my first reaction "serves him right"? Or do I remember, like the angels, to pray for his salvation?

CLOSING PRAYER

Father, I pray that you will not send chastisements too heavy for my strength, but send your angels to preserve me from all temptations of the enemy.

Don't listen even to an angel preaching heresy

St. Paul warned the Galatians not to listen even to an angel from Heaven if he preached any gospel other than what they had already heard. Could a heavenly angel actually do that? No, says St. Vincent of Lerins. But St. Paul means that, even if the impossible did happen, we should never deviate from the one gospel.

These people were wandering around in provinces and cities, carrying their venal errors with them. Some of them had found their way to Galatia, and when the Galatians heard them, they felt sick of the truth and vomited up the manna of Apostolic and Catholic doctrine. They were delighted with the garbage of heretical novelty.

The apostle then had to exercise the authority of his office and deliver his sentence with the utmost severity. "But even if we, or an angel from Heaven, should preach to you a gospel contrary to that which we preached to you, let him be accursed" (Gal. 1:8).

Why does he say "even if *we*"? Why not "even if *I*"?

He means even if Peter, or Andrew, or John—in short, the whole company of the apostles—should preach something contrary to what we have preached to you, let him be accursed.

What tremendous severity! He spares neither himself nor his fellow apostles, so he may preserve unaltered the faith that was first delivered. Nor is this all. He goes on: "*Even if an angel from Heaven* should preach to you a gospel contrary to that which we preached to you, let him be accursed." For the preservation of the faith as it was delivered, it was not enough just to refer to human beings: he had to take in angels as well. "Even if we, or an angel from Heaven." Not that the holy angels of Heaven are capable of sinning now. But what he means is this: "Even if what *cannot* happen *did* happen—if any one, whoever he may be, should attempt to alter the faith once for all delivered, let him be accursed."

—St. Vincent of Lerins, *Commonitory*, 8

Do I seek the help of the angels in the discernment of spirits? Do I recognize that not even an angel will dare to contradict the teaching of Christ's Church?

Guardian Angel, protect me with your power, and keep me in the light of divine truth.

Angels are bound to the gospel

The Donatists were a schismatic sect that called itself the only true Church. St. Augustine warns that no one—not even an angel—can truly preach any gospel but the gospel Christ preached to us.

You were kind enough to tell us about the letter sent to you by a Donatist priest—although, with the spirit of a true Catholic, you hold it in contempt. So, to help you in seeking his welfare (assuming that his folly isn't incurable), we beg you to forward to him the following reply.

He wrote that an angel had told him to declare to you the episcopal succession of the Christianity of your town—to you, mind you, who hold the Christianity not of your own town only, nor of Africa only, but of the whole world: the Christianity that has been published, and is now published to all nations.

This proves that they don't think it's important that they themselves are not ashamed of being cut off, and that they aren't doing anything to come back together with us while it's still possible. They're not happy unless they do their best to cut others off, and bring them to share their own fate, as dried-up branches fit for the flames.

So, even if you had yourself been visited by that angel he says appeared to him (which we think was just a cunning fiction), and even if the angel had said to you the very words he says he was told to say to you—even in that case it would have been your duty to remember the words of the Apostle: "But even if we, or an angel from Heaven, should preach to you a gospel contrary to that which we preached to you, let him be accursed" (Gal. 1:8).

–St. Augustine, *Letter 53*, 1.1

Am I careful to seek the help of the *holy* angels? Do I take care to address my angel directly as "*my* guardian angel" or "Angel of God"?

CLOSING PRAYER

My Guardian Angel, all you holy angels, protect me from the works and the deceptions of malicious spirits.

Helping a heretic escape false angels

When asked for advice on dealing with a heretic who claimed to have revelations from angels, St. Augustine gave this sensible advice. If the angel is leading away from Catholic truth, it's a false angel. But don't despise him: instead, let him know how much you love him and want him back in the Church.

The Apostle Paul says somewhere that even Satan transforms himself into an angel of light, so it is not strange that his servants should disguise themselves as ministers of righteousness (2 Cor. 11:13-15). So if your correspondent really did see an angel teaching him error, and wanting to separate Christians from the Catholic unity, he has met an angel of Satan transforming himself into an angel of light. On the other hand, if he has lied to you, and he did not see such a vision, then he himself is a servant of Satan disguising himself as a minister of righteousness.

Yet if he is not completely stubborn and perverse beyond all correction, then if he thinks about what we have said, he may still be delivered from misleading others and from being misled himself. Since you gave me the opportunity, I have met him without any hostility, remembering what the Apostle said about people like him: "Have nothing to do with stupid, senseless controversies; you know that they breed quarrels. And the Lord's servant must not be quarrelsome but kindly to everyone, an apt teacher, forbearing, correcting his opponents with gentleness. God may perhaps grant that they will repent and come to know the truth, and they may escape from the snare of the devil, after being captured by him to do his will" (2 Tim. 2:23-26). So if I have said anything hard to him, let him know that it does not come from the bitterness of argument, but from love that intensely desires him to come back to the right path.

–St. Augustine, Letter 53

IN GOD'S PRESENCE, CONSIDER . . .

How would St. Augustine's advice help me deal with non-Catholics in my everyday life? How would I help them escape the false angels without getting mired in a "stupid senseless controversy"?

CLOSING PRAYER

Have pity, O Lord God, lest they who pass by trample on the unfledged bird; and send your angel to restore it to its nest, that it may live until it can fly.

Judge the message, not the messenger

St. Clement of Alexandria tells us that even the devil can speak the truth when it suits his purposes. It's a hard thing to learn, but we have to judge the message by its content, not by the messenger.

It's true that the main purpose of the pruning hook is pruning. But we also use it to separate twigs that have got tangled, and to cut the thorns that have grown along with the vines when they're not very easy to reach. All these things have to do with pruning.

In the same way, we are made principally for the knowledge of God. But we also measure land, practice agriculture, and philosophize. The first promotes life, the second living well, and the third the study of things that can be demonstrated.

Now, let those who say that philosophy was invented by the devil know this, that the Scripture says the devil is transformed into an angel of light (2 Cor. 11:14). What is he doing when he's transformed into an angel of light? Plainly he's about to prophesy. But if he prophesies as an angel of light, he will speak what is true. If he prophesies what is angelical, what belongs to the light, then he prophesies what does us good when he is transformed into an angel of light—even though he is not really an angel of light, but an apostate. How could he deceive anyone, unless he drew the lover of knowledge into fellowship with him, and then drew him into falsehood afterwards? We'll find that he knows the truth—he may not understand it, but he is not ignorant of it.

So philosophy is not false, even if it is a thief and a liar who speaks the truth by changing the way he works. And we should not condemn what is said on account of who says it (though we have to keep that in mind in the case of those who claim to be prophets now). We have to look at what is said to see whether it sticks to the truth.

—St. Clement of Alexandria, *Stromata*, 6.8

IN GOD'S PRESENCE, CONSIDER . . .

How easily do I accept the truth from someone I don't like? How do I know how to recognize the truth even when it comes from the mouth of a demon?

CLOSING PRAYER

Remember, Lord, all who rightly interpret the Word of your truth. Send your angels to protect them from the deceit of the evil one.

Keep the creed all your life

St. Cyril of Jerusalem advises his students to memorize the creed word for word, and to keep it fresh in their memories all their lives. If you know your creed, he says, you know everything important about the Christian faith.

But as a learner, and in your profession of faith, take and hold only that faith which the Church delivers to you, and which is established from all Scripture.

Not everyone can read Scripture: some are uneducated, and others are too busy. Therefore we encompass all the whole doctrine of the faith in a few articles, so that the soul may not perish for lack of instruction. I want you to remember these articles word for word, and repeat it diligently among yourselves. Do not write it on paper, but get it by memory and engrave it on your heart as if it were on a monument.

I want you to keep this creed all through your life as a provision for your journey, and never receive any other creed besides this—even if I myself should change and contradict what I am teaching you now, or even if some opposing angel, transformed into an angel of light, should try to lead you astray. "But even if we, or an angel from Heaven, should preach to you a gospel contrary to that which we preached to you, let him be accursed" (Gal. 1:8).

—St. Cyril of Jerusalem, *Catechetical Lecture* 5, 6

IN GOD'S PRESENCE, CONSIDER . . .

Who are the "angels of light" who might try to persuade me to accept a different creed? How can I recognize them?

CLOSING PRAYER

Guardian Angel, keep the truth of the creed in my mind, and help me distinguish false spirits who would lead me away from the True Faith.

Let false hope perish

Continuing his meditation on Job's cursing the day he was born and the night he was conceived, St. Gregory the Great sees the curse as a renunciation of everything Satan offers to us.

This holy man (Job) mourned, in his own sorrows, the condition of the whole human race. He saw nothing that was in any way particular to himself in his own particular suffering. It's very appropriate for him to bring back to mind the original cause of sin, and to soften the pain inflicted on him by thinking about its justice.

He can look at humankind, and see where we fell from, and where we have fallen to, and exclaim, "Let the day perish wherein I was born, and the night which said, 'A man-child is conceived'" (Job 3:3).

It's as if he were saying, in so many words, "Let the hope perish that the apostate angel held out to me—who, when he disguised himself as day, was shining with the promise of a divine nature, but then showed himself as night and brought a cloud over the light of our immortality. Let our old enemy perish, who showed us the light of promises, but gave us the darkness of sin—who presented himself as day by his wheedling, but led us into a night of utter darkness by closing our hearts with blindness."

—St. Gregory the Great, Moralia in Job, 4.6

IN GOD'S PRESENCE, CONSIDER . . .
Do I renounce Satan and all his works every day?

CLOSING PRAYER
Lord, I renounce Satan and all his evil works, all his empty promises, and all his worldly magnificence.

Against Principalities and Powers

As long as we're sinners, says St. Augustine, we're slaves to the devil and his angels. Our life on earth is a struggle against their dominion.

The Lord sent his lambs into the midst of wolves—that is, righteous men into the midst of sinners, to preach the gospel received in the time of man from the inestimable divine Wisdom, so that he might call us from sin to righteousness.

But what the Apostle says, that our struggle is not against flesh and blood, but against Principalities and Powers (Eph. 6:12), and the other things that have been quoted, this means that the devil and his angels, like us, have fallen and lapsed by sin, and have secured possession of earthly things—that is, sinful human beings, who, as long as we are sinners, are under their yoke; just as when we shall be righteous, we shall be under the yoke of righteousness. And we contend against them, so that passing over to righteousness we may be freed from their dominion.

–St. Augustine, *Disputation Against Fortunatus*, 23

IN GOD'S PRESENCE, CONSIDER . . .

Do I struggle against the evil Principalities and Powers as much as I should? Or do I often end up letting them have their way?

CLOSING PRAYER

Compassionate and merciful God, do not withhold your aid from me in my struggle with the devil.

Angels don't stand between us and Christ

Like many Christian interpreters, St. Augustine sees Psalm 24 as a description of Christ's triumphal ascent into Heaven. Angels are powerful beings and have their role in managing the world, he says, but we don't worship them. Only the Lord is King of Glory.

"Who is this King of glory?" (Ps. 24:10).

What, you too, "prince of the power of the air" (Eph. 2:2)—you marvel and ask, "Who is this King of glory?"

"The Lord of hosts, he is the King of glory."

Yes, his body is now made alive again. He who was tempted marches above you; he who was tempted by the angel, the deceiver, goes above all angels.

So none of you had better put himself in front of us and stand in our way, trying to make us worship him as a god. Neither Principalities, nor Angels, nor Powers, will separate us from the love of Christ (Rom. 8:38-39).

It is good to trust in the Lord, rather than to trust in a prince. "Let him who boasts, boast of the Lord" (1 Cor. 1:31). Angels certainly are powers in the administration of this world, but the Lord of hosts, he is the King of glory.

—St. Augustine, *Exposition on Psalm 24*, 10

IN GOD'S PRESENCE, CONSIDER . . .

Do I recognize that when I prevail over temptation, I inherit greater glory? Do I ask the angels to minister to me as they ministered to Christ in the desert of temptation?

CLOSING PRAYER

Angel of God, come to me when I am tempted. Give me light, wisdom, hope, strength, and joy to sustain me in my every struggle.

Lord, who is like you?

Don't listen to anyone who tells you to worship idols, or nature, or even angels, says St. Augustine. God alone made all these things and they are nothing without him. Instead of worshiping angels, we should worship God as Creator of the angels.

"All my bones shall say, O Lord, who is like you?" (Ps. 35:10).

Who can say anything worthy of these words? I think they can only be pronounced, not explained.

Why do you seek this or that? What is like your Lord? You have him right in front of you. The unrighteous have shown me delights, but nothing like your law, O Lord!

There have been persecutors who have said, "Worship Saturn" or "Worship Mercury." I do not worship idols, he says: "Lord, who is like you?" They have eyes, but do not see. They have ears, but do not hear. Lord, who is like you, who made the eye to see, the ear to hear?

But I do not worship idols, he says, because a workman made them. "Worship a tree or mountain; did a workman make them, too?" Here too, Lord, who is like you? They show me earthly things, but you are Creator of the earth.

Then they might turn from these to the higher creation, and say to me, "Worship the moon, worship the sun, who with his light, as a great lamp in the heavens, makes the day." Here also I plainly say, "Lord, who is like you?" You made the moon and the stars; you set the sun alight to rule the day; you put the heavens together.

But there are many better things that are invisible. Perhaps someone will say to me, "Worship angels, adore angels." And here also will I say, "Lord, who is like you?" Even the angels you have created. The angels are nothing except by seeing you. It is better to possess you with them, than to fall from you by worshiping them.

–St. Augustine, *Exposition on Psalm 35*, 6

IN GOD'S PRESENCE, CONSIDER . . .

Do I make time in my prayer to praise the Lord for the wonder of creation—beginning with the angels? Do I recognize that praise is the purest form of prayer and the surest protection against idolatry?

CLOSING PRAYER

Let me be yours, O Lord of all the angels, for I worship no other God than you, and name no other name than yours.

Giving the devil his due

Each of us, says Rufinus of Aquileia, will get the reward we have earned in the final judgment. And that goes for the devil, too, who—along with all his angels—has earned the eternal fire.

In addition, I believe in a judgment to come, in which everyone will receive the reward he earned in his bodily life, according to what he has done, whether good or evil.

And if the reward for us humans is to be according to our works, imagine how much more this will be true in the case of the devil, who is the universal cause of sin. Of the devil himself our belief is what is written in the Gospel: that both he and all his angels will receive as their portion the eternal fire, and with him those who do his works—that is, who become the accusers of their brethren.

So if anyone denies that the devil is to be subjected to the eternal fires, may he have his part with him in the eternal fire, so that he may know by experience the fact that he now denies.

—Rufinus of Aquileia, *Apology*, 5

IN GOD'S PRESENCE, CONSIDER . . .

Do I accept what God has revealed, and what the Church teaches about the devil and about Hell?

CLOSING PRAYER

Lord, protect me from evil, save me from the fires of Hell. May my life be judged worthy of Heaven where I wish to spend eternity with your angels and saints.

Learn to recognize Satan in disguise

Satan can transform himself into an angel of light, says St. Augustine. If he does, we need to rely on the help of God to keep us on the right path, and to teach us to see through Satan's disguise.

It's very important to be able to see and know when Satan has transformed himself into an angel of light; otherwise, by deceiving us that way, he could seduce us into doing real damage.

There's no danger to our religion when he only deceives our bodily senses, and doesn't turn our minds from the true and correct judgment that guides our life of faith. Even if he pretends to be good and does or says things that a good angel would say, and he fools us that way, the mistake isn't dangerous; it can't kill our Christian faith.

But when he starts to lead us into his own ways with this strange trickery, then we really have to be on the alert to recognize him and not follow him. How few of us can avoid his deadly schemes, unless God guides and saves us!

But the fact that it's so difficult to recognize Satan's tricks is actually useful in one way: it reminds us that no one can put his hope in himself, or in any other person. Everyone who belongs to God should throw his hope in with God. Certainly no religious person would deny that this is the best way for us.

–St. Augustine, *Enchiridion*, chapter 16

IN GOD'S PRESENCE, CONSIDER . . .

What tools has God given us to distinguish the deceptions of Satan? How do I make use of them?

CLOSING PRAYER

Lord, humble the enemies of your Church, and put Satan behind us.

Angels don't want our worship

Some human beings are called "gods" even in the Bible, says St. Augustine—although of course only metaphorically. But Scripture never calls angels gods even metaphorically, so that we will understand that angels desire that we should not worship them, but the God whom they and we serve.

So that no one may think that there is no living and intelligent nature that delights in the pagan sacrifices, the Apostle adds, "what pagans sacrifice they offer to demons and not to God. I do not want you to be partners with demons" (1 Cor. 10:20).

So if we never find in the divine words that the holy angels are called "gods," I think the best reason is so that humans may not be persuaded by the name to offer that ministry and service of religion to the holy angels that the angels would not wish humans to pay at all to anyone but God, who is God of both angels and human beings.

Thus they are much more correctly called *angels*, which in our language is *messengers*, so that, by the name of their function, not their substance, we may clearly understand that they want us to worship the God whom they announce.

– St. Augustine, Exposition on Ps. 136, 3

IN GOD'S PRESENCE, CONSIDER . . .

Are there some strong desires or interests in my life that would tend to make me a partner with demons?

CLOSING PRAYER

Remember me when I am backsliding, Lord, and send in your divine mercy, your angels to help me.

Angels want us to worship God, not them

The Name of God is wonderful and powerful, says St. John Chrysostom. It's the only name a Christian can invoke. It's fine to ask the angels for help, but if we pray to them as if they were gods, they'll throw our prayers away, because all they want is the honor of God.

There is nothing equal to this Name. Everywhere it is wonderful. "Your name is oil poured out," it says (Song 1:3). Whoever speaks it is filled with perfume immediately. "No one," it is said, "can say 'Jesus is Lord' except by the Holy Spirit" (1 Cor. 12:3). That is how great this name is.

If you say, "In the name of the Father, and of the Son, and of the Holy Ghost," you've said everything. Look what great things you've done! You've *created a man,* and done everything else that goes with baptism!

The Name is just as formidable in commanding diseases. That's why the devil introduced the custom of using the names of angels, because he envied us the honor. Incantations with angels' names are for the demons! Even if it's the name of an angel, or an archangel, or one of the Cherubim, do not allow it. Those powers will not accept it if you call on them that way. They will throw away your prayers when they see their Master dishonored.

–St. John Chrysostom, *Homily 9 on Colossians*

IN GOD'S PRESENCE, CONSIDER . . .

How do I honor the Name of God? Do I treat God's name as something holy every day?

CLOSING PRAYER

Lord, you are far above every Principality, and Power, and Might, and Dominion, and every name that is named, not only in this world, but in the world that is to come.

Worship God, not angels

St. Augustine explains why we don't worship angels. Just as Paul and Barnabas refused to be worshiped when pagan Greeks tried to pay them divine honors, so the good angels have only one desire: to lead us to God. The only angels who desired worship were the ones who were cast out of Heaven.

See what holy men do—men who are like the angels. If you find some holy man who serves God and try to worship him instead of God, he won't let you. He refuses to take the honor due to God for himself. He doesn't want to be like God to you, but to be under God with you. This is what the holy Apostles Paul and Barnabas did.

These good men refused to be worshiped by people who wanted to treat them as gods. They insisted that only God could be worshiped. Only God could be adored. Only God could be offered sacrifices.

In the same way, the holy angels seek only the glory of the God they love. They try to lead and prompt everyone they love to contemplate God. Because they are messengers, they bring God's message, not their own. And because they are soldiers, they seek only the glory of their Captain. If they seek their own glory, they're condemned as usurpers. That's what happened to the devil and his angels: he claimed divine honor for himself and all his demons. He filled pagan temples and persuaded people to make him idols and sacrifice to him.

–St. Augustine, *Exposition on Psalm 97*, 10

IN GOD'S PRESENCE, CONSIDER . . .

Am I allowing the angels who surround me to lead me to God?

CLOSING PRAYER

Lord, teach me to trust that your holy angels desire only to lead me to you, and let me desire to follow where they lead.

Don't be surprised by demons' tricks

The evil angels can put on a good show, says St. Augustine. But that doesn't mean they're better than we are. We should remember that we who are on the side of God accomplish far greater miracles every day.

It is easy for the most worthless spirits to do things with their ethereal bodies that astonish souls weighed down by earthly bodies—even the souls of the better inclined. Earthly bodies themselves, once they are trained in skill and practice, can show us such great marvels in theater shows that those who never saw such things hardly believe them when they are told about them. Then why should it be hard for the devil and his angels, with their ethereal bodies, to make from corporeal elements things at which the flesh marvels? Why should it be hard for them, by hidden inspirations, to delude our senses, awake or asleep, or to drive us into a frenzy?

Though you may be better than a stage performer in life and character, you may gaze at the most worthless performer walking on a rope, or doing things with the motions of his body that are hard to believe—and yet you probably do not wish to do those things, or think that the performer is better than you are because he can do them. In the same way, if you are a faithful and pious soul, you may see the miracles of the demons, and the weakness of the flesh may make you shudder at them—yet for all that you will not deplore your own lack of power to do those things, or think that the demons are better than you are because they can do them. No, if you are a pious soul, you are in the company of the holy. And the holy, human or good angels, accomplish wonders through the power of God, to whom all things are subject, that are far greater, and quite the reverse of deceptive.

–St. Augustine, *On the Trinity*, 4.11

IN GOD'S PRESENCE, CONSIDER . . .

Do I allow the demons to distract me from holiness with glittery things like money and status?

CLOSING PRAYER

Lord, keep me thankful for your precious and heavenly gifts to me, and preserve me from the temptations set before me by the demonic powers.

Demons can't really give us prosperity

Pagans complained that neglecting their gods made Rome decline. St. Augustine replies that, even if it were true, it's far better to face adversity than to worship demons. But it's not true. Only God can really make us prosperous.

What beings are really propitiated by practicing such abominations in worship? Because Christianity has exposed the perversity and trickery of those devils (and it is also by their power that magic deceives people's minds), and because it has brought out the distinction between the holy angels and these malignant enemies, and has warned people to be on their guard against them, and even showed how it can be done—because of these things, Christianity is called an enemy of the State! As if any amount of adversity wouldn't be better than gaining prosperity by the aid of demons—even if worldly prosperity could be gained that way.

Yet it pleased God to keep us from being confused in this matter. In the age of comparative darkness of the Old Testament, in which the New Testament is hidden, God distinguished the first nation that worshiped the true God and despised false Gods by such prosperity in this world, that anyone can see from their case that prosperity is not at the disposal of devils, but only of him whom angels serve and devils fear.

–St. Augustine, *Letter 138*, 4

When I look for material prosperity, do I end up making deals with the demons? Do I compromise my Christian faith?

Guardian Angel, always remind me that adversity is far better than the help of demons. Guard me from temptation, and lead me to trust in God for my true prosperity.

Let them laugh

Even devils can sometimes perform apparent miracles, says St. Augustine, and if a rumor started that one of their own "philosophers" had done the miracles in the Scriptures, you would hear the same people who laugh at the Bible shouting in triumph.

If these objectors refuse to believe any narrative of a divine miracle, they must be refuted by another line of argument. In that case, they must not single out one particular miracle to be objected to, and called in question as incredible, but to denounce as incredible all narratives in which miracles of the same kind, or more remarkable ones, are recorded.

And yet, suppose what is written concerning Jonah were said to have been done by Apuleius of Madaura or Apollonius of Tyana—who, they boast, though unsupported by reliable testimony, performed many wonders. And even the devils do some works like those done by the holy angels—not in truth, but in appearance, and not by wisdom, but obviously by subtlety. What if some such event were narrated in connection with these men to whom they give the flattering name of magicians or philosophers? Then we should hear from their mouths sounds not of derision, but of triumph.

Well, fine—let them laugh at our Scriptures; let them laugh as much as they can, when they see themselves daily becoming fewer in number, while some are removed by death, and others by their embracing the Christian faith, and when all those things are being fulfilled which were predicted by the prophets who long ago laughed at them, and said that they would fight and bark against the truth in vain, and would gradually come over to our side; and who not only transmitted these statements to us, their descendants, for our learning, but promised that they should be fulfilled in our experience.

—St. Augustine, *Letter 102*

IN GOD'S PRESENCE, CONSIDER . . .

How do I react when someone derides Scripture? Am I tempted to explain away the angels and miracles in the Bible, as if they were embarrassments? Or do I have the patience to react calmly, reasonably, and tolerantly, the way St. Augustine does?

CLOSING PRAYER

Guardian Angel, keep the truth of God's word always before my eyes, and give me your assistance in spreading the truth to others around me.

Worshiping idols is worshiping demons

St. Augustine says that the only reason demons seduced us into worshiping them was because they knew that worship belongs to God alone.

The false gods, that is to say, the demons, which are lying angels, would never have required a temple, priesthood, sacrifice, and the other things connected with these from their worshipers, whom they deceive, had they not known that these things were due to the one true God.

When, therefore, these things are presented to God according to his inspiration and teaching, it is true religion; but when they are given to demons in compliance with their impious pride, it is baneful superstition. Accordingly, those who know the Christian Scriptures of both the Old and the New Testaments do not blame the profane rites of pagans on the mere ground of their building temples, appointing priests, and offering sacrifices, but on the ground of their doing all this for idols and demons.

As to idols, indeed, who doubts that they are completely devoid of perception? And yet, when they are placed in these temples and set on high on thrones of honor, so that they may be waited upon by suppliants and worshipers praying and offering sacrifices, then even these idols, though devoid both of feeling and of life, so affect weak minds, just because they appear to have the members and senses of a living being, that they appear to live and breathe, especially under the added influence of the profound veneration with which the multitude freely renders such costly service.

–St. Augustine, *Letter 102*

IN GOD'S PRESENCE, CONSIDER . . .

What are the demons I worship—the things that take me away from the worship of the one true God?

CLOSING PRAYER

Holy Guardian Angel, keep me from the worship of demons, and lead me to desire, as you do, only the true bliss of the divine vision.

Angels want us to be immortal and happy

The angels want us to be as happy as they are, says St. Augustine. That's why they refuse to let us worship them, but direct all our worship to God, the source of their own happiness.

The angels look on us miserable mortals compassionately and tenderly, and wish us to become immortal and happy—these blessed and immortal spirits, who inhabit celestial dwellings, and rejoice in the communications of their Creator's fullness, firm in his eternity, assured in his truth, holy by his grace. So it is very right that they do not desire us to sacrifice to themselves. For they know that they themselves are, along with us, his sacrifice.

For we and they together are the one city of God, to which it is said in the psalm, "Glorious things are spoken of you, O city of God" (Ps. 87:3)—the human part visiting here below, the angelic helping us from above. And it was from that heavenly city, in which God's will is the intelligible and unchangeable law—from that heavenly council-chamber (for they sit in counsel watching us)—that this Holy Scripture came down to us by the ministry of angels, in which it is written, "Whoever sacrifices to any god, save to the Lord only, shall be utterly destroyed" (Ex. 22:20).

This Scripture, this law, these precepts, have been confirmed by such miracles, that it is clear enough to whom these immortal and blessed spirits, who desire us to be like themselves, wish us to sacrifice.

–St. Augustine, *City of God*, 10.7

The angels put all their effort into directing our praises toward God. Do I do the same for other people, or am I happy to absorb a good bit of the praise for myself?

CLOSING PRAYER

Holy Guardian Angel, you love us with an unwavering love. Teach me to look upon others with the same constancy in charity.

Satan takes on all shapes

In St. Augustine's time, there were still many pagans who tried to find enlightenment in strange, sometimes even hallucinogenic, rituals. If you see angels when you're out of your mind, says St. Augustine, remember that Satan can look like an angel, but he still wants to hurt you.

As to those who perform these filthy cleansings by sacrilegious rites, and see in their initiated state (as Porphyry tells us further on, though we may question this vision) certain wonderfully lovely appearances of angels or gods, this is what the Apostle refers to when he speaks of Satan transforming himself into an angel of light (2 Cor. 11:14).

For these are the delusive appearances of that spirit who longs to entangle wretched souls in the deceptive worship of many and false gods, and to turn them aside from the true worship of the true God, by whom alone they are cleansed and healed, and who (as they used to say about Proteus) turns himself into all shapes—all of them equally hurtful, whether he assaults us as an enemy, or takes on the disguise of a friend.

–St. Augustine, *City of God*, 10.10

IN GOD'S PRESENCE, CONSIDER . . .

Do I understand that evil spirits make use of occult practices to manipulate human beings? Do I avoid those practices—fortune tellers, horoscopes, tarot readers, and so on—at all costs?

CLOSING PRAYER

Lord, deliver me from the evil one and his hosts; because yours is the kingdom, the power, the strength, the might, and the dominion in Heaven and on earth, now and always.

Make no sacrifices to angels

The more a being loves God, says St. Augustine, the less that being wants any of the worship due to God alone. That's why, although angels are incomparably more powerful and pure than we are, we never worship them.

As for the spiritual part of creation, it is either pious or impious: the pious being people and angels who are righteous, and who serve God in the right way; the impious being wicked people and angels, whom we also call devils.

Now, it's obvious that sacrifice must not be offered to a spiritual creature, even a righteous one, because the more pious and submissive to God any creature is, the less he presumes to aspire to the honor that he knows belongs to God alone.

Then how much worse it is to sacrifice to devils—that is, to a wicked spiritual creature—which, living in the comparatively dark heaven nearest the earth, as in the prison assigned to him in the air, is doomed to eternal punishment.

—St. Augustine, *Letter 102*

IN GOD'S PRESENCE, CONSIDER . . .

If an objective observer could see into my mind, would he see me offering sacrifice to devils, like greed or anger?

CLOSING PRAYER

Sanctify my soul, body, and spirit, Lord, and cast out the demons of worldly desires.

Only devils receive sacrifices

Even if you think you're worshiping angels, says St. Augustine, the only beings that receive your sacrifice are devils. The angels who love God could never accept the honor that belongs only to their Lord.

Some people say they are offering sacrifices to the higher celestial powers, which are not devils, and imagine that the only difference between themselves and us is the name: they call those powers gods, and we call them angels. But the only beings that really present themselves to those people, who are given over to be tossed around by many deceptions, are the devils, who find delight in the errors of humanity—and in a sense are nourished by those errors.

For the holy angels do not approve of any sacrifice except what is offered, according to the teaching of true wisdom and true religion, to the one true God, whom they serve in holy fellowship.

Impious presumption—in people or in angels—demands or desires the honors due to God alone for itself. But pious humility—in people or in angels—declines those honors when they are offered, and declares that they only belong to God. And we have some very notable examples of this conspicuously set forth in our sacred books.

–St. Augustine, *Letter 102*

IN GOD'S PRESENCE, CONSIDER . . .

If I'm flattered or honored immoderately, do I remember to follow the holy angels and put the honor where it really belongs?

CLOSING PRAYER

Guardian Angel, keep the love of God always before my mind, and lead me to praise the name of the Lord without boldness or pride.

How to earn the angels' help

Magical incantations won't earn you the help of the angels, says St. Augustine. What does earn us their help is trying to live a life as pure and good as theirs. If we do that, we can live among the angels on earth, even though our eyes can't see them.

We must certainly not try, through the supposed mediation of demons, to make use of the good will or help of the gods, or rather of the good angels. Instead, we earn their help by resembling them in their having a good will, through which we are with them, and live with them, and worship the same God with them, although we cannot see them with the eyes of our flesh.

We are not distant from them in place, but in merit of life, caused by our miserable unlikeness to them in will, and by the weakness of our character. For the mere fact that we live on earth under the conditions of life in the flesh does not prevent our fellowship with them. It is only prevented when we, in the impurity of our hearts, pay attention to earthly things. But in this present time, while we are being healed so that we may eventually be like them, we are brought near to them by faith, if by their assistance we believe that the God who is their blessedness is also ours.

–St. Augustine, *City of God*, 8.25

IN GOD'S PRESENCE, CONSIDER . . .

How would my life be different if I took the life of the angels as my model? What would I do differently today?

CLOSING PRAYER

My Guardian Angel, never leave me unprotected and preserve me from the misfortune of offending God.

Are Christians atheists?

One of the most common charges against the first Christians was that they were atheists! Well, says St. Justin Martyr, we are atheists—if you mean that we refuse to worship the demons who masquerade as gods in the pagan mythology. But we worship the only true God.

Since ancient times evil demons, making apparitions of themselves, both defiled women and corrupted boys, and showed such fearful sights to men, that those who did not use their reason in judging of the actions that were done were struck with terror. Carried away by fear, and not knowing that these were demons, they called them gods, and gave to each the name which each of the demons chose for himself.

When Socrates tried to bring these things to light by true reason and examination, and to deliver humanity from the demons, then the demons themselves, by means of men who rejoiced in iniquity, plotted his death as an atheist and a sacrilegious person, on the charge that he was introducing new gods.

They do the same thing in our case. For not only among the Greeks did the *Logos*, reason, prevail to condemn these things through Socrates, but also among the barbarians they were condemned by the *Logos* himself, who took shape, and became man, and was called Jesus Christ. In obedience to him, we not only deny that they who did such things as these are gods, but assert that they are wicked and impious demons, whose actions will not bear comparison with those even of men desirous of virtue.

This is why we are called atheists. And we confess that we *are* atheists, as far as gods of this sort are concerned. But not with respect to the most true God. We worship and adore him, and the Son who came forth from him and taught us these things—he and the host of the other good angels who follow and are made like him—and the prophetic Spirit. We know them in reason and truth, and declare what we have been taught without grudging to everyone who wishes to learn.

–St. Justin Maryr, *First Apology*, 5-6

IN GOD'S PRESENCE, CONSIDER . . .

Have I really renounced all the demons masquerading as gods? Or are there some false gods of today who can claim my allegiance?

CLOSING PRAYER

Guardian Angel, teach me to distinguish the false spirits from the true, and always to renounce whatever is not for my eternal good.

Satan does not control the Earth

Satan told Christ that he controlled all the kingdoms of the Earth. But he lied, says St. Irenaeus. God controls all the governments of the world, not Satan.

Since the authorities that exist "have been instituted by God" (Rom. 13:1), the devil obviously lied when he said, "These have been delivered to me, and I give them to whom I will" (Luke 4:6).

Kings are appointed by the law of the same Being who calls us all into existence, and those kings are adapted for the people who are placed under their government at that time. Some of them are given for the correction and the benefit of their subjects, and for the preservation of justice; but others, for the purposes of fear and punishment and rebuke. Still others, if we deserve it, are for deception, disgrace, and pride. The just judgment of God, as I have observed already, passes equally upon all.

The devil, however, since he is the apostate angel, can only go as far as he did at the beginning: he can deceive and lead astray the human mind into disobeying the commandments of God, and gradually darken the hearts of those who would try to serve him, until they forget the true God, and adore the devil as God.

–St. Irenaeus, *Against Heresies*, 5.24

Am I obedient to the lawful governments, at least as far as I can be and stay consistent with moral law? Do I remember to pray for the help of the angels who guard the governments that have power over me?

Lord Jesus Christ, strengthen the angels who guard all nations, and grant that the Church may always have peace with their governments.

Act like a demon, become a demon

People were often superstitious in St. John Chrysostom's day, and many of the uneducated were afraid of ghosts. St. John says that it's not dying a violent death that makes you an evil spirit: it's acting like an evil spirit.

Here, before I go on, I want to remove a wrong impression from your minds. For it is a fact that many of the less instructed think that the souls of those who die a violent death become wandering spirits. But this is not so. I repeat: it is *not so.*

It isn't the souls of those who die a violent death that become demons, but rather the souls of those who live in sin; not that their nature is changed, but that in their desires they imitate the evil nature of demons. Showing this very thing to the Jews, Christ said, "You are of your father the devil" (John 8:44). He said that they were the children of the devil, not because they were changed into a nature like his, but because they did the kinds of things he did. For the same reason he adds, "and your will is to do your father's desires." Also John says: "You brood of vipers! Who warned you to flee from the wrath to come? Bear fruit that befits repentance, and do not presume to say to yourselves, 'We have Abraham as our father'" (Matt. 3:7-9).

The Scripture, therefore, usually bases the laws of relationship, not on natural origin, but on good or evil disposition; and if anyone acts like or does the same things as a certain group, the Scripture declares him to be their "son" or their "brother."

–John Chrysostom, Four Discourses, *Chiefly on the Parable of the Rich Man and Lazarus,* Discourse 2, chapter 1

IN GOD'S PRESENCE, CONSIDER . . .

Angel or demon: which one do I resemble most today?

CLOSING PRAYER

Lord, send your Spirit to free me from every influence of the devil.

Pride makes you think you're an angel

It's easy to get all puffed up with even the humblest honor, says Sulpitius Severus. If the Church puts you in a position of responsibility, you may think you're some sort of angel. But you're not. You're just making a fool of yourself.

But when I think about these things, it occurs to me how unhappy and weak we are. Who is there among us who isn't elated with pride right away, or puffed up with vanity, if one miserable fellow has greeted us humbly, or one woman has given us foolish and flattering compliments? Then what happens? Even if you don't have any conscious feeling of sanctity, the flattery—or perhaps some fool's mistake—makes you think you're very holy indeed! And then, if you get frequent gifts, you'll start to think they come to you because of God's own generosity, since everything you need is given to you even while you sleep.

But then, if some signs of any power happen to fall on you, no matter how little—well, you think you're no less than an angel!

And even if you aren't distinguished from anyone else, either by what you do or what you're capable of, what happens if you're just made a cleric? Instantly you put long fringes on your robe, and you're delighted by the way everyone greets you. You're puffed up when people visit, and you go wandering around everywhere. Even if you used to travel on foot, or at most rode a donkey—now you're proudly riding on foaming steeds. You used to be happy in your humble cell, but now you build a lofty fretted ceiling. You put up lots of rooms, and you install carved doors and painted wardrobes. You won't wear cheap clothes anymore, but you have to have soft garments. You order the dear widows to weave an embroidered cloak for you, and the friendly virgins to weave you a flowing robe.

But I'll leave it to Jerome to describe these things more sarcastically.

—Sulpitius Severus, Dialogue 1, 21

IN GOD'S PRESENCE, CONSIDER . . .

What in my life gives me the most pride? Is that pride leading me away from what God really wants for me? Do I have the humility to see how far I am from the angels?

CLOSING PRAYER

Lord, you know my weakness. Through the ministry of your holy angels, deliver me from the evil one and his pride.

Strength in weakness

The devil has the perfection of an angel, says St. Augustine, and that makes him proud. Our weakness and mortality should help us overcome pride and confess that we can do nothing without God.

Man offended by a kind of strength, so it had to be corrected by weakness. We offended by a certain pride, so it had to be chastened by humility.

All proud people call themselves strong. But "many will come from east and west and sit at table with Abraham, Isaac, and Jacob in the kingdom of Heaven" (Matt. 8:11). Why will they be allowed to sit at that table? *Because they would not be strong.* What do we mean by "would not be strong"? They were afraid to assume their own merits. They did *not* seek to establish their own righteousness, and they *did* submit themselves to the righteousness of God.

Look: you're mortal; and you carry with you a body of flesh that is rotting away. And you will fall like one of the princes. You will die like men, and will fall like the devil. What good does the remedial discipline of mortality do you? The devil is proud, because he does not have a mortal body, since he is an angel. But you have received a mortal body—but even this does you no good: such a great weakness does not humble you. You will fall like one of the princes.

So this is the first grace of God's gift, to bring us to confess our weakness, so that whatever good we can do, whatever ability we have, we may be that in God. "Let him who boasts, boast of the Lord" (1 Cor. 1:31). "When I am weak," the apostle says, "then am I strong" (2 Cor. 12:10).

—St. Augustine, *Exposition on Psalm 39*, 15

Have there been problems in my life lately that I just can't overcome without help? Do I have the wisdom to seek the help of the angels?

CLOSING PRAYER

Lord, do not withhold your heavenly aid from me, for I am unable to overcome what is opposed to me. Send your angels to save me, Lord, from everything that is against me.

Sinners are Satan's graves

When our sins let Satan into our hearts, says St. Gregory the Great, our hearts become so many graves for the doomed spirit, who is bound for eternal death—and ready to take us with him.

There is a great difference between the natures of human beings and angels. But those who are bound together by one and the same guilt in sin are caught in the same punishment.

The prophet conveys this in a few short words when he says, "Assyria is there, and all her company, their graves round about her" (Ezek. 32:22). Now, whom does he mean by "Assyria," that proud king, except the old enemy who fell by pride? Because he draws so many into sin, he descends with all his multitude into the dungeons of hell. Graves are a shelter for the dead—and who suffered a more bitter death than he who, setting his Creator at naught, gave up life? And when human hearts let him remain in this state of death, surely they become his graves. So his graves are "round about" him, because all the people in whose souls he buries himself by their affections will be joined to him hereafter by torments.

–St. Gregory the Great, *Moralia in Job*, 9.103

IN GOD'S PRESENCE, CONSIDER . . .

Is my heart letting Satan in to bury himself? What secret sins are opening the door to him?

CLOSING PRAYER

Grant me your power, Lord, to avoid the attacks of the evil one, and give me an acceptable defense before the judgment seat.

Angels suggest, but we choose

Quoting two very early Christian writers, Origen tells us that an evil angel might suggest an evil thought, and a good angel a good thought. But in either case we have free will: we can choose to do evil or good.

That certain thoughts are suggested to our hearts either by good or evil angels, is shown both by the angel that accompanied Tobias (in the book of Tobit), and by the language of the prophet, where he says, "The angel who talked with me said" (Zech. 1:9).

The book of the *Shepherd* declares the same, saying that each individual is attended by two angels; that whenever good thoughts arise in our hearts, they are suggested by the good angel; but when the other kind arise, they are instigated by the evil angel.

The same is declared by Barnabas in his epistle, where he says there are two ways, one of light and one of darkness, over which he asserts that certain angels are placed—the angels of God over the way of light, the angels of Satan over the way of darkness.

But we should not think that any other result follows from what is suggested to our heart, whether good or bad, except a stirring and an incitement instigating us either to good or evil. For it is quite within our reach, when an evil power has begun to incite us to evil, to cast the wicked suggestions away from us, and to resist the vile inducements, and to do nothing that is at all deserving of blame. And, on the other hand, it is possible, when a divine power calls us to better things, not to obey the call. In either case, our own free will remains.

−Origen, *De Principiis*, 3.2.4

Do I know that "the devil made me do it" is an unacceptable excuse? Do I listen for the voice of the good angels?

CLOSING PRAYER

My Guardian Angel, whenever I stray, stir up a desire of repentance in me, and intercede with God for my pardon.

Don't blame the devil for your sin

It's true that the devil tempts us to sin, says St. Cyril of Jerusalem. But the sin itself is entirely our own doing. We have the power to give in or to resist.

But you may say, "What can sin be? Is it a living thing? An angel? An evil spirit? What is this working inside us?"

It is not an enemy from outside fighting with you, but a shoot of evil growing from inside you. "Let your eyes look directly forward" (Prov. 4:25), and lust does not exist. Keep what is yours, and do not take what is someone else's, and there is an end to theft. Remember the judgment, and neither fornication, nor adultery, nor murder, nor any other unrighteousness will prevail in you. But as soon as you forget God, you start to think up wickedness and do evil.

But nature is not the only cause of this evil. There is another who miserably urges us on to it—the devil. He urges everyone, but he prevails only over those who listen to him. If you indulgently allow yourself to think of lust, through your imagination, it will strike its roots into you, and captivate your mind, and drag you down into the pit of evils. And don't say, "I'm a believer, so it won't gain control over me, even if my mind dwells on the objects of lust." Don't you know that even a rock is split after a while by a root that clings to it for a long time? Don't let the seed in: it will break your faith in pieces. Root out the problem before it blooms, or, because you were lazy at the beginning, you may have to attack it with axes and fire later.

—St. Cyril of Jerusalem, *Catechetical Lecture 2*, 2

IN GOD'S PRESENCE, CONSIDER . . .

What small sins do I let the devil persuade me to indulge in—sins that might be growing roots? A little bit of gluttony? A smidgen of lust?

CLOSING PRAYER

Lord, protect me from the snares of the Evil One, make the evil odor of my soul fragrant again, and purify me with the sanctifying power of your Holy Spirit.

The Old and New Testaments agree

In the two Seraphim Isaiah saw in the heavenly court, St. Augustine sees a symbol of the two Testaments of Scripture—both of them singing "Holy, holy, holy" in perfect tune.

Hear this as well: "Out of Zion, the perfection of beauty, God shines forth" (Ps. 50:2). The psalm clearly agrees with the Gospel, which says, "to all nations, beginning from Jerusalem" (Luke 24:47).

"Out of Zion, the perfection of beauty" means that the beauty of his gospel begins there. From there he began to be preached, beautiful in form beyond all humanity. That agrees with the words of the Lord, who says, "beginning from Jerusalem." New things are in tune with old, and old things are in tune with new. The two Seraphim say to one another, "Holy, holy, holy is the Lord of hosts" (Isa. 6:3). The two Testaments (Old and New) are both in tune, and the two Testaments have one voice. Let the voice of the Testaments be heard—not the voice of disinherited pretenders.

—St. Augustine, *Exposition on Psalm 50, 4*

IN GOD'S PRESENCE, CONSIDER . . .

Am I sensitive to the role the angels have played through all the history of salvation, in the Old Testament and the New Testament?

CLOSING PRAYER

Lord, bless me and keep me, and help me to receive your word as it is delivered by the angels— as Moses did, as the prophets did, as John the seer did.

Angels will proclaim the gospel to the end

In Origen's time, some heretical sects said that the God of the Old Testament was not the same as the God of the New. But Origen says there is only one gospel, and angels will proclaim it to every nation even to the end of time.

But the beginning of the gospel is nothing but the whole Old Testament. John (the Baptist) is, in this respect, a type of the Old Testament, or, if we regard the connection of the New Testament with the Old, John represents the termination of the Old. Mark himself says: "The beginning of the gospel of Jesus Christ, the Son of God. As it is written in Isaiah the prophet, 'Behold, I send my messenger before thy face, who shall prepare thy way; the voice of one crying in the wilderness: Prepare the way of the Lord, make his paths straight'" (Mark 1:1-3).

And here I must wonder how the heretics can connect the two Testaments with two different Gods. These words, even if there were no others, are enough to convict them of their error. How can John be the beginning of the gospel if they suppose he belongs to a different God, if he belongs to the demiurge, and, as they hold, is not acquainted with the new deity?

And the angels are not entrusted with just one evangelical ministry—and that a short one, the one addressed to the shepherds—for at the end an exalted and flying angel, having the gospel, will preach it to every nation, for the good Father has not entirely deserted those who have fallen away from him. John, son of Zebedee, says in his Apocalypse: "Then I saw another angel flying in midheaven, with an eternal gospel to proclaim to those who dwell on earth, to every nation and tribe and tongue and people; and he said with a loud voice, 'Fear God and give him glory, for the hour of his judgment has come; and worship him who made heaven and earth, the sea and the fountains of water'" (Rev. 14:6-7).

—Origen, *Commentary on John,* 1.14

IN GOD'S PRESENCE, CONSIDER . . .

How am I helping the angels spread the gospel?

CLOSING PRAYER

Remember, in your mercy and compassion, all who have not heard your Word, and send your messengers to proclaim it to them.

Christ was made man, not angel

St. Gregory the Great says that Christ was made man because he came to save us, not the fallen angels. By not taking on their nature, he rejected Satan and his followers.

Our old enemy does actually see the coming of the Redeemer. But, because he is restricted by the darkness of his pride, he never comes back to pardon with the elect.

This is why it is written, "For surely it is not with angels that he is concerned but with the descendants of Abraham" (Heb. 2:16).

In fact, this is why our Redeemer was not made an angel, but was made man. He needed to be made of the same nature as that which he redeemed; so he could let the lost angel go immediately, by not taking on his nature, and restore humanity by taking our nature into himself.

–St. Gregory the Great, *Moralia in Job*, 4.8

IN GOD'S PRESENCE, CONSIDER . . .

Christ took on my nature, not the nature of the angels. How much effort do I put into trying to imitate Christ?

CLOSING PRAYER

Savior, Redeemer, and Benefactor, when you came to redeem me from the shame of my transgressions, you were made a human being like me. Teach me to imitate your humility, so that I may also be counted as a child of God.

God passed the angels to become one of us

Why did it take the whole Old Testament to prepare humanity for Christ? Simply because the truth of the Incarnation was so incomprehensibly wonderful, says St. John Chrysostom. God passed by all the orders of angels to become a lowly human being.

The truth of the Incarnation was very hard to receive. God's extraordinary mercy and the greatness of his condescension were simply amazing, and needed much preparation to be accepted.

God is indescribable, unintelligible, invisible, incomprehensible. He holds the ends of the earth in his hands. He looks on the world and makes it tremble. He touches the mountains and makes them smoke. Even the Cherubim couldn't bear the weight of his condescension, but veiled their faces in the shelter of their wings.

Think what a great thing it was to hear and learn that this God who surpasses all understanding, and baffles all calculation, had passed by Angels, Archangels, and all the spiritual powers above, and deigned to become a human being, to take flesh made of earth and clay, and enter the womb of a virgin, and be carried there for nine months, and be nourished with milk, and suffer everything that can happen to a man.

—St. John Chrysostom, *Homily on "Father, If It Be Possible..."*

IN GOD'S PRESENCE, CONSIDER . . .

How must the Incarnation have looked from the angels' point of view? Would thinking of it from that point of view help me see how much God has given me?

CLOSING PRAYER

With the heavenly powers I give you thanks, Lord, because you have granted me your great grace that cannot be repaid. You took on our human nature, that you might bestow life on us through your divinity. You raised our ruined state. You roused up our mortality. You blotted out our guilt. You enlightened our intelligence. You condemned our enemy, and you caused our insignificant and feeble nature to triumph.

The angels are evangelists, too

Origen suggests that, if we call the Gospel writers evangelists (a Greek word that means "messengers of good news"), then surely we ought to call the angels evangelists as well, since they were the first who brought the good news.

If there are some people who are honored with the ministry of evangelists, and if Jesus himself brings news of good things and preaches the Gospel to the poor, surely those messengers who were made spirits by God, those who are a flame of fire, ministers of the Father of all, cannot have been excluded from being evangelists also.

Thus an angel standing over the shepherds made a bright light shine round about them, and said: "Be not afraid; for behold, I bring you good news of a great joy which will come to all the people; for to you is born this day in the city of David a Savior, who is Christ the Lord" (Luke 2:10-11).

And at a time when there was no knowledge among humanity of the mystery of the Gospel, those who were greater than human and inhabitants of Heaven, the army of God, praised God, saying, "Glory to God in the highest, and on earth peace among men with whom he is pleased!" (Luke 2:14). And having said this, the angels go away from the shepherds into Heaven, leaving us to gather how the joy preached to us through the birth of Jesus Christ is glory in the highest to God; they humbled themselves even to the ground, and then returned to their place of rest, to glorify God in the highest through Jesus Christ.

But the angels also wonder at the peace which is to be brought about on account of Jesus on the earth, that seat of war, on which Lucifer, star of the morning, fell from Heaven, to be warred against and destroyed by Jesus.

–Origen, *Commentary on John*, 1.13

IN GOD'S PRESENCE, CONSIDER . . .

What am I doing to pass on the message the angels first brought to us?

CLOSING PRAYER

Count me worthy, Lord, to be your angel on earth, and to make known your Word without condemnation.

The angels learned the gospel along with us

Introducing the Gospel of John to his flock, St. John Chrysostom tells them they are about to hear what the angels themselves didn't know until it was revealed to us and them—the full truth of the Gospel.

All Heaven is his stage. His theater is the inhabited world. All the angels are his audience—and all of us who are angels already, or want to become angels. For only such people can hear the harmony truly, and show it in their works. But the rest are like little children who hear but don't understand what they're hearing, because they're thinking about candy and toys: stuck in merriment and luxury, living only for wealth and power and pleasure, they sometimes hear what is said, but they display nothing great or noble in what they do. They don't make themselves part of the clay that forms bricks for the Church.

Beside this Apostle the powers from above are standing, marveling at the beauty of his soul, and his understanding, and the blooming virtue that drew Christ himself to him, and won him the grace of the Spirit. He has made his soul ready, as if it were a well-made lyre with golden strings, and given it up to the spirit to play something great and divine.

Since this is no longer just the fisherman, the son of Zebedee, but the One who knows the deep things of God (1 Cor. 2:10)—I mean the Holy Spirit—that plays this lyre, let us listen. For he will not speak to us as a man, but he will say what he says from the depths of the Spirit, from those secret things that even the angels didn't know before they happened. They also have learned what we know from the voice of John with us, and even by us—as another Apostle declared: "that through the church the manifold wisdom of God might now be made known to the Principalities and Powers in the heavenly places" (Eph. 3:10).

—St. John Chrysostom, *Homily 1 on the Gospel of John*

IN GOD'S PRESENCE, CONSIDER . . .

Do I make time to listen to the message that the angels were so eager to hear?

CLOSING PRAYER

You are the Gospel and the light, Savior and keeper of my soul and body.

Angels saw the Son when we did

The angels, says St. John Chrysostom, did not know the mystery of the Son of God until it was revealed to the Church. This, as St. Paul says, is a great mystery, and the beginning of our being made like the angels.

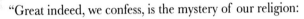

"Great indeed, we confess, is the mystery of our religion:

He was manifested in the flesh,
vindicated in the Spirit,
seen by angels,
preached among the nations,
believed on in the world,
taken up in glory" (1 Tim. 3:16).

The Church is the pillar of the world. Consider this mystery, and you may be struck with awe: for it is indeed a great mystery, and a mystery of godliness, and that without controversy or question, for it is beyond all doubt. Since in his (Paul's) directions to the priests he had required nothing like what is found in Leviticus he refers the whole matter to Another, saying, "He was manifested in the flesh."

The Creator was seen incarnate. "He was vindicated in the Spirit." As it is said, Wisdom is justified by her children—or, because Christ practiced no guile, as the prophet says, "although he had done no violence, and there was no deceit in his mouth" (Isa. 53:9). "Seen by angels." So that angels together with us saw the Son of God, not having before seen him. Great, truly great, was this mystery!

–St. John Chrysostom, *Homily 11 on 1 Timothy*

God gave his revelation to both angels and human beings. Do I recognize their company when I hear God's word proclaimed?

God and Lord of all, let me join my praise to the praise of all creation: the sun, the moon, and all the choir of the stars; earth, sea, and all that is in them; spirits of the just and of prophets; souls of martyrs and of apostles; Angels, Archangels, Thrones, Dominions, Principalities, and Authorities, and dread Powers; and the many-eyed Cherubim, and the six-winged Seraphim.

Mary alone saw the glory of the archangel

Mary, the Blessed Virgin, had a privilege no one else in history has ever had, says St. Gregory the Wonder-Worker: she saw the archangel Gabriel in all his glory.

Most of the holy fathers, and the patriarchs, and the prophets desired to see Christ and to be eyewitnesses of him. But they did not reach that goal. In visions, some of them saw him figuratively and dimly. Others had the privilege of hearing the divine voice through the cloud, and were favored with visions of holy angels.

But only to Mary, the pure virgin, did the archangel Gabriel show himself luminously, bringing her the happy greeting, "Hail, you who are full of grace!"

And that was how she received the word. And in due time, as the body ran its course, she brought forth the priceless pearl.–Origen, *Letter to Gregory*, 3

–St. Gregory Thaumaturgus, *Homily 1 on the Annunciation to the Holy Virgin Mary*

IN GOD'S PRESENCE, CONSIDER . . .

Am I ready to receive news of God's plan for me, the way Mary willingly received the news the archangel brought her?

CLOSING PRAYER

Holy angel, St. Gabriel, you came from Heaven to address Our Lady as your queen. May we too recognize her queenship, give her due reverence, and know her powerful maternal care in our lives.

Undoing Eve's damage

The Annunciation, says St. Irenaeus, is more than good news. In her obedience to the word from a good angel, Mary undoes the effects of Eve's disobedience at the persuasion of a wicked angel.

Eve was betrothed to a man, and was unhappily deceived.

The Virgin Mary was betrothed to a man as well. The truth happily declared to her by the angel shows that the Lord was coming to what belonged to him, and sustaining them by means of that creation which he himself supports. He was reenacting that disobedience that had happened in connection with a tree through the obedience he showed on the tree. And the effects of Eve's deception were being done away with.

Just as Eve was led astray by an angel, so that she fled from God when she had disobeyed his word, so Mary heard from an angel the glad news that she would bear God in obedience to his word. Though Eve disobeyed God, Mary was persuaded to obey God, so that she might advocate for the virgin Eve.

Thus, just as the human race fell into bondage by means of a virgin, so it is rescued by a virgin. One virgin's disobedience is balanced in the scale by the other virgin's obedience.

–St. Irenaeus, *Against Heresies*, 5.19.1

IN GOD'S PRESENCE, CONSIDER . . .

Which of the two angels more often persuades me—Gabriel or Satan?

CLOSING PRAYER

God, you were pleased that your Word, when the angel delivered his message, should take flesh in the womb of the Blessed Virgin Mary. Give ear to my humble petitions, and grant that I, who truly believe her to be Mother of God, may be helped by her prayers.

We add our praise to Gabriel's

St. Gregory the Wonder-Worker invites us to join our voices to the angel Gabriel's. When we look at what graces were given to Mary, we can only say along with Gabriel, "Hail, O favored one, the Lord is with you!"

David and Isaiah and all the prophets foretold the Lord's becoming man in all their preaching. But you, Holy Virgin—you alone shall receive the mystery unknown by them. Learn, and do not wonder how this can happen to you. For he who made man out of virgin soil, the very same will now do as he wishes for the salvation of his creature.

New radiance of eternal light gleams forth for us now in the inspired harmony of these words. Now is it right and fitting for me to wonder like the Holy Virgin, whom the angel appropriately first greeted thus: "Hail, O favored one"—because with her all the treasures of grace are made alive. Among all nations she alone was both virgin and mother and without knowledge of man, holy in body and soul. Among all nations she alone was made worthy to bring forth God; alone she carried in her the One who carries everything by his Word.

And not only is it right to marvel at the beauty of the Holy Mother of God, but also at the excellence of her spirit. Therefore let us also come, my friends, and discharge our debt according to our ability. Following the voice of the archangel, let us cry aloud: "Hail, O favored one, the Lord is with you!"

–St. Gregory Thaumaturgus, *Homily Concerning the Mother of God*, 20-23

IN GOD'S PRESENCE, CONSIDER . . .

Have I made the Holy Virgin, Queen of Angels, a regular part of my prayer life?

CLOSING PRAYER

All-holy, pure, most glorious, and most blessed Lady, Queen of the heavenly hose, help me to be like the angels in devoting my whole life to Christ my God.

The perplexity of Gabriel

We find it easy to imagine how amazed Mary was by the Annunciation. But what was Gabriel thinking? St. Gregory, known as the Wonder-Worker, imagines Gabriel's perplexity when he's given his assignment. The mystery of the Incarnation is as baffling to archangels as it is to humans (1 Peter 1:12).

"Speak in the ears of my rational Ark" (God said to Gabriel), "to prepare a way for me in her hearing. But do not disturb or trouble the soul of the Virgin. Show yourself in a way befitting that sanctuary, and greet her first with the voice of gladness. Address Mary with this salutation: 'Hail, O favored one,' so that I may show compassion for Eve in her fall."

The archangel heard these things, and thought them over—which was only reasonable. "This is a strange thing," he thought. "What has just been said is beyond comprehension. He who is dreaded by the Cherubim, he who cannot be looked on by the Seraphim, he who is incomprehensible to all the heavenly powers—is he saying that he will be connected this way with a virgin? Is he announcing that he will come in person? And more, does he make himself available to her hearing? Is he who condemned Eve eager to give Eve's daughter such honor? For he says, 'to prepare a way for me in her hearing.' Can the womb contain him who cannot be contained in space? This is certainly a fearful mystery."

–St. Gregory Thaumaturgus (Wonder-Worker), *Homily 3*

IN GOD'S PRESENCE, CONSIDER . . .

When I see the Incarnation from Gabriel's point of view, does it give me a fresh appreciation for the magnitude of God's grace?

CLOSING PRAYER

Let me join my prayer to the prayers of Gabriel and all the angels who ministered to the Son in Heaven. They saw him on earth when he was serving us, washing our feet, cleansing our souls. Blessed be his lowliness!

Hail, O favored one

If we imitate the virtues of the Blessed Virgin Mary, says St. Gregory Thaumaturgus, then we, too, will be included in that angelic salutation, "Hail, O favored one!"

With what spiritual song or word shall we honor her who is most glorious among the angels? She is planted in the house of God like a fruitful olive that the Holy Spirit overshadowed; and by means of her we are called sons and heirs of the kingdom of Christ. She is the ever-blooming paradise of incorruptibility, in which is planted the tree that gives life, and that provides the fruits of immortality to all. She is the boast and glory of virgins, and the exultation of mothers. She is the sure support of the believing, and the help of the pious. She is the vesture of light, and the dwelling place of virtue. She is the ever-flowing fountain, from which the water of life sprang and produced the Lord's incarnate manifestation. She is the monument of righteousness; and all who become lovers of her, and set their affections on virgin-like innocence and purity, will enjoy the grace of angels.

All who keep themselves from wine and intoxication, and from the wanton enjoyments of strong drink, will be made glad with the products of the life-bearing plant. All who have kept the lamp of virginity alight will be privileged to receive the unfading crown of immortality. All who have possessed themselves of the stainless robe of temperance will be received into the mystical bride-chamber of righteousness. All who have come nearer the angelic degree than others will also enter into the more real enjoyment of their Lord's beatitude. All who have possessed the illuminating oil of understanding, and the pure incense of conscience, will inherit the promise of spiritual favor and the spiritual adoption. All who worthily observe the festival of the Annunciation of the Virgin Mary, the mother of God, acquire as their proper recompense the fuller interest in the message, "Hail, O favored one, the Lord is with you!" (Luke 1:28).

—St. Gregory Thaumaturgus, *Homily 2 on the Annunciation*

IN GOD'S PRESENCE, CONSIDER . . .

What could I change in my life to be a better imitator of Mary's virtues, so that I can be worthy of that same angelic greeting?

CLOSING PRAYER

O Mother of our Lord Jesus Christ, whom the archangel Gabriel called the "favored one," beseech for me the only-begotten Son, who was born of you, to forgive me my offenses and my sins, through your intercession for me, O holy Mother.

Why did the angel wait to tell Joseph?

St. John Chrysostom answers an obvious question: why didn't the angel tell Joseph about the coming birth of Jesus at the same time he told Mary? In his explanation, he points out the value of discretion, not just truth, in choosing what we say and when we say it.

It's worth asking why the angel didn't speak sooner, before the husband had such thoughts, but came when he thought about it, and not until then—for it is said, "as he considered this," the angel comes (Matt. 1:20). And yet to her he declared the good tidings even before she conceived. Here's another difficulty; for even though the angel had not spoken, why was the Virgin silent, who had been informed by the angel; and why, when she saw her betrothed husband in trouble, did she not put an end to his perplexity?

Well, then—for we must explain the first difficulty first—why didn't the angel speak before Joseph became troubled? What was the reason? It was so that Joseph wouldn't be unbelieving, and the same happen to him that happened to Zechariah (Luke 1:18-20). For when the thing was visible, belief was easy from then on; but when it had not yet begun, it was not as easy to receive the angel's saying.

This is why the angel didn't speak at the first, and for the same reason the Virgin too held her peace. She didn't think her betrothed husband would believe her when she told him something no one had ever heard of before. She was afraid she'd provoke him even more, as though she were concealing a sin she had committed. After all, if she herself, who was to receive so great a favor, reacted more or less like an ordinary human being, and said, "How shall this be, since I have no husband?" (Luke 1:34), he would have doubted much more—and especially when hearing it from the woman who was under suspicion.

That's why the Virgin says nothing to him, but the angel presents himself to him when the time is right.

—St. John Chrysostom, *Homily 4 on Matthew*, 8

Angels never err in discretion because they are always attentive to God. How can I make sure I am attentive to God during all of my human interactions?

Holy angels, my world is so big and I have no attention for it. Help me to have a mind that is always attentive to divine things, even when I am busy in the earthly work that needs to be done.

Praised by angels, born in poverty

Although as God he was without beginning, says St. Gregory the Wonder-Worker, Christ's life on earth began the way every child's life begins. The God whom Cherubim praise was a child who shared our misery so he could lift us out of it.

Turn, congregations, and come—let us all praise him who is born of the Virgin. Praise him because, although he was the glory and image of the Divinity before the ages, he still came to suffer poverty along with us. Although he was the power and image of God beyond all magnificence, he still took on the form of a slave. Although he puts on light as a garment, he still lived a life as wretched as ours. Although he is hymned by the Cherubim and by countless angels, he still lived as a citizen on earth. Although he existed before all existence and makes all creation alive, he was born of the Holy Virgin, so that he might make what he had first created live again. Although he shared the beginning-less life of God the Father, Christ, our God, began life as a human being, so that he could lift fallen humanity up to the beginning-less beginning of the Divinity.

−St. Gregory Thaumaturgus, *Homily Concerning the Mother of God*, 5-6

IN GOD'S PRESENCE, CONSIDER . . .

Jesus said, "Blessed are the poor," and the angels praised him in his poverty. Do I live a praiseworthy detachment from possessions?

CLOSING PRAYER

Lord, let me imitate your humble life, and gain the approval of the angels, by serving your creatures the way you served them.

Angels were the first to preach Christ

When a priest at your parish church preaches Christ, says St. Cyril of Alexandria, he joins his voice to the voices of the original shepherds, who learned the good news of Christ's coming from the angels themselves.

The company of the holy prophets had foretold that, in due time, he would be born in the flesh, and that he would put on our likeness. Now that this hope had been fulfilled, the rational powers of Heaven brought the happy news of his appearance in the world to shepherds at Bethlehem—the first to receive the knowledge of the mystery. And this is a type that corresponds to the reality: for Christ reveals himself to the *spiritual* shepherds, so that they can preach him to the rest—just as the holy angels taught Christ's mystery to the shepherds, who then ran to bring the happy news to their neighbors.

Angels, then, are the first to preach him, and declare his glory, God miraculously born of a woman in the flesh.

So when you see the child wrapped in swaddling clothes, do not let your thought stop at his birth in the flesh. Rise to contemplate his Godlike glory. Elevate your mind; climb up to Heaven. Then you will see him in the highest exaltation, with transcendent glory. You will see him lifted up on a throne. You will hear the Seraphim praising him in hymns, and saying that "heaven and earth are full of his glory."

Indeed, this has even happened on earth. For the glory of God shone to the shepherds, and a multitude of the heavenly host told Christ's glory. Many holy prophets were born from time to time, but none of them ever was glorified by angels' voices—for they were men, like us. But Christ was not like them: he *is* God and Lord. He was the one who sent the holy prophets. As the psalmist says, "Who in the clouds shall be compared to the Lord, and who shall be likened to the Lord among the sons of God?"

–St. Cyril of Alexandria, *Commentary on Luke*, 2:8-18

IN GOD'S PRESENCE, CONSIDER . . .

No one can praise God adequately. But do I set aside some time in my prayer life just to praise God for his goodness and show my gratitude?

CLOSING PRAYER

"Holy, holy, holy is the Lord of hosts; the whole earth is full of his glory" (Isa. 6:3).

The best news ever

The birth of Christ, says St. John Chrysostom, is simply the best news ever. In an instant the world is changed, and we're made close friends with the angels.

What news could ever be as good as this? God on Earth—man in Heaven—and all mixed together: angels joined the choirs of men; men had fellowship with the angels, and with the other powers above! We see the long war ended, and God and our nature reconciled—the devil brought to shame, demons in flight, death destroyed, Paradise opened, the curse blotted out, sin put out of the way, error driven off, truth returning, the word of godliness planted everywhere, and flourishing in its growth, the city of those above planted on the earth, those powers in safe association with us, and angels always visiting earth, and hope abundant for things to come!

–St. John Chrysostom, Homily 1 on Matthew, 3

IN GOD'S PRESENCE, CONSIDER . . .

In the Lord's Incarnation, we are led to see "the angels of God ascending and descending upon the Son of Man" (Jn. 1:51). Do I gratefully and eagerly take up this gift?

CLOSING PRAYER

Angel of God, you know the plan of salvation, the means by which God has divinized human flesh. Help me to live in my body the way the Lord lived in his, that I may know glory with him and with you forever.

Christ gives us the peace of the angels

Christ, says St. Cyril of Alexandria, takes away the sin that came between us and the Father. Now we can have the same peace that the angels know in Heaven—the peace the angels proclaimed to the shepherds when Jesus Christ was born.

So do not look upon him who was laid in the manger merely as a baby, but in our poverty see him who as God is rich, and in the measure of our humanity him who excels the inhabitants of Heaven, and who therefore is glorified even by the holy angels.

And how noble was the hymn, "Glory to God in the highest, and on earth peace among men with whom he is pleased!" (Luke 2:14). For the Angels and Archangels, Thrones and Dominions, and high above them the Seraphim, preserving their settled order, are at peace with God. They never transgress his good pleasure in any way, but are firmly established in righteousness and holiness. But we, wretched beings, by setting up our own lusts in opposition to the will of our Lord, had put ourselves into the position of his enemies.

But Christ has got rid of all this. He is our peace; he has united us by himself to God the Father. He has taken sin away from between us—sin, the cause of the enmity—and so justifies us by faith, and makes us holy and without blame, and calls near to him those who were far off. And besides this, he has created the two people into one new man, thus making peace and reconciling both in one body to the Father. For it pleased God the Father to form all things into one new whole in him, and to bind together things below and things above, and to make those in Heaven and those on Earth into one flock.

Christ, therefore, has been made for us both Peace and Goodwill.

—St. Cyril of Alexandria, *Commentary on Luke*, Sermon 2

IN GOD'S PRESENCE, CONSIDER . . .

Christ gives me the chance to live a life like the angels' life, with my will always in harmony with God's. How well am I taking him up on that offer?

CLOSING PRAYER

Lord, let me not be cast out from your presence as the rebellious angels were, but as your servant let me find grace and mercy.

A little child, Commander of angels

St. Ephrem the Syrian meditates on what it meant for the Lord of all to be a human child. Even as a baby crawling on the floor, Christ was in command of all the multitudes of angels.

When it bore him, the sea was calm. How could the lap of Joseph bear him?

The womb of hell conceived him and burst open. How could the womb of Mary contain him?

He broke open the stone that was over his grave by his might. How could Mary's arm hold him?

You came to a low estate, so that you might raise all to life. Glory be to you from all who are made alive by you!

Who can speak of the Son of the Hidden One, who came down and clothed himself with a body in the womb? He came forth and sucked milk as a child; the Lord of all crawled around with little children. They saw him as a little child in the street; in secret angels surrounded him in fear. He was cheerful with the little ones as a child; he was awe-inspiring with the angels as a Commander. He was too-awe-inspiring for John to loose the buckle of his sandal; he was gentle to sinners who kissed his feet.

The angels saw him as angels see; each human being saw him according to the measure of his own knowledge. Each one saw the One greater than all according to the measure of his discernment. Only he and the Father have the full measure of knowledge, so as to know him as he is.

—St. Ephrem the Syrian, *Rhythm 3*

How does imagining Jesus as a child playing in the street affect my relationship with the Son of God? When I see a child playing today, can I imagine that child as the Commander of legions of angels?

Lord Jesus Christ, you were in command of countless myriads of angels, yet you came to us as a helpless child. Teach me that same humility, so that with you I may rise to glory.

The Lord of hosts is with us

As the psalm says, not just an angel, not just a host of angels, but the Lord of all the angels is with us—the Lord who came to make us equal to the angels. What can we possibly fear, St. Augustine asks, if we have the Lord himself on our side?

The Lord of hosts is with us;
the God of Jacob is our refuge (Ps. 46:7).

Not any man, not any power, not, in short, an angel, or any creature either earthly or heavenly, but the Lord of hosts is with us; the God of Jacob is our refuge. He who sent angels, came after angels, came so that angels might serve him, came to make human beings equal to angels.

What powerful grace! If God is for us, who can be against us? "The Lord of hosts is with us." What Lord of hosts is with us? As I say, "If God is for us, who is against us? He who did not spare his own Son but gave him up for us all, will he not also give us all things with him?" (Rom. 8:31-32).

Let us be secure, then, and cultivate a good conscience in tranquility of heart with the bread of the Lord.

—St. Augustine, *Exposition on Psalm 46*, 10

Is my heart tranquil, or is my conscience troubled? Will knowing that God himself—who made beings as powerful as angels—fights on my side help me overcome my troubles?

Help me to remain in peace, Lord, knowing that not only is my angel with me, but you who created that angel, are with me as well.

Angels join us in Christmas praise

In a hymn for the Christmas vigil, St. Ephrem the Syrian expresses his aston-
ishment that angels and archangels joined with human beings to praise Christ.
In our Christmas hymns, we are the companions of the Seraphim.

On his feast day, let us tell of the birth of the First-Born.

On his day, he gives us secret comforts. If the wicked king at his feast, in memory of his own birthday, gave the gift of wrath, the head (of John the Baptist) on a platter, how much more will the Blessed give blessings to us when we sing praises at his feast!

Let us not suppose that this evening is like any other evening. The reward of our wakefulness—his feast—exceeds a hundred times every other day. This feast makes war on sleep this evening. Speaking of it makes war on silence. Adorned with every blessing, it is the highest of all feasts, and of every joy.

Today the angels and archangels came down to sing a new song on earth. In this mystery they come down and rejoice with those who keep the vigil. Blasphemy was everywhere, but they gave praise. Blessed be the birth by which—Look!—the world resounds with anthems of praise!

For this is the night that brought together the Watchers on high with the keepers of the vigil. The Watchers came to make more watchers in the midst of creation. Look! Those who keep the vigil become friends of the watchers! Those who sing praise become companions of the Seraphim! Blessed be anyone who becomes the harp of Christ's praise—and Christ's grace becomes his reward.

–St. Ephrem the Syrian, *Hymns on the Nativity*, 14

IN GOD'S PRESENCE, CONSIDER . . .

When Christmas is coming, do I find my place in the drama of salvation as the angels found their place at the Annunciation, at the crib, on the road with the Magi, and among the shepherds in the fields?

CLOSING PRAYER

Angels whom we have heard on high, teach us to praise the God come down from Heaven
to take on our lowliness.

"Increased in wisdom and stature"

What does it mean when Luke says that the child Jesus "increased in wisdom and stature"? St. Athanasius says that the Word of God could not grow any more perfect; but the human body grew, and as Jesus grew older the people around him understood his wisdom more and more.

"And Jesus increased in wisdom and in stature, and in favor with God and man" (Luke 2:52).

If he "increases" in being the Word, what more can he become than Word and Wisdom and Son and God's power? The Word is all these things. Anyone who shares even one ray of all this light, so to speak, becomes all-perfect among mortals, and equal to angels.

Angels, and Archangels, and Dominions, and all the Powers, and Thrones, share in the Word, and by sharing in the Word always see the face of the Father. He supplies perfection to others! How can he "increase" more than they do? Angels even ministered at his Nativity—and this passage from Luke comes later than that.

How could anyone even think it? How could Wisdom advance in wisdom?

No, he did not "increase" as the Word, but he did as a man, since it is human to increase. Thus the Evangelist, choosing his words carefully, mentions that he increased "in stature." As Word and God he is not measured in stature: stature belongs to bodies. So the increase is of the body; and when it increased, the manifestation of the Godhead also increased, to those who saw it.

—St. Athanasius, *Discourse 3 Against the Arians*

IN GOD'S PRESENCE, CONSIDER . . .

If I spent some time meditating on the human growth of Jesus, might that help me see the wisdom of the Word, without whom not even the angels can see the face of the Father?

CLOSING PRAYER

Lord Jesus Christ, let me share one ray of your light, so that I may at the last become equal to the angels.

"Angel" was his job, not his nature

Some even in the time of Christ thought John the Baptist was a heavenly angel in the form of a man. The word "angel" is from the Greek word for "messenger," and Greek makes no distinction between "angel" and "messenger." Thus St. Cyril has to explain that "messenger" is John's job description, not his nature.

There was already a rumor going around that the holy Baptist was not really a man by nature, but one of the holy angels in Heaven, making use of a human body and sent by God to preach. As evidence for this inference they pointed out that God had said, "Behold, I send my *messenger*" (in Greek, *angelon*) "to prepare the way before me" (Mal. 3:1).

But those who imagine that John was an angel are wrong. They do not realize that the name "messenger" refers to ministry rather than to essence, even as in the history of the blessed Job "messengers" one after the other run to announce his various sufferings, and minister to those incurable afflictions. The very wise Paul explains something like this about the angels: "Are they not all ministering spirits sent forth to serve, for the sake of those who are to obtain salvation?" (Heb. 1:14).

John the blessed Baptist, then, is called an *angel* or *messenger* by the mouth of the Lord, not because he is actually by nature an angel, but because he is sent to announce and cry aloud, "Prepare the way of the Lord."

–St. Cyril of Alexandria, *Commentary on John*, 1.7

IN GOD'S PRESENCE, CONSIDER . . .

How well am I doing my job as God's angel—that is, as his messenger of the Gospel?

CLOSING PRAYER

Lord, send me forth into the world as your angel to proclaim the gospel of your kingdom.

The threefold temptation of Christ

St. Augustine gives us an analysis of the temptation of Christ, showing how Satan tried to appeal to Christ's hunger, his vanity, and his curiosity.

The temptation of the Lord Man was threefold:

1. By food: that is, by the lust of the flesh, where he suggests, "command these stones to become loaves of bread" (Matt. 4:3).

2. By vain boasting, where, when stationed on a mountain, all the kingdoms of this earth are shown him, and promised if he would worship (Matt. 4:8-9).

3. By curiosity, where, from the pinnacle of the temple, he is advised to throw himself down to see whether he would be held up by angels (Matt. 4:6).

Thus, after the enemy could not prevail on him with any of these temptations, it says, "when the devil had ended every temptation (Luke 4:13).

–St. Augustine, *Exposition on Psalm 8*, 13

IN GOD'S PRESENCE, CONSIDER . . .

How do I respond when the devil's temptations strike at my hunger, my vanity, or my curiosity? Can I think of any such temptations recently that I either did or did not overcome?

CLOSING PRAYER

Preserve me, Lord, from the malice and craftiness of the evil one, for the sake of your holy name.

At his humblest, Christ was served by angels

There's no contradiction, says St. Ambrose, between saying that Christ was humble and saying that he was Lord of all the powers of Heaven. The Incarnation, though it made him a humble human being, did not affect his divinity.

Let us not be troubled if we find the Son of Man called mighty in one place, and yet read in another that the Lord of glory was crucified. What might is greater than sovereignty over the powers of Heaven? But this sovereignty was in the hands of him who ruled over Thrones, Principalities, and Angels. For, although he was among the wild beasts, as it is written, yet angels ministered to him. So you can see the difference between what belongs to the Incarnation, and what belongs to sovereignty. As far as his flesh is concerned, he endures the assault of wild beasts; as far as his Godhead is concerned, he is adored by angels.

—St. Ambrose, *Exposition of the Christian Faith*, 3.4

IN GOD'S PRESENCE, CONSIDER . . .

Do I follow Christ in humility here on earth, so that I may follow him in glory to Heaven? Do I serve him constantly as the angels do?

CLOSING PRAYER

Sow in me the good seed of humility, Lord, and teach me to serve you as constantly as your angels do.

Demons recognize Christ but don't know him

Christ revealed enough of himself to the demons so that they would fear and obey him, says St. Augustine. But they didn't know him the way he is known by the holy angels, who love his righteousness and share his eternal life.

The devils themselves knew this manifestation of God so well that they said to the Lord, though he was clothed with the infirmity of flesh, "What have you to do with us, Jesus of Nazareth? Have you come to destroy us?" (Mark 1:24).

From these words, it is clear that they had great knowledge, and no charity. They feared his power to punish, and did not love his righteousness. He let them know as much as he pleased, and he was pleased to let them know as much as was necessary. But he did not make himself known the same way as he does to the holy angels, who know him as the Word of God, and rejoice in his eternity, which they share. He made himself known only as much as was needed to terrify the beings from whose tyranny he was going to free those who were predestined to his kingdom and the glory of it, eternally true and truly eternal.

He made himself known to the demons, therefore, by some worldly effects of his power, and evidences of his mysterious presence, which were more easily discerned by the angelic senses even of wicked spirits than by human infirmity.

But when he judged it advisable to suppress these signs gradually, and to retire into deeper obscurity, the prince of the demons was not sure he was the Christ, and tried to find out by tempting him, as much as he permitted himself to be tempted, so that he might make the humanity he wore an example for us to imitate. But after that temptation, when, as Scripture says (Matt. 4:3-11), he was ministered to by the angels who are good and holy, and therefore objects of terror to the impure spirits, he revealed more and more distinctly to the demons how great he was, so that, even though the infirmity of his flesh might seem contemptible, none dared to resist his authority.

–St. Augustine, *City of God,* 9.21

IN GOD'S PRESENCE, CONSIDER . . .

Do I know Christ as my joy and my life, the way the angels do? Or do I only recognize him, the way the demons do? How can I know Christ better?

CLOSING PRAYER

Holy angels, my protectors, you will what God wills, on Earth as in Heaven. Guard me from the snares of the one who was a murderer from the beginning, and who seeks my demise. In your care I will always know safety.

Christ was made less than the angels

Arguing against heretics who denied that the Son was equal to the Father, St. Ambrose marvels at the pride of people who would judge God. Yet the most wonderful thing of all is not that the Son is equal to the Father, but that he made himself less than the angels for our sake.

They say he is inferior: I ask, who has measured it? Who has such an extravagantly proud heart, as to place the Father and the Son before his judgment seat to decide upon which is the greater? "My heart is not haughty, nor are my eyes raised unto vanity," says David. King David feared to raise his heart in pride in human affairs, but we raise ours even in opposition to the divine secrets.

Who shall decide about the Son of God? Thrones, Dominions, Angels, Powers? But Archangels give attendance and serve him, Cherubim and Seraphim minister to him and praise him. Who then decides about the Son of God, on reading that the Father himself knows the Son, but will not judge him? For no one knows the Son but the Father (Matt. 11:27). "Knows," it says, not "judges." It is one thing to know, another to judge. The Father has knowledge in himself. The Son has no power superior to himself. And again: No one knows the Father but the Son; and he himself knows the Father, as the Father knows him.

But you say that he said he was inferior. He said also he was a stone (Luke 20:17-18). You say more, and yet you impiously attack him. I say less and with reverence add to His honor. You say he is inferior, and confess him to be above the angels. I say he is *less* than the angels, yet do not take from his honor; for I do not refute his Godhead, but I do proclaim his pity.

—St. Ambrose, *Exposition of the Christian Faith*, 5.18

When I recognize the glory of the angels, how much more I will appreciate the Lord's incarnation. He is greater than the angels, yet he made himself less for my sake.

CLOSING PRAYER

Let the Cherubim who carried up the Son in glory praise him with me. He left his glory, and toiled and found the sheep that was lost. Thanks be to him!

Let the Seraphim praise him with me also. They who had proclaimed the Son holy watched as he was reviled by those who denied him. He bore their contempt and taught us to praise. Glory be to Christ!

MIKE AQUILINA   187

God leads us past the angels to himself

The angels are immortal and blessed, says St. Augustine, but it's not their nature that we will share in Heaven. By becoming a man, God leads us to share the nature of the Trinity, which is the very source of the angels' immortality and blessedness.

I do not say that Christ is Mediator because he is the Word, for as the Word he is supremely blessed and supremely immortal, and therefore far from miserable mortals. But he is Mediator because he is man. By his humanity he shows us that we need not seek other mediators to lead us step by step to that blessed and beatific good, but that the blessed and beatific God, having himself become a partaker of our humanity, has given us ready access to participation in his divinity. In delivering us from our mortality and misery, he does not lead us to the immortal and blessed angels, so that we should become immortal and blessed by participating in their nature, but he leads us straight to that Trinity, by participating in which the angels themselves are blessed.

Therefore, when Christ chose to be in the form of a servant, and lower than the angels, so that he might be our Mediator, he remained higher than the angels, in the form of God—who is himself at once the way of life on earth and life itself in Heaven.

–St. Augustine, *City of God*, 9.15

IN GOD'S PRESENCE, CONSIDER . . .

Even the angels in Heaven are blessed only because they participate in the nature of Christ. How do I share the nature of Christ here on earth? Do I serve as He served?

CLOSING PRAYER

Blessed are you, O holy angels, whose charity does not grow weary with our human crimes. We thank you for keeping the earth habitable by always dwelling within it.

Lower than the angels, but served by them

*When Christ was a humble Galilean carpenter, says St. Ambrose, he was still
Lord of all the angels. The Incarnation took nothing away from his divinity.*

So the Son of God was made lower than not only the Father, but angels
as well. Do you think that dishonors him? Then is the Son, as God, less than his
angels who serve him and minister to him?

You see how, when you try to diminish his honor, you run into the blasphemy
of exalting the nature of angels above the Son of God. But the servant is not
above his master (Matt. 10:24). Again, angels ministered to him even after his
Incarnation, just to make sure you would acknowledge that he suffered no loss
of majesty because of his bodily nature. For God could not submit to any loss of
himself, while the nature he has taken of the Virgin neither adds to nor takes away
from his divine power.

–St. Ambrose, *Exposition of the Christian Faith*, 2.8

IN GOD'S PRESENCE, CONSIDER . . .

The angels knew and served Christ even when he was a humble carpenter's son. Do
I recognize Christ and serve him in the humblest people I see—the poor, the forgotten,
the homeless?

CLOSING PRAYER

*Lord Jesus Christ, show forth a plain sign of your majesty, that all on earth may serve you
as faithfully as your angels serve you.*

Even Jesus relied on the angels

When he was in the flesh, Jesus himself took his Father's orders through the angels, says Dionysius the Areopagite. Though he himself was the cause of their existence, Jesus kept himself within the limits assigned to mankind.

The angels were the first ones initiated in the divine mystery of the love of Jesus for humanity. Then the gift of that knowledge passed through them to us.

For example, the most divine Gabriel taught Zechariah the priest that the son who would be born to him—by divine grace, when he had no hope of a son—would be a prophet of the work of the Lord Jesus, God incarnate, which would be shown in the world for its own salvation, as becomes God's goodness.

Gabriel also revealed to Mary how she would bear the supremely divine mystery of the ineffable God made flesh.

Another angel taught Joseph how the things that had been promised to his ancestor David would really be fulfilled.

Another brought the glad news to the shepherds, who were purified by their separation from the crowd and their quiet life; and with that angel a multitude of the heavenly host announced that often-sung doxology to us on earth.

Now let us rise to the highest manifestations of light in Scripture: we see that even Jesus himself, who was the cause of these heavenly beings' very existence, kept within the limits of mankind when he had become a man, and subjected himself to the will of God the Father through angels. Through the mediation of angels God announced to Joseph that the Son must leave for Egypt, as the Father had arranged; and the return from Egypt to Judea was announced in the same way. And through angels we see Jesus subjecting himself to his father's decrees.

–Dionysius the Areopagite, *Heavenly Hierarchy*, 4.4

IN GOD'S PRESENCE, CONSIDER . . .

Jesus had no need of the angels' ministry; he accepted it in order to lead us by example. Am I following that example by relying on the angels to lead me to God?

CLOSING PRAYER

Dear Jesus, you received the ministry of angels in the desert and in the garden. Help us to benefit from their ministry in the deserts and gardens of our own lives.

Ninety-nine angels and one lost sheep

St. Cyril of Alexandria suggests an interpretation of Christ's famous parable of the lost sheep: the ninety-nine who were not lost are the angels in Heaven, and the one lost sheep is humanity, which had been lost to sin but is now brought back with great rejoicing.

"What man of you, having a hundred sheep, if he has lost one of them, does not leave the ninety-nine in the wilderness, and go after the one which is lost, until he finds it?" (Luke 15:4). And if he happens to find it, I tell you truly, he rejoices more over it than over the ninety-nine that never went astray. For the multitude of rational created beings that form Christ's flock in Heaven and on earth is innumerable, and so great that it even mounts up to a perfect number. For this is what is meant by the term "a hundred."

So the companies of the holy angels are the ninety-nine—for, as I said, they are many—but the flock on earth is one, but yet useful to complete the number, and also sought for by Christ. Then did he seek it as what was lost, or as what had not yet been lost? But it is plain that what is lost is sought for. Then how had it been lost? By being brought down into sin: by wandering from the divine will, and going far astray from the universal Shepherd.

−St. Cyril of Alexandria, *Commentary on Luke*, Fragment from Sermon 21

IN GOD'S PRESENCE, CONSIDER . . .

Am I working with the guardian angels to gather the lost sheep of Christ?

CLOSING PRAYER

Guardian angels, bring back the straying, enlighten the darkened, and bring them all into the way of salvation.

Is it an angel? Judge by its fruits

Satan, St. Paul tells us, disguises himself as an angel of light, and his ministers will call themselves apostles of Christ. How will we know the genuine article? St. Cyril of Alexandria repeats Christ's advice: examine the fruit.

Again, Christ somewhere says, "Beware of those who come to you in sheep's clothing but inwardly are ravenous wolves" (Matt. 7:15). See again, Christ commands that those who come to us must be distinguished not by their clothing, but by what they really are. "For the tree is known by its fruit," he says (Matt. 12:33); and just as it is ignorance and folly for us to expect to find our favorite kinds of fruits on thorns, like grapes or figs, so it is ridiculous for us to imagine that we can find anything admirable—I mean the nobleness of virtue—in hypocrites and the profane.

Would you like to see how true this is? Would you like to see who the wolves are that clothe themselves in the sheep's skin? Look at the writings of the holy Apostles: hear what they say of certain men: "For such men are false apostles, deceitful workmen, disguising themselves as apostles of Christ. And no wonder, for even Satan disguises himself as an angel of light. So it is not strange if his servants also disguise themselves as servants of righteousness" (2 Cor. 11:13-15).

We may well call these people thorns and briers. There is no particle of sweetness in them, but everything that is bitter and of an evil nature—for the fig does not grow on thorns—nor will one find anything pleasant in them, for grapes are not produced on briers. We must decide, then, the character of the teacher, not by appearances, but by the acts of each one's life.

—Cyril of Alexandria, *Commentary on Luke*, Sermon 33

I say I'm a Christian, but in the sight of the angels, do I look more like grapes and figs, or thorns and briers?

Guardian Angel, help me yield fruit thirty or a hundred times in Christ's Church.

Who is the vinedresser?

In the parable of the fig tree, the vinedresser begs the owner not to cut down the tree until it has one more chance. Is that vinedresser the angel who guarded Israel throughout the Old Testament? Or is it the Son interceding with the Father? St. Cyril of Alexandria thinks either interpretation is reasonable.

But the vinedresser begged him, saying, "Let it alone, sir, this year also, till I dig about it and put on manure. And if it bears fruit next year, well and good; but if not, you can cut it down" (Luke 13:8-9).

Now we need to ask who is to be understood by the vinedresser. If you decided to say that it is the angel who was appointed by God as the guardian of the synagogue of the Jews, you might be giving one appropriate interpretation. For we remember that the prophet Zechariah wrote, that one of the holy angels stood offering supplications for Jerusalem, and saying, "O Lord of hosts, how long will you have no mercy on Jerusalem and the cities of Judah, against which you have had indignation these seventy years?" (Zech. 1:12). And it is written also in Exodus, that when the ruler of the land of the Egyptians with his warriors was pursuing after the Israelites, and was already upon the point of engaging with them in battle, the angel of God stood between the camp of the Israelites and of the Egyptians, and the Egyptians did not come near the Israelites all the night. There is therefore nothing wrong in supposing here also that the holy angel who was the guardian of the synagogue offered supplications in its behalf, and prayed for a respite, in case, yielding to better influence, it might yet bring forth fruit.

But if anyone should say that the vinedresser is the Son, this view also has some reason on its side. For he is our "advocate with the Father" and "the expiation for our sins" (1 John 2:1-2), and the husbandman of our souls. He constantly prunes away whatever injures us, and fills us with rational and holy seeds, so that we may bring forth fruits for him.

—St. Cyril of Alexandria, *Commentary on Luke*, Sermon 96

IN GOD'S PRESENCE, CONSIDER . . .

In Christ and in his angels, I've been given everything I need now to grow and bear fruit abundantly. What fruit will the owner of the land find when he comes back to check?

CLOSING PRAYER

Guardian Angel of my parish church, Guardian angel of my diocese, guide us to healthy growth, so that we may bear fruit for Christ.

The Cross brings us together with the angels

Our sin is what keeps us from being fit citizens of Heaven. But the Cross over-comes that, says St. John Chrysostom. Because of the Cross, we are now part of the same community with the angels.

The Cross destroyed the hostility of God toward humanity. It brought about the reconciliation; it made earth Heaven, associated human beings with angels, pulled down the fortress of death, destroyed the power of sin, saved the world from error, brought back the truth, destroyed temples, overturned altars, suppressed the sacrifices, established virtue, founded the churches.

The Cross is the will of the Father, the glory of the Son, the rejoicing of the Spirit, and the boast of Paul—for, as he says, "far be it from me to glory except in the cross of our Lord Jesus Christ" (Gal. 6:14). The Cross is brighter than the sun, more brilliant than the sunbeam. Even when the sun is darkened, the Cross shines brightly—and the sun is darkened not because it has gone out, but because it is overpowered by the brilliance of the Cross.

The Cross has broken our chains. It has made the prison of death useless. It is the demonstration of the love of God.

—St. John Chrysostom, *Homily on "Father, If It Be Possible..."*

IN GOD'S PRESENCE, CONSIDER . . .

Am I living with the angels, a citizen of the new kingdom? Or am I still tied to the old world of sin and death?

CLOSING PRAYER

Lord Jesus Christ, render me worthy of the splendid glory of your kingdom, and of glad-ness with your holy angels, and of confidence before you, that I may stand at your right hand.

Angels glory in the Cross

The cross was the most shameful method of execution the ancient world could think of. But angels glory in the Cross of Christ, says St. Cyril of Jerusalem, because it was the instrument of our salvation.

We can never get tired of hearing about our crowned Lord—and least of all in this most holy Golgotha. For while others only hear, we can see and touch as well.

Let no one be tired! Take your armor against your adversaries in the cause of the Cross itself. Set up the faith of the Cross as a trophy against the deniers. When you're going to argue with unbelievers about the Cross of Christ, first make the sign of Christ's Cross with your hand—the denier will be silent.

Don't be ashamed to confess the Cross. Angels glory in it: they say, "We know that you seek Jesus who was crucified" (Matt. 28:5). Angel! Couldn't you have said, "I know you seek my Master"? No: he says boldly, "I know that you seek Jesus who was crucified." The Cross is a crown, not a dishonor.

—St. Cyril of Jerusalem, *Catechetical Lecture 13*, 22

IN GOD'S PRESENCE, CONSIDER . . .

Is the Sign of the Cross a regular part of my life? Or am I sometimes ashamed to acknowledge in public the sign that the angels glory in?

CLOSING PRAYER

Holy angels, the sign of Christ's crucifixion is your glory. Teach me to make it my glory as well, so that I may never be ashamed to acknowledge Jesus who was crucified.

Redeemed from the devil and his angels

In St. Augustine's time, the Roman Empire was crumbling, and barbarian attacks were the worst fear of every civilized family. (Later, St. Augustine himself would die as the Vandals were destroying his own city.) But Christ, he says, redeemed us from a far worse danger than barbarian captivity.

Brethren, if the ancient prophets, our fathers, sighed after the Jerusalem above even before the Lord Jesus Christ came in the flesh, before he rose from the dead, think how much we ought to long for the place to which he has gone before us, and which he never left. For the Lord did not come to us in such a way that he left the angels. He both stayed for them and came to us. For them he remained in majesty; for us he came in the flesh.

But where were we? If he is our Redeemer, then we were held captives. But where were we held, that he should come to redeem us as captives? Were we held among barbarians?

No, worse than any barbarians are the devil and his angels. Before our time, they had possession of the human race. From them he redeemed us, giving for us not gold or silver, but his own blood.

–St. Augustine, Exposition on Ps. 126, 1

IN GOD'S PRESENCE, CONSIDER . . .

Jesus is standing by with my price—but am I ready to walk out of my captivity? Or do I enjoy the company of my demons too much?

CLOSING PRAYER

Lord, I renounce the devil and all his empty promises. Send your angels to protect me, and guide me to the perfect redemption.

No angel was worthy

In Revelation, an angel holds a scroll and asks, "Who is worthy to open the scroll and break its seals?" St. Victorinus says that the scroll is the Old Testament, and to open it is to overcome death—something no angel could do. Only Christ could accomplish it.

"And I saw in the right hand of him who was seated on the throne a scroll written within and on the back, sealed with seven seals" (Rev. 5:1). This book signifies the Old Testament, which has been given into the hands of our Lord Jesus Christ, who received judgment from the Father.

"And I saw a strong angel proclaiming with a loud voice, 'Who is worthy to open the scroll and break its seals?' And no one in Heaven or on Earth or under the Earth was able to open the scroll" (Rev. 5:2-3).

Now to open the scroll is to overcome death for humanity. There was no one found worthy to do this—neither among the angels of Heaven, nor among men in Earth, nor among the souls of the saints in rest. Only Christ the Son of God alone was worthy, whom he says that he saw as "a Lamb standing, as though it had been slain, with seven horns" (Rev. 5:6).

—St. Victorinus, *Commentary on Revelation*

IN GOD'S PRESENCE, CONSIDER . . .

Do I read the Old Testament, which even the angels could not unseal, in light of the New—with the knowledge of how Christ has opened the meaning of it?

CLOSING PRAYER

Lord, I thank you that you have given us the truth that even the angels in Heaven could not have unsealed without you. Though I am mortal with a frail nature, teach me to be delighted with the sweetness of your oracles.

Angels could not set us free

Though angels have often come to aid God's faithful people, says St. Gregory the Great, they could not redeem us from sin. Only God himself could accomplish that.

"It (wisdom) cannot be gotten for gold" (Job 28:15).

What does "gold" mean here but the holy angels? They are called "gold" because they persist in the original innocence in which they were created. They shine with the beauty of righteousness, and they are stained with no impurity of sins—not in the very least.

But none of the angels were to be sent in place of this Wisdom as the Redeemer of the human race. To keep us from placing our hope on any of those angels—who, as we have been taught, have often come to our aid—it is said that wisdom "cannot be gotten for gold." This is as though it said plainly, "Wisdom itself will be made manifest to redeem humanity from sin." No angel is sent in place of him: the creature must be set free by the Creator.'

–St. Gregory the Great, Moralia in Job, 18.71

IN GOD'S PRESENCE, CONSIDER . . .

Though I can never equal the angels here on earth, do I strive to shine with the beauty of righteousness?

CLOSING PRAYER

Lord, strengthen me with your Spirit, and send your angels to protect me; for I trust not in my own righteousness, but in your abundant mercy.

The angels wondered at the risen Christ

Christ rose to Heaven in his glorified body, says St. Cyril of Alexandria. He imagines how the angels must have wondered at the sight: the God of all creation appearing in human form, with scars from the nails still in his hands!

Thus the only-begotten Word of God returned to the heavens, with the flesh united to him.

How strange was the sight in Heaven! The throng of angels marveled when they saw the King of earth and the Lord of might in a form like ours. And they said, "Who is this that comes from Edom (meaning from the earth) in crimsoned garments from Bozrah?"—the interpretation of which is *flesh*, as being a narrowing and pressing (Isa. 63:1).

Then too they inquired, "What are these wounds in the middle of your hands?"

He answered, "With these was I wounded in the house of my beloved."

After his return to life from the dead, when he showed his hands to Thomas (for very good reasons), Christ told him to handle both the prints of the nails, and the holes bored in his side. In the same way, when arrived in Heaven, he gave full proof to the holy angels, that Israel was justly cast out and fallen from being of his family. For this reason, he showed his garment stained with blood, and the wounds in his hands, and not as though he could not put them away; for when he rose from the dead, he put off corruption, and with it all its marks and attributes: he retained them therefore, that the manifold wisdom of God, which he wrought in Christ, might now be made known by the Church, according to the plan of salvation, to Principalities and Powers.

—St. Cyril of Alexandria, *Commentary on Luke*, Sermon 12

IN GOD'S PRESENCE, CONSIDER . . .

The angels themselves marveled at what Christ had done for the salvation of humanity. When I see the spectacle from their point of view, does it help me realize just how much God has done for me?

CLOSING PRAYER

Rise, Lord, and let your enemies be scattered, and let all who hate your holy name be put to flight.

The Resurrection amazed even the angels

The angels, says St. Ambrose, were amazed by the Resurrection. Even the hosts of Heaven could not understand the wonderful mystery of our salvation until Christ himself revealed it.

Why should we be surprised if by their worldly wisdom men failed to comprehend the mystery of God the Father and the Lord Jesus Christ, in whom all the treasures of wisdom and knowledge are hidden (Col. 2:3); that mystery which not even angels have been able to know except by revelation?

For who could by pure imagination, and not by faith, follow the Lord Jesus, first descending from the highest heaven to the shades below, and then rising again from Hades to the heavenly places; in a moment self-emptied, so that he might dwell among us, and yet never made less than he was, the Son being ever in the Father and the Father in the Son?

Angels, too, stood spellbound in wonder at the heavenly mystery. The Lord rose again, and the heights of Heaven could not bear the glory of his rising from the dead. Just now, as far as his flesh was concerned, he had been confined in the narrow limits of a tomb. Even the heavenly hosts doubted and were amazed. For a Conqueror came, adorned with wondrous spoils. The Lord was in his holy Temple. Before Him went angels and archangels, marveling at the prey wrested from death.

—St. Ambrose, Exposition of the Christian Faith, 4.1

IN GOD'S PRESENCE, CONSIDER . . .

To know the mysteries of Christ, even angels have need of Revelation. Do I take every opportunity to hear the revealed Word of God—by paying attention to the readings and the homily at Mass and by reading often in Scripture?

CLOSING PRAYER

Guardian Angel, keep the love of God's word and my need of God's Revelation always before my eyes.

Angels proclaim the Resurrection

The women who came to the tomb where Jesus had been buried were granted a vision of angels. Why were they given this privilege? It was because of their deep love for Christ, says St. Cyril of Alexandria.

The women came to the sepulcher, and when they could not find the body of Christ—for he had risen—they were much perplexed. And what happened then? For the sake of their love for Christ, and their earnest zeal in it, they were counted worthy of seeing holy angels, who even told them the joyful tidings, and became the heralds of the Resurrection, saying, "Why do you seek the living among the dead? He is not here, but is risen" (Luke 24:5).

For the Word of God always lives, and is by his own nature Life: but when he humbled himself to emptying, and submitted to be made like to us, he tasted death. But this proved to be the death of death: he rose from the dead, to be the way by which *we* return to incorruption, rather than himself.

And let no one look among the dead for him who always lives; for he is not here—not with death, that is, and in the tomb. So where is he? In Heaven, plainly, and in godlike glory. And to make the women's faith in these things even firmer, the angels recall to their minds what Christ had said, that he "must be delivered into the hands of sinful men, and be crucified, and on the third day rise" (Luke 24:7).

Angels brought the joyful tidings of the nativity to the shepherds in Bethlehem, and now they tell of his resurrection: and Heaven yields its service to proclaim him, and the hosts of the spirits above attend the Son as God, even when he had become flesh.

–St. Cyril of Alexandria, *Commentary on Luke*, Fragment of Sermon 154

IN GOD'S PRESENCE, CONSIDER . . .

St. Cyril says that the way to be counted worthy of seeing angels is through earnest love for Christ. How can I show more zeal in love for Christ?

CLOSING PRAYER

Holy angel who guarded the tomb of our Lord, holy angels who proclaimed his birth, help me to see the truth of these mysteries. Reflect them in my life and reveal them in my words.

Who is the King of glory?

St. Ambrose imagines the twenty-fourth psalm as the dialog of the angels when Christ rose from the dead. He points out that even angels, though they possess great knowledge, can advance step by step just as we do.

When the angels saw the Lord of all approaching, the first and only Vanquisher of death, they told their leaders to lift up the gates, saying in adoration, "Lift up your heads, O gates! and be lifted up, O ancient doors! that the King of glory may come in" (Ps. 24:7).

Yet there were still, even among the hosts of Heaven, some that were amazed, overcome with astonishment at such pomp and glory as they had never yet seen. So they asked, "Who is the King of glory?" (Ps. 24:8). But since the angels, like us, acquire their knowledge step by step, and are capable of advancement, they certainly must show differences of power and understanding. For God alone is above and beyond the limits imposed by gradual advance, since he possesses every perfection from everlasting.

Then others—namely those who had been present at his Resurrection, those who had seen or who already recognized him—answered, "The Lord, strong and mighty, the Lord, mighty in battle!" (Ps. 24:8).

Then, again, sang the multitude of angels, in triumphal chorus, "Lift up your heads, O gates! and be lifted up, O ancient doors! that the King of glory may come in" (Ps. 24:9).

—St. Ambrose, *Exposition of the Christian Faith*, 4.1

IN GOD'S PRESENCE, CONSIDER . . .

Even the angels can grow in wisdom and understanding. Do I try as hard as I should to keep growing in understanding of Christ's truth?

CLOSING PRAYER

Lord, guide me and teach me, so that I may grow daily in understanding, even as our angels do in Heaven.

The angels announce the Ascension

Angels tell the gaping disciples that "this Jesus" has been taken into Heaven. St. Augustine says that the angels are emphasizing that it is the very same Jesus whose body they saw broken on the Cross and buried in the tomb—the same Jesus who will come again, but who, even in Heaven, is always with them.

"God has gone up with a shout, the Lord with the sound of a trumpet" (Ps. 46:5).

The disciples wondered in joy, seeing him whose death they had mourned going up into Heaven.

Angels preached the Ascension of the Lord. They saw the disciples when their Lord ascended, lingering in wonder, confused, saying nothing but rejoicing in their hearts, and then came the sound of the trumpet, the clear voice of the angels: "Men of Galilee, why do you stand looking into Heaven? This Jesus..." (Acts 1:11)—as if they didn't know it was the same Jesus. Hadn't they just seen him in front of them? Hadn't they heard him speaking with them? In fact, they didn't just see him with them: they had touched his arms. So didn't they know by themselves that it was the same Jesus?

But they were out of their minds with wonder and joyous celebration; and that's why the angels specifically said *"this Jesus."* It was as if they were saying, "If you believe him, this is the same Jesus who was crucified, and your feet stumbled—who was dead and buried, and you thought your hope was lost. This is the *same Jesus.* He has gone up before you. He will come in the same way you have seen him go into Heaven. His body is taken away from your sight, it's true, but God is not separated from your hearts. See him going up. Believe in him when he isn't here. Hope for his coming. But yet, through his secret mercy, *feel him present.* For although he ascended into Heaven and was taken away from your sight, yet he promised you, "Lo, I am with you always, to the close of the age" (Matt. 28:20).

—St. Augustine, *Exposition on Psalm 47*, 6

IN GOD'S PRESENCE, CONSIDER . . .

Do I go to the angels for help in understanding the mysteries of Christ's life? Do I ask my guardian angel to accompany me as I pray the rosary or read the Scriptures?

CLOSING PRAYER

Angel of God, open my eyes, that I may see the Lord's mysteries as you do.

Angels announced the first and second coming

Angels announced the first coming of Christ in the Incarnation, says St. Leo the Great, and angels have foretold the second coming as well—so that we would know what power Christ would come with.

But when the disciples' eyes, turned up in earnest wonder, had followed the Lord ascending into Heaven, two angels stood by them in robes shining with brightness, saying, "Men of Galilee, why do you stand looking into Heaven? This Jesus, who was taken up from you into Heaven, will come in the same way as you saw him go into Heaven" (Acts 1:11).

By those words, all the children of the Church were taught to believe that Jesus Christ will come visibly in the same flesh with which he ascended, and not to doubt that all things are subject to him, when the ministry of angels had waited on him from the beginning of his birth.

An angel announced to the Blessed Virgin that Christ would be conceived by the Holy Spirit. The voice of heavenly beings sang of his birth to the shepherds. Messengers from above were the first to tell that he had been raised from the dead. Finally, the angels were sent to foretell his coming in the flesh to judge the world, so that we might understand what great powers will come with him when he comes as Judge, when such great ones ministered to him even when he was being judged.

–St. Leo the Great, *Sermon 74*, 4

IN GOD'S PRESENCE, CONSIDER . . .

Am I ready to hear St. Gabriel blow his trumpet? If the Judgment were scheduled for this time tomorrow, what would I do in the next twenty-four hours to get ready?

CLOSING PRAYER

Lord, when your angels once more announce the Judgment, do not deal with me according to my sins, but according to your mercy.

Angels can't understand the mysteries of salvation

St. Ephrem the Syrian imagines the angels looking all over for God the Son. They look for him in Heaven, and find him on earth—but they look for him on earth, and find him in Heaven.

It is not only for weak beings that the sight of you is too great, or the searching out of you is concealed. The senses of the body, since they stand in so much need of the senses in our inmost imagination, do not grasp even the smallest things they look for.

Let us then ask the angels near your gate. Though the angels stand before you with praises, yet they do not know which way to look to see you. They sought you above in the height; they saw you in the depth. They looked for you in Heaven, and saw you in the deep. They looked for you with the Worshipful One, and found you among the creatures. They came down to you and gave praise.

When they looked into how you had appeared among created things, they could not understand as they ran up and down where to stop looking for you. For they saw you in the depth, and they saw you on high. They saw you in the tomb, dead, and they found you a Raiser of the dead. They were amazed; they were astonished; they had no strength left.

—St. Ephrem the Syrian, Rhythm 4

IN GOD'S PRESENCE, CONSIDER . . .

Where do I look for Christ? Do I remember to look in the depths as well as the heights—even as the angels had to learn?

CLOSING PRAYER

Glorious Hidden One, even your smallest mystery is a fountain of mysteries! As you taught your angels, teach me to look downward as well as upward and find you in the humblest of your creatures.

A glorious subjection

All things are made subject to Christ—but what kind of subjection is this? Not ignoble slavery, says St. Ambrose, but a glorious service of the Good. We are subject the way the angels are subject.

Are not all things now subject to him? Are not the choirs of the saints made subject? Are not the angels, who ministered to him when on the earth (Matt. 4:11)? Are not the Archangels who were sent to Mary to foretell the coming of the Lord? Are not all the heavenly hosts? Are not the Cherubim and Seraphim, are not Thrones and Dominions and Powers that worship and praise him?

But how are they brought into subjection? In the way that the Lord himself has said: "Take my yoke upon you" (Matt. 11:29). It is not the fierce who bear the yoke, but the humble and the gentle. This clearly is no degrading subjection for us, but a glorious one: "that at the name of Jesus every knee should bow, in Heaven and on Earth and under the Earth, and every tongue confess that Jesus Christ is Lord, to the glory of God the Father" (Phil. 2:10-11).

—St. Ambrose, *Exposition of the Christian Faith*, 5.13

IN GOD'S PRESENCE, CONSIDER . . .

Do I take on Christ's glorious subjection willingly, like the good angels? Or am I straining at the yoke, like the devil and his angels, still trying to have my own way?

CLOSING PRAYER

St. Michael the Archangel, teach me to say, as you said, "I will serve."

Only the truth can conquer

Angels don't lie, says St. Ephrem the Syrian. The message they bring from God is true. And the message we read in the Gospel is true. If it were not, it could not have been established all over the world.

Why did Gabriel not deceive Daniel and say that he was God (Dan. 8:17)? Why did the Seraph not deceive Isaiah and say that he was the Son of God (Isa. 6:6)?

Because he was an angel, he did not lie.

The Apostle speaks truly and did not deceive us. He asserted and revealed that Christ was greater than all.

Hear what I say: If this were not the truth, it would have been refuted and come to an end. Only the truth can increase in the east, and spread to the west, and lay hold on the north, and clasp the south. Into the depth it went down and conquered. It went up and dwelt on high.

–St. Ephrem the Syrian, *Rhythm 61*

IN GOD'S PRESENCE, CONSIDER . . .

Do I make a real effort to be as truthful as the angels of Heaven?

CLOSING PRAYER

Guardian Angel, guard me from falsehood at all times, and teach me to love truth as you do.

Angels saw Christ in the flesh

Theodoret of Cyrus imagines a dialogue between Orthodoxos, the champion of orthodox Christianity, and Eranistes, whose name we might translate as "Mishmash," because he takes his opinions from all the heresies, and explains that angels cannot see God directly, but when Christ rose they did see him in the flesh.

Eranistes: Then the substance of God was not seen by those who beheld those revelations?

Orthodoxos: No! Who is mad enough to dare to say so?

Eranistes: Yet it is said that they saw.

Orthodoxos: Yes, it is said; but using reverent reason, and relying on the divine Scriptures, which exclaim distinctly, "No one has ever seen God" (John 1:18), we say that they did not see the divine Nature, but certain visions adapted to their capacity.

Eranistes: That is what we say.

Orthodoxos: And we should understand the same thing of the angels when we hear that they "always behold the face of my Father" (Matt. 18:10). What they see is not the divine substance—which cannot be circumscribed, comprehended, or understood, and which embraces the universe—but some glory made comparable with their nature.

Eranistes: We acknowledge that.

Orthodoxos: After the Incarnation, however, he was seen also by angels, as the divine Apostle says—not, however, by similitude of glory, but using the true and living covering of the flesh as a kind of screen. "God," says the Apostle, "was manifested in the flesh, vindicated in the Spirit, seen by angels" (1 Tim. 3:16).

—Theodoret of Cyrus, *Dialogue 1*

Angels saw Christ in the flesh after the Incarnation. Where do I look to see Christ in the flesh today?

Guardian Angel, you saw Christ in the flesh when he came to us in the Incarnation. Teach me to recognize Christ in the flesh in the poor, the sick, and the distressed everywhere.

A prayer for help from the angels

St. Gildas the Wise lived in the time after the legendary King Arthur, when barbarians were destroying his native Britain. Here he prays God to send him help from all the angels.

Help, unity of trinity,
   have pity, trinity of unity;
Help me, I pray, thus placed
   as in the peril of a great sea,
So that the plague of this year
   will not draw me with it, nor the vanity of the world.
And this very prayer I make to the high
   powers of the heavenly warfare,
that they will not leave me to be harried by enemies,
   but defend me with their strong armor;
that before me in the battle will go
   those armies of the heavenly warfare,
Cherubim and Seraphim with their thousands,
   Gabriel and Michael with like ones.
May Thrones, Powers, Archangels,
   Principalities, Dominions, Angels,
defend me with their thick array,
   and be strong to overthrow my enemies.

—St. Gildas the Wise, *Lorica*

IN GOD'S PRESENCE, CONSIDER . . .

When troubles surround me, do I remember that God has an army of angels ready to help me if I ask for their help?

CLOSING PRAYER

May Christ make with me a strong covenant, he whose terror scares away the foul throngs.

Know your angels

A very early Christian writing, The Shepherd of Hermas, gives us the famous image of the good and bad angels competing for our attention. In a vision, a glorious shepherd explains to the author that you can tell the angels apart by the suggestions they give you.

"Hear now," he said, "about faith. There are two angels with each person—one of righteousness, and the other of wickedness."

And I said to him, "How, sir, am I to know the powers of these? For both angels live with me."

"Hear," he said, "and understand them. The angel of righteousness is gentle and modest, meek and peaceful. So when he comes into your heart, immediately he talks to you of righteousness, purity, chastity, contentment, and of every righteous deed and glorious virtue. When all these come into your heart, know that the angel of righteousness is with you. These are the deeds of the angel of righteousness. Trust him, then, and his works.

"Now look at the works of the angel of wickedness. First, he is angry, and bitter, and foolish, and his works are evil, and ruin the servants of God. So when he comes into your heart, know him by his works."

And I said to him, "How, sir, I shall perceive him? I do not know."

"Hear and understand," he said. "When anger comes upon you, or harshness, know that he is in you; and you will also know that he is in you when you are attacked by a longing for many business deals, and the richest delicacies, and drunken revels, and various luxuries, and improper things, and by a lust for women, and by overreaching, and pride, and blustering, and by whatever is like these. When these come into your heart, know that the angel of wickedness is in you.

"These, then, are the actions of both angels. Understand them, and trust the angel of righteousness; but go away from the angel of iniquity, because his instruction is bad in every deed."

—*The Shepherd of Hermas*, book 2, commandment 8

IN GOD'S PRESENCE, CONSIDER . . .

Am I aware at all times that my life is influenced by both good and evil spirits? Do I pray for the gift of discernment of spirits?

CLOSING PRAYER

My Guardian Angel, fortify my weakness and shield me from the many temptations of the evil one.

We're surrounded by protection we can't see

During a tense time in Milan, St. Ambrose reminds his flock of a story from the Old Testament. The king of Syria wanted to attack Israel, and decided to silence the powerful prophet Elisha first. Elisha's servant feared the army coming against them, but Elisha showed him the angelic hosts arrayed for their protection.

Now here's an example from the Old Testament.

Elisha was being pursued by the king of Syria, who sent an army to capture him. He was surrounded on every side. His servant started to be afraid, because he was a servant—that is, his mind wasn't free, and he didn't have the freedom to do his own will.

The holy prophet prayed that his eyes might be opened, and said, "Look! See how many more are on our side than on theirs!" And he looked up and saw thousands of angels (2 Kings 6:12-17).

So, as you see, the servants of Christ are protected by invisible beings rather than visible ones. And when they surround you with their protection, it's your prayers that have called them to protect you. For you've read that those men who came looking for Elisha, when they entered Samaria, found the very man they wanted to capture—yet they were not able to hurt him at all. Instead, they were saved by the very man they came for.

—St. Ambrose, *Sermon Against Auxentius on the Giving Up of the Basilicas*, 11

IN GOD'S PRESENCE, CONSIDER . . .

Do I have the faith to trust in the ministry of the angels, even when I can't see it at work?

CLOSING PRAYER

Lord, give me eyes to see the powers you have placed at my service.

Martyrs like a legion of angels

In a very dangerous time for orthodox Christians and the whole Roman Empire, St. Ambrose reminds us that we always have helpers to protect us. Just as Elisha could count on a legion of angels, we have the legions of the martyrs on our side.

Thanks be to you, Lord Jesus, that at this time, when your Church requires greater guardianship, you have raised up for us the spirits of the holy martyrs.

Let all be well aware what kind of champions I want: the kind who act as protectors, not assailants. These are the ones I have obtained for you, holy people—a benefit to all, and a hurt to none. These are the defenders I want; these are my soldiers—not the world's soldiers, but Christ's. Let them come, then, and see my bodyguard: I don't deny that I am surrounded by such weapons as these. "Some boast of chariots, and some of horses; but we boast of the name of the Lord our God" (Ps. 20:7).

The lesson from Holy Scripture relates how Elisha, when surrounded by the army of the Syrians, told his trembling servant not to fear, "for those who are with us are more than those who are with them" (2 Kings 6:16). And in order to convince Gehazi of this, he prayed that his eyes might be opened, and when this was done he saw a countless host of angels present with the prophet.

And we're conscious of their presence, though we don't see them. Our eyes were kept closed, as long as the bodies of the saints lay hid in their graves. Now God has opened our eyes, and we have seen the aids which had so often helped us. Before, we didn't see them, although we did have them.

And so, as though the Lord said to our trembling hearts, "See what great martyrs I have given you," just so, "We all, with unveiled face," are "beholding the glory of the Lord" (2 Cor. 3:18). As far as the suffering of the martyrs is concerned, it's past; as far as their working for us goes, it's present.

–St. Ambrose, *Letter 22*, 10-11

IN GOD'S PRESENCE, CONSIDER . . .

Do I strive to imitate the holy martyrs? And, in the spirit of Ambrose, do I pray for angelic protection even for my enemies?

CLOSING PRAYER

Father, I join my prayers with the prayers of the holy angels and all the saints for every soul in tribulation and distress.

Everyone has a guardian angel

Even children of adultery, says one of the characters in St. Methodius's Banquet of the Ten Virgins, have guardian angels caring for them, because, as human beings, they are "copies and living pictures of Christ."

Nature could not accomplish such a great work in such a little time without divine help. Who gave the bones their fixed nature? Who bound the soft members with muscles, to be extended and relaxed at the joints? Who made channels for the blood, and a soft windpipe for the breath? What other god could have made the humors ferment, mixing them with blood and forming the soft flesh out of the earth? No one but the Supreme Artist, who makes us human, the rational and living image of himself. He forms it like wax in the womb from a tiny moist seed.

By whose providence is it that the fetus is not drowned when shut up in the connected vessels? And after it is brought forth into the light, who changes it from a weak, tiny thing to size, beauty, and strength? As I said, it can only be God, the Supreme Artist, making copies and living pictures of Christ by his creative power.

This is why the inspired Scriptures tell us that even those who are begotten by adultery are committed to guardian angels.

—St. Methodius, *Banquet of the Ten Virgins*, 2.6

IN GOD'S PRESENCE, CONSIDER . . .

If I have to deal with someone I don't like, have I tried praying to that person's guardian angel?

CLOSING PRAYER

Blessed guardian angels, spread your wings over all who need your care, and lead them safely to rest in the Lord.

When do we get guardian angels?

Origen, one of the Church's earliest theologians, tries to work out the truth about guardian angels. When are they assigned to us? He finds several passages in Scripture that seem to indicate we have them from birth.

We might ask at what time those who are called "their angels" assume guardianship of the little ones pointed out by Christ. Did they receive this commission to discharge concerning them, when, by "the washing of regeneration" (Tit. 3:5), through which they were born as new-born babes, they "long for the pure spiritual milk" (1 Pet. 2:2) which is without guile, and no longer are in subjection to any wicked power? Or were they appointed from birth, according to the foreknowledge and predestination of God, over those whom God also foreknew, and foreordained to be conformed to the glory of the Christ? (Rom. 8:29).

With reference to the view that they have angels from birth, we might quote, "he who had set me apart before I was born" (Gal. 1:15), and "Upon thee I have leaned from my birth," and "you are he who took me from my mother's womb" (Ps. 71:6), and, in the epistle of Jude, "To them that are beloved in God the Father and are kept for Jesus Christ, being called" (Jude 1)—"kept" meaning kept completely by the angels who keep them.

–Origen, *Commentary on Matthew*, 13.27

IN GOD'S PRESENCE, CONSIDER . . .

Have I cultivated a real relationship with my guardian angel, who knows me more intimately than anyone in my family?

CLOSING PRAYER

Guardian Angel, stay near me, and at the end of my life deliver my soul so that, with you, I may praise the goodness of God forever.

Angels guide the unborn child

Even Roman superstition, says Tertullian, admitted that the unborn child was a human being—otherwise why would all those mythical goddesses have been assigned to guide the embryo? Christians know that the developing fetus is a living human, and Tertullian believes that the angels guide its development.

Now the entire process of sowing, forming, and completing the human embryo in the womb is no doubt regulated by some power, which in all this serves the will of God, whatever may be the method which it is appointed to employ.

Even the superstition of Rome, by carefully attending to these points, imagined the goddess "Alemona" to nourish the fetus in the womb; as well as "Nona" and "Decima," called after the most critical months of gestation; and "Partula," to manage and direct parturition; and "Lucina," to bring the child to the birth and light of day.

We, on our part, believe that the angels do this work for God. The embryo therefore becomes a human being in the womb from the moment that its form is completed. The law of Moses, indeed, punishes with due penalties the man who shall cause abortion, inasmuch as there exists already the rudiment of a human being, which has imputed to it even now the condition of life and death, since it is already liable to the issues of both, although, by living still in the mother, it for the most part shares its own state with the mother.

—Tertullian, *Treatise on the Soul*, 37

IN GOD'S PRESENCE, CONSIDER . . .

Is there something I could be doing to help the angels in their mission of protecting unborn children? Are there pregnant mothers who need help in my community?

CLOSING PRAYER

Lord, send your angels to protect all your children, and grant their parents the strength to care for your precious creation.

Only the virtuous earn angel guides

Lazarus, the poor man in Jesus' parable (Luke 16:19-31) never cursed his evil fate or blamed God for the unfairness of life. How do we know? Because, says St. John Chrysostom, at the end of his life he earned an honor guard of angels.

But the poor man who was left at his gate didn't grieve, or blaspheme, or complain. He didn't say to himself, as many do, "Why is this happening to me? This man living in wickedness and cruelty and inhumanity enjoys far more than he needs, and endures no trouble nor any of the unexpected reverses that often happen in human affairs. He enjoys unmixed pleasure, while I don't even have a chance to get the food I need. To this man, who squanders all his substance on parasites and flatterers and wine—to him all good things flow like a river; while I live as an object to be stared at—an object of shame and derision. I'm starving to death. Is this Providence? Does Justice really rule human affairs?"

He didn't say any of these things, nor did he have them in his mind. How do we know that? From the fact that guardian angels surrounded him at his death, and bore him away to Abraham's bosom. If he had been a blasphemer, he wouldn't have gained this glory.

So most people wonder at this man merely because of his poverty; but I go on to show that he endured these ninefold afflictions, not for punishment, but so that he might become more glorious. And that's exactly what happened.

–St. John Chrysostom, *Four Discourses, Chiefly on the Parable of the Rich Man and Lazarus*, Discourse 1, chapter 9

IN GOD'S PRESENCE, CONSIDER . . .

When life really seems unfair, do I have the strength to trust that God's angels are guiding me according to the divine plan?

CLOSING PRAYER

Lord Jesus Christ, you voluntarily endured your life-giving death on the Cross. Grant me patience to endure this brief life so that your angels may surround me at my death and bear me away to you.

Angels hear our prayers

Why do we pray when God already knows what we need? Perhaps, says St. Augustine, we pray so that the angels can receive their instructions about us.

When the Apostle says, "let your requests be made known to God" (Phil. 4:6), we should not think this means that, when we do so, they become known to God. He certainly knew them before we spoke them. But we should understand it in this sense: that our requests are to be made known to ourselves in the presence of God by patient waiting on him, not in the presence of other people by pretentious worship.

Or perhaps so that they might also be made known to the angels that are in the presence of God, so that these beings may in some way present them to God, and consult him about them, and either openly or secretly bring us what they have learned is his will by listening to his commandment—for they must fulfill his will according to what they have learned there is their duty. For the angel said to Tobias, "And so, when you and your daughter-in-law Sarah prayed, I brought a reminder of your prayer before the Holy One" (Tob. 12:12).

—St. Augustine, *Letter 130*, 9

IN GOD'S PRESENCE, CONSIDER . . .

How much of my prayer is pretentious worship, and how much is really patient waiting on God? Do I pray to be heard by angels, or to be heard by other people?

CLOSING PRAYER

Faithful spirits who always adore the divinity, teach me to love, so that one day I may join you in Heaven for all eternity.

When angels hear us, God hears us in them

God does work miracles, St. Augustine says, but all according to his unchanging will. We can look at everything that happens as a miracle of God. And whenever we pray to the angels, it's God working in the angels who hears our prayers.

Although we don't usually think about the standing miracle of this visible world, because it's always in front of us, yet, when we start to think about it, it's a greater miracle than the rarest and most unheard-of marvels. Man himself is a greater miracle than any miracle done by means of man.

Therefore God, who made the visible heaven and earth, does not disdain to work visible miracles in heaven or earth, so that through them he may awaken the soul immersed in visible things to worship him, the Invisible. But the place and time of these miracles depend on his unchangeable will, in which future things are ordered as if they were already accomplished. For he moves temporal things without himself moving in time. He does not see the future one way and the past in a different way. Nor does he listen to those who are praying now differently from the way he sees those who will pray. For even when his angels hear us, it is God himself who hears us in them, as he does in his true temple not made with hands, as he does in those people who are his saints. And his answers, though they happen in time, have been arranged by his eternal decision.

–St. Augustine, *City of God*, 10.12

IN GOD'S PRESENCE, CONSIDER . . .

Do I trust that God has a plan for me, and that my angel knows that plan? Do I go to my guardian angel, so that I may walk the sure paths God has arranged for me in his providence since the beginning of time?

CLOSING PRAYER

Guardian Angel, by your God-given power, you can search my heart and know me. Help me form the prayers in my heart, and join me in those prayers, that they may be pleasing to God, and I may do his will.

Angels visit when you're alone

Sulpitius Severus visited the holy hermits of the desert in Egypt. They told him a story of one particular hermit who was so intent on his devotion that he never allowed any human visitors at all. He told the one man who had visited him in all those years, that if you are frequently visited by mortals, the angels won't visit you.

I visited two monasteries of St. Anthony, which are at the present day occupied by his disciples. I also went to that place in which the most blessed Paul, the first of the hermits, had his abode. I saw the Red Sea and the ridges of Mount Sinai, the top of which almost touches heaven, and cannot be reached by any human effort.

They said that an anchorite was living somewhere within its recesses. I tried very hard to see him for a long time, but I couldn't. He had been removed from all human fellowship for nearly fifty years, and wore no clothes, but was covered with bristles growing on his own body—though, by divine gift, he didn't know of his own nakedness. Though pious men often wanted to visit him, rushing into the pathless wilderness, he shunned all meeting with his kind.

About five years before I got there, they said, he had granted an interview to only one man; and I believe that man obtained the favor through the power of his faith. The two of them talked together for quite a while. They said that when the man asked why he shunned all human contact so carefully, the recluse replied that the man who was frequently visited by mortals like himself could not often be visited by angels. From this, not without reason, the report had spread, and was accepted by multitudes, that that holy man enjoyed angelic fellowship.

—Sulpitius Severus, *Dialogue 1*, 17

IN GOD'S PRESENCE, CONSIDER . . .

Do I find enough opportunities to be alone for prayer and contemplation? Do I acknowledge the presence of my angel?

CLOSING PRAYER

Guardian Angel, may I know peace through your companionship. May I pray well through your instruction.

In solitude, but not alone

St. Ambrose recognizes that, when he seems to be completely alone, he is never alone. Mary was visited by an angel when she was alone, and when we read the Scriptures God walks with us in paradise.

Since you also take pleasure in receiving my letters, by means of which, although separated from each other, we discourse together as if present, I will for the future more frequently converse with you by letter when I am alone. For I am never less alone than when I seem to be so, nor ever less at leisure than in the intervals of labor. Then I can summon anyone I wish, and visit with whoever I love most or find most sympathetic; no one interrupts or intrudes upon us. That's when I feel closer to you, and when I confer with you in the Scriptures, and when we converse together more at length.

Mary was alone when addressed by the angel, alone when the Holy Spirit came upon her, and the power of the Most High overshadowed her. She was alone when she effected the salvation of the world, and conceived the Redemption of the universe. Peter was alone when the mystery of the sanctification of the Gentiles all over the world was made known to him. When Adam was alone, he didn't fall, because his mind stayed with God. But when the woman was joined to him, he lost his power of sticking with the heavenly precepts, and therefore he hid himself when God walked in Paradise.

And even now, while I read the sacred Scriptures, God walks in Paradise. The book of Genesis, in which the virtues of the Patriarchs sprout, is Paradise; Deuteronomy, in which the precepts of the Law grow, is also Paradise, where the tree of life brings forth good fruit, and diffuses over all nations the precepts of eternal hope.

—St. Ambrose, *Letter 49*

IN GOD'S PRESENCE, CONSIDER . . .

When I have time to myself, do I turn to my angel and read Scripture with this divinely appointed supernatural help?

CLOSING PRAYER

Holy Angel, God's messenger and my guardian, keep the divine Word in my mind, in my heart, and on my lips all the days of my life.

The Lord always delivers

The Lord sent an angel to rescue Peter from prison. Then why didn't he send an angel to rescue him from being crucified? Not because the Lord failed to deliver him, says St. Augustine, but because the delivery was even more complete.

Fear not: only do what he commands; and if the Lord does not deliver you bodily, he will deliver you spiritually.

He delivered Peter, when the angel came to him in prison, and said, "Get up quickly" (Acts 12:7)—and suddenly his chains were loosed, and he followed the angel, and the Lord delivered him.

Had Peter lost righteousness when he did not deliver him from the cross?

But didn't he deliver him then? Yes, even then he delivered him. Did his long life make Peter unrighteous? Perhaps Peter heard him more at last than at first, when truly he delivered him out of all his troubles. For when the Lord first delivered him, how many things he had to suffer afterwards! But at last he sent him where he could suffer no evil.

—St. Augustine, *Exposition on Psalm 34*, 21

IN GOD'S PRESENCE, CONSIDER . . .

When bad things happen to me, do I trust that God is still planning my salvation? Do I recognize that he always sends his angels to give me what I need—even when that's not what I want?

CLOSING PRAYER

By the ministry of your angels, deliver me from my troubles, Lord, and drive away the spirit of weakness in me.

God acts in the angels

Whether God acts directly or through the angels, says St. Augustine, it is God acting. An angel does God's will; and even though we cannot see God directly, we can see God acting in any created being that does God's will.

The fathers of the New Testament saw your mysteries revealed, and they preached the secret things revealed to them. Nevertheless, they said that they themselves saw only through a glass, darkly, but that seeing face to face is reserved to a future time, when what the Apostle himself speaks of has come (1 Cor. 13:12). "When Christ who is our life appears, then you also will appear with him in glory" (Col. 3:4)

Seeing face to face is reserved for that time, of which John also speaks: "Beloved, we are God's children now; it does not yet appear what we shall be, but we know that when he appears we shall be like him, for we shall see him as he is" (1 John 3:2).

So although then our ancestors did not see you as you are, face to face—although that vision is reserved until the resurrection—yet, even though they were angels who presented themselves, it is you who "ordain victories for Jacob" (Ps. 44:4). You are not only present by your own Self; but when you appear in any created beings, you are the one who commands by them. Whether you do it yourself for your servants' salvation, or whether they do it because you command it, it is your doing.

–St. Augustine, *Exposition on Psalm 44, 4*

IN GOD'S PRESENCE, CONSIDER . . .

Do I respect God's wisdom as he uses the things of creation to mediate himself to me? Do I accept the proper place he has given the angels in my life?

CLOSING PRAYER

In whatever I do, Lord, make me an instrument of your will, so that others can recognize the ministry of your angels in my life.

Remember the angels that surround you

Angels are literally everywhere, says St. Hilary of Poitiers—even within us. Whenever we're tempted toward evil, we should remember that there are witnesses who will know what we do and be ashamed of us if we do wrong.

Everything is filled with the angels of God, even if it seems empty. There's nowhere they don't live as they go around doing their service.

People are often deterred from committing some sin they've been thinking of because they're afraid someone might come back suddenly. But how should Christians act—and not just act, but even think and wish—when we remember that a number of spiritual powers live in every part of us? When some evil desire overcomes us, shouldn't we tremble at the presence of all the choirs of angels surrounding us?

–St. Hilary of Poitiers, *Homily on Psalm 118*

IN GOD'S PRESENCE, CONSIDER . . .

Does the knowledge that multitudes of angels surround me—and even live within me—help me deal with the temptations I face every day?

CLOSING PRAYER

Angels of God, keep me in mind of your presence throughout the day, especially when I come face to face with temptation.

Whoever is holy pushes us on to God

Our happiness will never be found in another person or in an angel, says St. Augustine. Proud angels and proud people will be glad to have us put our hope in them, but the truly holy push us forward toward God.

For if we find our happiness complete in one another, we stop short along the road, and place our hope of happiness in a person or an angel.

Now the proud person and the proud angel arrogate this to themselves, and are glad to have the hope of others fixed upon them. But, on the contrary, the holy man and the holy angel, even when we are weary and anxious to stay with them and rest in them, set themselves to build up our energies with the provision they have received from God for us or for themselves; and then urge us thus refreshed to go on our way towards God, in the enjoyment of whom we find our common happiness.

For even the Apostle exclaims, "Was Paul crucified for you? Or were you baptized in the name of Paul?" (1 Cor. 1:13), and again: "So neither he who plants nor he who waters is anything, but only God who gives the growth" (1 Cor. 3:7). And the angel admonishes the man who is about to worship him, that he should rather worship Him who is his Master, and under whom he himself is a fellow-servant (Rev. 19:10).

–St. Augustine, *On Christian Doctrine*, 1.33

IN GOD'S PRESENCE, CONSIDER . . .

The holy angels always strive to lead me beyond themselves to their Creator. Do I do the same? Do the people who know me move on toward God?

CLOSING PRAYER

Holy angels who surround me, teach me to imitate you in humility, so that all who know me may be led toward their Creator.

Angels help the holy

A legend of an especially holy Egyptian monk shows us the strength of the early Christians' faith in angels. It seemed only natural that an especially holy man would be given angelic aid in overcoming an obstacle to his holiness.

Since I have already mentioned the monasteries of Egypt, this may be a good place to give a short account of them. They were probably founded at a very early period, but they were greatly enlarged and expanded by a devout man whose name was Ammoun.

It is said that Ammoun never saw himself naked: he used to say, "It is not appropriate for a monk to see even his own body exposed." Once he wanted to cross a river, but he was unwilling to undress. So he prayed to God to allow him to cross without having to break his resolution. And immediately an angel transported him to the other side of the river.

–Socrates Scholasticus, *Ecclesiastical History*, 4.23

IN GOD'S PRESENCE, CONSIDER . . .

Are there any principles of purity that I feel so strongly about that I would ask for angelic help in sticking to my resolutions? Should there be?

CLOSING PRAYER

Guardian Angel, I give you humble thanks for the charity and zeal with which you protect me, and I ask you to help me preserve my innocence whenever I am in danger from temptation.

Encounters with angels

Two ancient anecdotes of Egyptian monks tell of their encounters with angels. Whether their visions were really angelic visits or merely dreams, the stories point out how real the heavenly hosts were to the early Christian monks. These devoted men simply expected that angels would be part of their daily lives.

Piammon and John presided over two celebrated Egyptian monasteries near Diolcus. They were presbyters who discharged their priesthood very carefully and reverently. It is said that one day, when Piammon was officiating as priest, he beheld an angel standing near the holy table and writing down in a book the names of the monks who were present, while he erased the names of those who were absent. John had received from God such power over sufferings and diseases, that he healed the gouty and restored the paralytic.

Another ascetic, Mark was, from his youth upwards, distinguished by extreme mildness and prudence; he committed the sacred Scriptures to memory, and manifested such eminent piety that Macarius himself, the presbyter of Celliae, declared that he had never given to him what priests present to the initiated at the holy table, but that an angel administered it to him whose hand up to the forearm he declares himself to have seen.

–Sozomen, *Ecclesiastical History*, 6.29

IN GOD'S PRESENCE, CONSIDER . . .

How often do I remember the angelic spirits who surround all of us?

CLOSING PRAYER

Pure and happy spirits sent by God to be our protectors, I owe my preservation to you a thousand times, and I humbly offer my thanks for your protection.

"By this symbol, conquer"

Many historians have told the story of Constantine's conversion. Sozomen says that angels explained his vision of the Cross to him. The story may be apocryphal, but it illustrates perfectly how completely the early Christians trusted in the protection of the angels.

We have been informed that Constantine was led to honor the Christian religion by the concurrence of several different events, particularly by the appearance of a sign from Heaven.

When he first formed the resolution of entering into a war against Maxentius, he was beset with doubts as to the means of carrying on his military operations, and as to the quarter whence he could look for assistance. In the midst of his perplexity, he saw, in a vision, the sight of the Cross shining in Heaven. He was amazed at the spectacle, but some holy angels who were standing by exclaimed, "Constantine! By this symbol, conquer!"

And it is said that Christ himself appeared to him, and showed him the symbol of the Cross, and commanded him to construct one like unto it, and to retain it as his help in battle, as it would insure the victory.

—Sozomen, *Ecclesiastical History*, 1.3

IN GOD'S PRESENCE, CONSIDER . . .

Even when I can't see or hear angels around me, do I have the faith to trust in their protection?

CLOSING PRAYER

Lord, ten thousand myriads of holy angels bless and adore your majesty. Join my insignificant voice with the Sanctus of Seraphim and Archangels.

Trust Christ, and the angels will defend you

When Satan dared Jesus to throw himself off a tower, he quoted Scripture, saying that the angels would guard him. But Christ, who is the Lord of angels, has no need of their protection. Instead, if we trust in him, he will send his angels to protect us.

"For it is written, 'He will give his angels charge of you, to guard you'" (Luke 4:10).

Satan then made use of these verses, as though the Savior were a common man. For being entirely darkness, and having his mind blinded, he did not understand the force of what was said, that the Psalm is spoken in the person of every just man who is aided by the Highest—that is, the God of Heaven. And besides this, he did not know that the Word, being God, was made man, and was himself now being tempted in accordance with the plan of salvation.

But it is monstrous for us, who accurately know the mystery, and believe that he is God and the Son of God, and that for our sakes he became man like unto us, to imagine that the verses were spoken of him. To say, "You have made the Most High your habitation" (Ps. 91:9), then, is not appropriate for the person of the Savior. For he is himself the Most High: the refuge of all, the hope of all, the all-powerful right hand of the Father. No evil will approach anyone who trusts him for defense. For he shall command the angels, who are ministering spirits, to guard the just.

For just as our fathers in the flesh, when they see that the path is rough and impassable, pick up their infants in their hands, so that their tender feet will not be hurt, being because they are yet unable to walk over the hard road, so also the rational powers do not permit those who are as yet unable to labor, and whose understanding is still childish, to toil beyond their strength, but snatch them out of every temptation.

–St. Cyril of Alexandria, *Commentary on Luke*, Sermon 12

IN GOD'S PRESENCE, CONSIDER . . .

Do I really trust that the angels are guarding me right now? How can I recognize their help, even when things seem to be going wrong?

CLOSING PRAYER

Guardian Angel, keep me from stumbling on my way, and preserve me in the true faith.

Trusting in the angels

When Constantinople was menaced by a Persian attack, the report of a message from the angels gave its citizens courage. In times of trouble, ancient Christians keenly felt the protecting presence of the angels.

When the emperor saw that the Persian was mustering his whole force, he made additional levies to his army, and put his whole trust in God for the victory.

And that the king was not without immediate benefit from this pious confidence the following circumstance proves. As the people of Constantinople were in great consternation, and worrying about how the war would come out, angels from God appeared to some persons in Bithynia who were traveling to Constantinople on their own affairs, and told them to tell the people not to be alarmed, but pray to God and be assured that the Romans would be conquerors. For they said that they themselves were appointed by God to defend them.

When this message was circulated it not only comforted the residents of the city, but rendered the soldiers more courageous.

—Socrates Scholasticus, *Ecclesiastical History*, 7.18

IN GOD'S PRESENCE, CONSIDER . . .

Do I trust in angels to deliver me from my own troubles?

CLOSING PRAYER

St. Michael the Archangel, be our defense against the wickedness and snares of the devil.

An army of angels

The Gothic leader Gainas tried to make himself master of the whole Roman Empire. Constantinople, the eastern capital, was in serious danger: most of the Roman army was too far away to help. But the barbarians were defeated—and popular opinion insisted that their defeat was due to angelic protection.

The city was accordingly quite inundated by the barbarians, and its residents were reduced to a condition equivalent to that of captives. Moreover, so great was the danger of the city that a comet of prodigious magnitude, reaching from heaven even to the earth, such as was never before seen, gave forewarning of it.

Gainas first most shamelessly attempted to make a seizure of the silver publicly offered for sale in the shops: but when the proprietors, advised beforehand by report of his intention, abstained from offering it on their counters, his thoughts were diverted to another object, which was to send an immense body of barbarians at night for the purpose of burning down the palace.

Then indeed it appeared distinctly that God had providential care over the city: for a multitude of angels appeared to the rebels, in the form of armed men of gigantic stature, before whom the barbarians, imagining them to be a large army of brave troops, turned away with terror and departed.

When this was reported to Gainas, it seemed to him quite incredible—for he knew that the greatest part of the Roman army was at a distance, dispersed as a garrison over the Eastern cities—and he sent others on the following night and repeatedly afterwards. Now as they constantly returned with the same statement— for the angels of God always presented themselves in the same form—he came with a great multitude, and at length became himself a spectator of the prodigy.

–Socrates Scholasticus, *Ecclesiastical History*, 6.6

IN GOD'S PRESENCE, CONSIDER . . .

When I'm really afraid of something, do I remember the angels who surround me?

CLOSING PRAYER

Holy angels, who adore God in myriads, defend me from the attacks of the enemy, so that I may praise God with you forever in Heaven.

Simeon the Pole-Sitter, an angel on earth

Simeon Stylites ("of the pillar") attempted to live the life of the angels on earth—by removing himself as far as possible from the earth, living on top of a column for thirty-seven years. In spite of his eccentricity, however, he was unquestioningly obedient to the leaders of the Church.

Simeon tried to realize the life of the heavenly hosts in the flesh. He lifted himself above the concerns of earth, and—overpowering the downward tendency of human nature—was intent on things above. Placed between earth and heaven, he held communion with God, and united with the angels in praising him; from earth, offering his intercessions on behalf of human beings, and from Heaven, drawing down upon them the divine favor.

When Simeon, that angel on earth, that citizen in the flesh of the heavenly Jerusalem, had devised this strange and hitherto unknown way of life, the inhabitants of the holy desert sent someone to him, charged with an injunction to render a reason for this strange habit—namely, why he abandoned the beaten path the saints had trodden, and pursued another altogether unknown to mankind. The injunction further demanded that he should come down and travel the road of the elect fathers. At the same time they gave orders that, if he should show a perfect readiness to come down, he should be given the freedom to follow out the course he had chosen, since his compliance would be sufficient proof that he persevered in this endurance of his under God's guidance. But if he should show repugnance, or be swayed by self-will, and refuse to be guided implicitly by the injunction, then he should be dragged down by force.

When the messenger came and announced the command of the fathers, Simeon, obeying the injunction, immediately put one foot forward. But then the messenger told him he was free to take his own course. "Be strong and play the man," he said. "The way you have chosen is from God."

—Evagrius Scholasticus, *Ecclesiastical History*, 1.13

IN GOD'S PRESENCE, CONSIDER . . .

Am I docile to the authority of the Church on earth? Do I realize that such docility is a mark of angelic life?

CLOSING PRAYER

Guardian Angel, help me to resist all temptations to disobedience. I want to live in communion with the Church, with all the holy angels, and with God.

The keys of heaven

Who has the authority to promise the keys of Heaven? Not an angel, says St.
Cyril of Alexandria, and not any of the other powers of Heaven. Responding to
heretics who doubted the divinity of Jesus, St. Cyril says that only God himself
can make a promise like that—even when God looks like a Galilean carpenter.

"And I tell you, you are Peter (that is, a rock), and on this rock I will build
my church, and the powers of death shall not prevail against it. I will give you
the keys of the kingdom of Heaven, and whatever you bind on Earth shall be
bound in Heaven, and whatever you loose on Earth shall be loosed in Heaven"
(Matthew 16:18-19). See how he makes himself at once the Lord of Heaven and
of Earth. For he promises things that exceed our nature, and surpass the measure
of humanity—in fact, they surpass even the measure of the angelic rank. They
are appropriate to be bestowed only by that Nature whose glory and sovereignty
transcend all.

First he says that the church belongs to him; the sacred Scriptures nevertheless distinctly ascribe it rather to God, and to him only, saying that it is "the church
of God." For they say that "Christ presented it to himself, having neither spot nor
stain, but holy rather, and blameless." As God, therefore, he says that it is his, and
indeed promises to found it, granting it to be unshaken, because he himself is the
Lord of powers. And next he says that he gives him the keys of Heaven. Then who
is it that thus pours forth language appropriate to God? Is it an angel? Is it some
other intelligent power—a Principality, or Throne, or Dominion? Is it one of the
holy Seraphs? Not at all. As I said before, such language belongs to Almighty God
alone, to whom belongs the sovereignty of Earth and Heaven.

So do not let these innovators divide the one Christ, so as to say that one Son
is the Word of God the Father, and that he who is of the seed of David is another
Son. For Peter mentions only one Christ, the Only-begotten who became man
and was made flesh.

–St. Cyril of Alexandria, *Commentary on Luke*, Sermon 49

IN GOD'S PRESENCE, CONSIDER . . .

Do I respect the earthly hierarchy which God has given extraordinary power in
Heaven as well? Do I recognize the gift God has given in letting men occupy the office of
angels?

CLOSING PRAYER

Lord, strengthen those in Holy Orders who serve the Church with the assistance of your
angels.

Friendship with angels is useless without charity

The struggles between Christians and the Donatist sect had become violent, and two Donatists had died, whom the Donatists called martyrs. St. Optatus of Milevis says they cannot be called martyrs, because they had abandoned charity, the one virtue without which not even communion with angels will do us any good.

Those men you call martyrs refused to recognize their brethren, and had no charity.

And don't say in their excuse that they were unwilling to hold communion with Betrayers, since it has been most clearly proved that they themselves were the sons of Betrayers. Therefore you have no way of excusing them, for it is quite obvious that they had no charity, without which we can't call what they did martyrdom. Martyrdom can't exist without charity. Without charity, the very greatest and most commanding virtue loses its effect; without it, the knowledge of all tongues is worthless; without it, even the fellowship of angels is of no use—as says the Apostle Paul:

"If I have the power of commanding mountains so as to move them from place to place, and if I speak with the tongues of all nations, even of angels, and if I deliver my body to the flames, and have no charity in me, I am nothing. I am like tinkling brass in the desert, so that the effect of my word will die away there, where there is no one to hear." (a paraphrase of 1 Cor. 13:1-3)

If someone as great as the blessed Paul, the Vessel of Election, declares that, even if he has commanding virtue and the company of angels, he is nothing without charity, then consider whether those people should not be called something very different from martyrs, who, having deserted charity, may perhaps, because of that desertion, have suffered something.

–St. Optatus of Milevis, *Against the Donatists*, Book 3

IN GOD'S PRESENCE, CONSIDER . . .

Where am I most lacking in charity? Have I tried to reach up to the angels without first being more charitable to the people I'm tempted to condemn?

CLOSING PRAYER

Lord, help me to heed the promptings of the guardian angels of people I find difficult— people who challenge me, people who oppose me. May the angels ensure that my dealings are always marked by supernatural charity.

Angels our fellow servants

St. Basil the Great replies to those who would make the Holy Spirit something less than God. They argue that the angels are sometimes also mentioned together with the Father and the Son; but St. Basil says that, in those cases, the angels are called as witnesses, as fellow servants under the same Lord.

Some people object that other beings mentioned along with the Father and the Son are certainly not always glorified together with them. The Apostle, for instance, in his charge to Timothy, associates the angels with them in the words, "In the presence of God and of Christ Jesus and of the elect angels I charge you" (1 Tim. 5:21). We are not for alienating the angels from the rest of creation, and yet, it is argued, we do not allow of their being counted with the Father and the Son.

To this I reply that possibly before a mild and gentle judge, and especially before One who by his leniency to those arraigned before him demonstrates the unimpeachable equity of his decisions, one might be willing to offer as witness even a fellow slave; but for a slave to be made free and called a son of God and quickened from death can only be brought about by the Lord, who has acquired natural kinship with us, and has been changed from the rank of a slave. How can we be made kin with God by one who is an alien? How can we be freed by one who is himself under the yoke of slavery? It follows that the mention of the Spirit and that of angels are not made under the same conditions. The Spirit is called on as Lord of life, and the angels as allies of their fellow slaves and faithful witnesses of the truth.

It is customary for the saints to deliver the commandments of God in the presence of witnesses, as also the Apostle himself says to Timothy, "and what you have heard from me before many witnesses entrust to faithful men who will be able to teach others also" (2 Tim. 2:2). Now he calls the angels to witness, for he knows that angels will be present with the Lord when he comes in the glory of his Father to judge the world in righteousness.

–St. Basil the Great, *On the Holy Spirit*, 13

IN GOD'S PRESENCE, CONSIDER . . .

Angels are witnesses of what I'm doing right now. Does remembering that change what I planned to do later on today?

CLOSING PRAYER

Holy angels who surround me, keep me in your sight, and keep your presence in my mind throughout the day.

The angel of the Lord driving us on

When misfortunes strike us, says St. Gregory the Great, we're very likely to despair—a tendency represented by the bad advice of Job's wife. But we need to remember that our sufferings can be useful in bringing us back to the right path.

"Then his wife said to him, 'Do you still hold fast your integrity? Curse God, and die'" (Job 2:9).

The wife, with her bad advice, is the carnal thought that prods at the mind. It often happens (as I've just said) that we are both harried by blows from outside and worn out by carnal prodding inside.

Thus Jeremiah mourns, saying, "In the street the sword bereaves; in the house it is like death" (Lam. 1:20). "The sword bereaves" when vengeance strikes and stabs at us from the outside; and "in the house it is like death" because we are lashed and yet the conscience is still not clear of the stains of inner temptation.

This David says, "Let them be like chaff before the wind, with the angel of the Lord driving them on!" (Ps. 35:5). Whoever is caught by the blast of temptation in the heart is lifted up like dust before the wind. And if the strictness of God strikes us in the middle of these blows, what else is it, except that the angel of the Lord is driving us on?

—St. Gregory the Great, *Moralia in Job*, 3.62

IN GOD'S PRESENCE, CONSIDER . . .

How easily do I give up when misfortune strikes? Do I recognize the angel of God in my misfortunes, driving me on toward Heaven?

CLOSING PRAYER

Lord, send your angels to strengthen me, so that I may resist evil thoughts even in adversity.

Sickness may be your angel in the way

In the Bible's most famous talking-animal story, Balaam is riding to curse Israel, but his ass sees an angel in the way, though Balaam doesn't. Sickness, says St. Gregory the Great, may be your angel in the way, stopping you from sinning and turning your mind back to God.

Remind the sick to think about how great health of the heart is in bodily suffering, which brings the mind back to knowing itself, and renews the memory of infirmity, which health for the most part throws away—so that the stricken flesh may remind the spirit, which is carried out of itself into elation, what condition it is subject to.

This is rightly shown to Balaam—if he had only been willing to follow the voice of God obediently—in the very obstruction of his journey. For Balaam is on his way to do what he plans to do, but the animal under him thwarts him. The ass, stopped by the prohibition, sees an angel that the human mind does not see. (Num. 22:21-35.)

In just the same way, the flesh is slowed down by afflictions. Then, from the pain it endures, it shows the mind that controls it the God whom the mind did not see, so that it stands in the way of the eagerness of the spirit, which is trying to advance in this world as if it were going on a journey, until it makes known to it the invisible one who stands in its way. Peter said it very well: he "was rebuked for his own transgression; a dumb ass spoke with human voice and restrained the prophet's madness" (2 Pet. 2:16). For a man really is rebuked as mad by a dumb beast of burden, when an elated mind is reminded by the afflicted flesh that it ought to keep the good of humility.

Remind the sick to think about how great a boon bodily affliction is. It both washes away committed sins and restrains those which might have been committed, which inflicts on the troubled mind wounds of penitence derived from outward stripes.

–St. Gregory the Great, Pastoral Rule, 3.12

IN GOD'S PRESENCE, CONSIDER . . .

When I'm suffering from illnesses and trials, do I look for an angel in my way? Do I try to use that trial to examine my life and see whether I'm going somewhere God doesn't want me to go?

CLOSING PRAYER

Holy angels, you are with us even in the trials of this life. Help me to have confidence in your presence and your mission. Help me to see each trial as an opportunity to draw closer to the Lord.

No one can hurt you

If you're a Christian, says St. John Chrysostom, no one can really hurt you—not even the devil himself. But more than that, you can't hurt anyone else.

Listen to me! I testify, and proclaim with a loud voice, more piercing even than the sound of a trumpet—and if it were possible to rise up on high and cry aloud, I would not shrink from doing it—no one of all the human beings that inhabit the earth has the power to hurt a Christian.

And why do I say human beings? Not even the evil spirit himself, the tyrant, the devil, can hurt us, unless we injure ourselves. Whatever anyone does against us, he does it in vain. Just as no human being could hurt an angel if he were on earth, so no human being can hurt another human being. And that human being will not be able to hurt another, as long as he is good.

What could be better than this—not to be able to be hurt, and not to be able to hurt another? For not being able to hurt another is just as important as not being able to be hurt. Someone like that is like an angel—in fact, like God. That's what God is like, except that he is like that by nature, whereas the human being is like that by moral choice. Neither one can be hurt by another, and neither one can hurt another.

—St. John Chrysostom, *Homily 51 on Acts*

IN GOD'S PRESENCE, CONSIDER . . .

Am I the sort of Christian who's really incapable of hurting anyone else—like an angel, or even like God? What hurts have I inflicted that I need to rectify?

CLOSING PRAYER

Guardian Angel, lead me always to desire the good of others the way you always desire my good.

Suffer a little while, be with angels forever

The Holy Spirit is called the Comforter, says St. Cyril of Jerusalem, because he does exactly that. How can the martyrs face horrible tortures without blinking? Because the Spirit has whispered in their ears, reminding them that they will soon be with the angels.

And the Spirit is called the Comforter, because he comforts us, and encourages us.

Often a man is outraged, dishonored, and hurt for Christ's sake. Tortures on every side—fire and sword—savage beasts—the deep pit. But the Holy Spirit softly whispers to him, "Wait for the Lord. What is happening to you now is trivial; what you're being given is great. Suffer a little while, and be with angels forever. 'The sufferings of this present time are not worth comparing with the glory that is to be revealed to us' (Rom. 8:18)."

He portrays the kingdom of Heaven to the man; he almost shows him the paradise of delight. And the martyrs, whose faces must necessarily be turned toward their judges, but whose spirits are already in paradise, despise the hardships they see in front of them.

—St. Cyril of Jerusalem, *Catechetical Lecture 16*, 20

IN GOD'S PRESENCE, CONSIDER . . .

If it helped martyrs face being torn apart by beasts, could remembering that God means me to share Heaven with angels, help me get through the mere annoyances of today?

CLOSING PRAYER

Father, I desire the company of angels eternally. I pray to you that your Spirit, the Comforter, may be sent down on me to strengthen me for your service.

Good deeds are like angels protecting us

Angels protecting Lot struck the men who would attack him blind, so that they could not find their way into his house. This, says St. Gregory the Great, is a good metaphor for the good deeds of the righteous, which strike their enemies blind so that they cannot find an opening of wickedness anywhere.

"They meet with darkness in the daytime, and grope at noonday as in the night" (Job 5:14).

The day of good deeds shines outwardly in a neighbor, but they "grope as in the night," because inwardly they are under the darkness of their jealous feeling. They busy themselves to find some points that they may reprimand—they seek out an opening for detraction. But since they cannot find one, they search around in blindness outside.

This is well set forth in that occasion, when because the angels were protecting Lot, the inhabitants of Sodom could not find the doorway in his house—as it is written, "Then they pressed hard against the man Lot, and drew near to break the door. But the men put forth their hands and brought Lot into the house to them, and shut the door. And they struck with blindness the men who were at the door of the house, both small and great, so that they wearied themselves groping for the door" (Gen. 19:9-11).

What does it mean that, when the wicked are up in arms against him, Lot is brought back into the house, and defended? It means that every righteous man, while he encounters the assaults of evil ones, is brought back into his interior, and stays there undismayed. But the men of Sodom cannot find the door in Lot's house, because the corrupters of souls detect no opening of accusation against the life of the righteous man. For, stricken with blindness, they go round and round the house, so to speak, under the influence of envy scrutinizing words and deeds. But because in the life of the just, strong and praiseworthy conduct confronts them from every direction, groping at random they feel nothing but the wall.

–St. Gregory the Great, *Moralia in Job*, 6.38

IN GOD'S PRESENCE, CONSIDER . . .

Am I so well surrounded by good deeds, like the angels that surrounded Lot, that the envious can find nothing to accuse me of?

CLOSING PRAYER

Guardian Angel, be with me throughout the day, and lead me to surround myself everywhere with good deeds as armor against the assaults of evil.

Good people are worth more than bad angels

Just as you'd rather have gold than fleas, even though fleas are higher on the scale of creation than gold, it's far better to be a good person than a bad angel, says St. Augustine.

Among existing beings that are not of God the Creator's essence, those that have life are ranked above those that have none; those that have the power of generation, or even of desiring, above those that lack it. And, among things that have life, those that feel are higher than those that have no feeling, as animals are ranked above trees. And, among the ones that feel, the intelligent are above those that do not have intelligence, as people (for example) are ranked above cattle. And, among the intelligent, the immortal, such as the angels, above the mortal, such as people.

These are the gradations according to the order of nature; but according to the usefulness each one of us finds in a thing, there are various standards of value, so that it turns out that we prefer some things that have no sensation to some sentient beings. And so strong is this preference, that, if we had the power, we would abolish the latter from nature altogether—either because we don't understand the place they hold in nature, or, though we know it, we would sacrifice them to our own convenience. For example, who wouldn't rather have bread in his house than mice, or rather have gold than fleas?

But there is little to wonder at in this, seeing that even when valued by humans themselves (whose nature is certainly of the highest dignity), more is often given for a horse than for a slave, for a jewel than for a maid.

But will and love matter so much in intelligent beings that, though in the order of nature angels rank above humans, yet, by the scale of justice, good people are worth more than bad angels.

–St. Augustine, *City of God*, 11.16

IN GOD'S PRESENCE, CONSIDER . . .

Am I honestly worth more than a bad angel? Am I working in that direction?

CLOSING PRAYER

My Guardian Angel, keep me away from every occasion of sin, and make me worthy of the aid you so generously give me.

Friendship makes angels rejoice and lulls demons

St. John Chrysostom compares friendship to the music of a harp or orchestra, where different notes produce a single harmony.

This is a wonderful thing to see: many in one, and one in many—just as the sounds are different in a harp, but the harmony is one, and all together they make one harmony and symphony

But the musician is the power of love. This is what plays the sweet melody, singing a song in which no note is out of tune. The angels rejoice at it, and the Lord, the God of angels. The whole audience in Heaven rises to hear it. The song even lulls the wrath of demons. It lulls the passions—in fact, it doesn't even allow them to rise, but makes a deep calm.

Just as in the theater everyone listens with a hush and keeps perfect silence while the orchestra is playing, so among friends, when love plays the chords, all the passions are calmed and laid to sleep, like wild beasts chained and tamed.

—St. John Chrysostom, *Homily 40 on Acts*

IN GOD'S PRESENCE, CONSIDER . . .

Is this a good description of my friendships? Do they calm demons and make angels rejoice? Or do they stir up trouble?

CLOSING PRAYER

Lord, let me hear the sweet harmony of your life-giving commandments, and with the joyful angels I will sing everlasting glory to you without ceasing.

Show the world how angels live

If we live the angelic life here on earth, says St. John Chrysostom, that will be our most powerful tool for evangelism. The people around us will see what the kingdom of Heaven looks like, and they'll want to be part of it.

Let's show them all a new kind of life. Let's make earth into Heaven, and by doing it show the Greeks what great blessings they're missing.

When they see how we treat each other, they'll be looking at the very face of the kingdom of Heaven. Then they'll say, "If the Christians have already turned into angels here, what will they be after they leave this world?"

That way they too will be reformed.

–St. John Chrysostom, *Homily on Matthew* 43:7

IN GOD'S PRESENCE, CONSIDER . . .

Could the people around me think I've turned into an angel already? What would have to change in my life before they thought of me that way?

CLOSING PRAYER

Guardian Angel, help me to live as you would live in the ordinary circumstances of every day—in my work and in my rest, with my family and with my neighbors.

Unlike angels, sometimes we're wrong

St. Augustine points out that St. Cyprian was wrong about some things—but he was wrong in the right way. It is angelic to refrain from judging those who have different opinions on obscure things, but the presumption of the devil to divide the Church over those differences.

It often happens that something is imperfectly revealed to the more learned, so that their patient and humble charity, from which comes the greater fruit, may be proved—either in the way in which they preserve unity when they hold different opinions on matters of comparative obscurity, or in the temper with which they receive the truth when they learn that it has been declared to be contrary to what they thought.

The blessed Cyprian shows us both of these ways. He shows us the first in the way in which he preserved unity with those from whom he differed in opinion. For he says, "Judging no one, and not depriving anyone of the right of communion if he differs from us." And he shows us the other in the way he could receive the truth when he found it to be different from what he thought it was. Though his letters are silent on the point, his good temper is still proclaimed by his merits. If there is no letter extant to prove it, it is witnessed by his crown of martyrdom; if the Council of bishops does not declare it, it is declared by the host of angels.

For it is a considerable proof of a very peaceful soul that he won the crown of martyrdom in that unity from which he would not separate, even though he differed from it. After all, we are only human; and one of the temptations to which humans are subject is that we should hold views that differ with the truth on some point. But if we have too great love for our own opinion, or too much jealousy of our betters, we may come even to the sacrilege of dividing the communion of the Church, and of founding heresy or schism, and that is a presumption worthy of the devil. But never to have an opinion that differs from the truth in any point is a perfection found only in the angels.

–St. Augustine, *On Baptism, Against the Donatists*, 2.5

IN GOD'S PRESENCE, CONSIDER . . .

Am I tempted toward the presumption of the devil when I see things in the Church I don't like? How could I be more of a force for unity?

CLOSING PRAYER

Guardian Angel, keep all presumption far from me, and lead me to accept the decisions of the Church in patient and humble charity.

Taste and see

The holy angels drink from the sweetness of God, says St. Ambrose—but the sweetness is hidden from you as long as you are captive to sin. As soon as all your hope is placed in the Lord, you taste what the angels taste.

With good reason, then, is the sweetness of God hidden to you. The law placed in your members, resisting the law of your mind, brings you into captivity. The holy angels drink from that sweetness, but it is hidden from you. You cannot drink and taste that sweetness, because you are a captive.

You would not have known lust if the law had not said, "You shall not lust." You heard, feared, tried to fight, could not win.

God forbids adultery. You have coveted another man's wife, but you do not go in to her. You have a chance—you have time, the right place, no witnesses— and yet you don't do it. Why not? *Because you fear the punishment.* But no one will know it! Well, won't God know it? So it's clear that, because God knows what you are about to do, you do not do it. But here you fear the threats of God. You do not love his commandments. Why don't you do it? Because you'll be thrown into hell fire if you do. The fire is what you fear.

Oh, if you loved chastity, you would not do it, even if you could go completely unpunished! If God said to you, "Go ahead, do it, I won't condemn you, I won't send you to hell, but I will withhold my face from you"—then, if you didn't do it because of *this* threat, it would be from the love of God that you refrained, not from the fear of judgment.

Charity works through you, when you act with your will. You taste the sweetness right away if you hope in the Lord.

–St. Augustine, *Sermon 95 on the New Testament*

IN GOD'S PRESENCE, CONSIDER . . .

How much of what keeps me in line is love, and how much is fear? Would I have less trouble with temptation if I remembered the sweetness that the angels taste?

CLOSING PRAYER

Lord, I am fearful and trembling when I stand before you. Make me worthy to taste your sweetness with your holy angels.

We dig our own ditch

When the rich man in Christ's parable begs that Lazarus give him just a little water, Abraham tells him that there's a great chasm between the righteous and the sinners. What does that mean? asks St. Asterius of Amasea. That the nature of our lives creates a vast separation between the righteous and unrighteous.

It is also worthwhile to examine intelligently how each of these men when dead was carried forth. The poor man, when he fell asleep, had angels as his guards and attendants who carried him, full of joyful expectation, to the place of rest. The rich man, Christ says, died and was buried.

It is not possible to improve the declaration of the Scriptures in any way. A single sentence adequately indicates the unhonored decease of the rich man. For the sinner when he dies is indeed buried, being earthly in body, and worldly in soul. He degrades the spiritual within him to the material by yielding to the enticements of the flesh, leaving behind no good memorial of his life, but, dying the death of beasts, is wrapped in unhonored forgetfulness.

After the rich man had begged him many times, and after hearing countless piteous appeals, Abraham was not moved by the laments of the suppliant. He did not take the one who was bitterly scourged away from his pain. Instead, with austere mind he confirmed the final judgment, saying that God had given each what he deserved. And he said to the rich man, "Since in life you lived in luxury through the calamities of others, what you are suffering is imposed upon you as the penalty of your sin. But to him who once had hardships, and was trampled on and endured in bitterness life in the flesh, there is allotted here a sweet and joyful existence."

I think this parable is a material representation of a spiritual truth. We should not imagine that there is in reality a ditch dug by angels. Instead Luke, by the similitude of a chasm, has represented for us the separation of those who have lived virtuously and those who have lived otherwise.

–St. Asterius of Amasea, *Sermon 1: The Rich Man and Lazarus*

IN GOD'S PRESENCE, CONSIDER . . .

Which side of the great chasm am I living on—the side with the holy angels, or the side with the fallen ones? What do I need to change to make sure I'm on the right side?

CLOSING PRAYER

Father, though I know I am unworthy, you have sent angels to assist me and serve me. I rely on their help because they come from you.

The yield is what counts

St. Peter, says St. Augustine, denied Christ, stood in his way, and misunderstood the New Covenant—yet he will judge angels. What matters most to Christ is not the thistles we had to uproot from our souls, but the yield we give him once the gospel is planted.

We see the same thing in the Gospel, where the devils confess that Christ is the Son of God in the words used by Peter, but with a very different heart. So, though the words were the same, Peter is praised for his faith, while the impiety of the devils is stopped. For Christ, not by human sense, but by divine knowledge, could inspect and infallibly distinguish the sources from which the words came.

Besides, there are multitudes who confess that Christ is the Son of the living God, without meriting the same approval as Peter—not only of those who shall say in that day, "Lord, Lord," and shall receive the sentence, "Depart from me," but also of those who shall be placed on the right hand. They may probably never have denied Christ even once; they may never have opposed his suffering for our salvation; they may never have forced the Gentiles to follow Jewish law; and yet they will not be honored equally with Peter, who, though he did all these things, will sit on one of the twelve thrones, and judge not only the twelve tribes, but the angels. So, again, many who have never desired another man's wife, or procured the death of the husband, as David did, will never reach the place which David nevertheless held in the divine favor.

There is a vast difference between what is in itself so undesirable that it must be utterly rejected, and the rich and plenteous harvest which may afterwards appear. For farmers are best pleased with the fields from which, after they may have pulled out big thistles, they receive a hundredfold; not with fields which have never had any thistles, but hardly bear thirtyfold.

−St. Augustine, *Reply to Faustus the Manichean*, 22.6c

IN GOD'S PRESENCE, CONSIDER . . .

When I confess that Christ is the Son of God, do I do it as Peter and the angels do, with love and awe? Or do I do it as the devils did, with cringing fear?

CLOSING PRAYER

Lord Jesus Christ, I confess that you are the Son of the living God, and I renounce the impiety of the devil and all his angels.

Repentance makes a new person

St. Augustine says that, when we repent of our sins, our "pain and tears" give birth to a new person, one who belongs in Heaven with Christ and the angels. We lose that heavenly citizenship when we relapse into our old sinful ways.

"What is man that you are mindful of him, and the son of man, that you care for him?" (Ps. 8:4).

Every son of man is a man, although not every man is a son of man. Adam, for instance, was a man, but not a son of man. From that we may be able to tell what the difference is here between "man" and "son of man": those who bear the image of the earthy man, who is not a son of man, are meant by the name of "men"; but those who bear the image of the heavenly Man should be called "sons of men."

The repentance of the old man begets this "son of man"—that is, the new man—with pain and tears. Although he is new, he is still called a "man of the flesh" while he is fed with milk: "I, brethren, could not address you as spiritual men, but as men of the flesh," says the apostle. And to show that they were not already regenerated, he adds, "as babes in Christ. I fed you with milk, not solid food." And when he relapses to the old life—as often happens—he hears in rebuke that he is a man: "are you not of the flesh, and behaving like ordinary men?" (1 Cor. 3:1-3).

This is why the "son of man" was first visited in the person of the Lord Man himself, born of the Virgin Mary. Because of the very weakness of the flesh that the Wisdom of God condescended to bear, and the humiliation of the Passion, the Psalm (8:5) justly says of him, "You have made him a little less than the angels. But I add that glorification in which he rose and ascended into Heaven: "you crown him with glory and honor. You have given him dominion over the works of your hands (Ps. 8:6).

—St. Augustine, *Exposition on Psalm 8*, 10-11

IN GOD'S PRESENCE, CONSIDER . . .

In spite of previous repentance, have I relapsed into old sins, rendering myself far lower than the angels and closer to the beasts?

CLOSING PRAYER

Lord, though I have sinned often, permit me to stand before you with your angels and implore your forgiveness for all my sins.

Missing the angels

We were created to be in fellowship with angels, says St. Gregory the Great. But our sin keeps us out of Heaven and bound to Earth. How can we help mourning what we've lost?

"But where shall wisdom be found? And where is the place of understanding? Man does not know the way to it, and it is not found in the land of the living" (Job 28:12-13). In this passage, what does the name "land" mean but the human soul?—about which the psalmist says, "my soul thirsts for you like a parched land" (Ps. 143:6).

But this wisdom cannot be found in the land of the living, because whoever is still fed with the pleasures of this life is cut off from the perception of the eternal Wisdom. Anyone with a truly wise mind, when banished from the eternal delights, would mourn over the blind condition of the exile he has fallen into.

This is why Solomon says "he who increases knowledge increases sorrow" (Eccles. 1:18). The more we begin to know what we have lost, the more we begin to mourn the sentence passed on us for our corruption. We see where we have fallen from and where we have fallen into; we see how we have come from the joys of Paradise into the woes of the present life—from the company of angels to worrying about necessities. We consider what a number of dangers we now lie exposed to, when we formerly disdained to stand without danger. We mourn the exile we are cursed to suffer, and sigh after the condition of heavenly glory that we might be enjoying safely if we did not have the urge to commit sin.

The psalmist rightly sees this and says, "I had said in my alarm, 'I am driven far from your sight'" (Ps. 31:22). After contemplating the interior joys of the vision of God, and the assembly in fellowship of the angels holding fast, he brought back his eyes to things beneath. He saw how he was laid low, when he was created so that he might stand in heavenly realms.

–St. Gregory the Great, *Moralia in Job*, 18.66

IN GOD'S PRESENCE, CONSIDER . . .

I may not be able to stand in Heaven with the angels yet, but do I remember their companionship and ask for their help?

CLOSING PRAYER

Guardian Angel, shelter me under your wings; light my path, and guide my steps.

Believe the angels if nothing else

At a time when Arian heretics threatened to take over the Church, St. Ambrose reminds us that the angels themselves have declared that Christ was divine, and that he was to be born of a virgin.

But if they will not believe the doctrines of the clergy, let them believe the revealed word of Christ. Let them believe the admonitions of angels who say, "For with God nothing shall be impossible." Let them give credit to the Creed of the Apostles, which the Roman Church has always kept and preserved undefiled.

Mary heard the voice of the angel before she had said, "How shall this be?" She didn't ask because she had no faith that God could do what he said. Afterwards she replied, "Behold the handmaid of the Lord, be it unto me according to thy word."

This is the virgin who conceived. This is the virgin who brought forth a Son. For thus it is written, "Behold a Virgin shall conceive and bear a Son"; declaring not only that she should conceive as a virgin, but also that she bring forth as a virgin.

–St. Ambrose, *Letter 42*, 5

IN GOD'S PRESENCE, CONSIDER . . .

When I hear the Word of God, am I willing to give the same assent that Mary gave? Do I remember that angels themselves have brought the Word to human beings?

CLOSING PRAYER

Lord, with your Blessed and Ever-Virgin Mother, Mary, Mother of God, let me listen to the Word you have sent your angels to proclaim.

Come back and make the angels glad

St. Pacian reminds us that you're never so far gone in sin that you can't re-pent. The angels are watching and waiting; when you come back, no matter how far you've strayed, the angels will rejoice.

The book of Revelation also threatens the seven Churches unless they should repent. Now, God wouldn't threaten those who *don't* repent, unless he pardoned those who *do*. God Himself says, "Remember then from what you have fallen," and "repent" (Rev. 2:5). And again, "When you return and mourn, then you shall be saved, and know where you have been."

And let no one think that any soul has become so vile and sinful that God has no more need of him. The Lord does not will that any of us should perish. Even those of little worth—even the very least—are sought after. If you don't believe me, look in the Gospel. The piece of silver is sought after, and when found is shown to the neighbors. The poor sheep, although he has to carry it back on his shoulders bending low, is not burdensome to the Shepherd. Over one sinner that repents the angels in Heaven rejoice, and the celestial choir is glad. Come, then, sinner; never stop asking! You see where there is joy over your return!

–St. Pacian, *Paraenesis*, 25

IN GOD'S PRESENCE, CONSIDER . . .

Am I tempted to despair of my sins? Have I confessed the sins that bother me most? Have I asked my guardian angel for help in keeping me from sin?

CLOSING PRAYER

Lord, do not despise me, in spite of all my sins; I know that I am not worthy, but I trust in the care of the angels you send to help me.

Even angels can't take away your sin

When the emperor Theodosius gave orders that resulted in a massacre in Thessalonica, St. Ambrose, bishop of the imperial capital of Milan, refused him communion until he made public penance. He warned the emperor that not even an angel can take away his sin. Only "tears and penitence" can do it.

And Scripture tells us that when the people were dying, on the very first day and at dinner time, David saw the angel that struck down the people, and he said, "Lo, I have sinned, and I have done wickedly; but these sheep, what have they done? Let your hand, I pray you, be against me and against my father's house" (2 Sam. 24:17). So the Lord repented, and commanded the angel to spare the people, and that David should offer sacrifice. In those days there were sacrifices for sin, but now we have the sacrifices of penitence. So by that humility he was made more acceptable to God. It's not surprising that a man should sin, but it is indeed blameable if he doesn't acknowledge his error, and humble himself before God.

I've written all this, not to confuse you, but so that these royal examples may lead you to put away this sin from your kingdom. You will do that if you humble your soul before God. You are a man. Temptation has come to you; vanquish it. Sin is only washed away by tears and penitence. Neither angel nor archangel can do it. The Lord himself—who alone can say "I am with you"—grants no remission of sin except to the penitent.

—St. Ambrose, *Letter 51*, 9-11

IN GOD'S PRESENCE, CONSIDER . . .

Am I regular in the practice of sacramental confession? Do I call upon my angel to help me when I examine my conscience?

CLOSING PRAYER

Guardian Angel, help me be sincerely penitent, as David was, as Peter was, so that the Lord may accept my repentance.

A glimpse of the chambers of the south

St. Gregory the Great reads "the chambers of the south" in Job as symbolic of the depths of Heaven. Just as the climate gets warmer the farther south we go, so the deeper we are in Heaven the more we are filled with the heat of the Holy Spirit.

"(W)ho made the Bear and Orion, the Pleiades and the chambers of the south" (Job 9:9).

"The chambers of the south" are those unseen orders of angels, and those unfathomed depths of the heavenly country, that are filled with the heat of the Holy Spirit. There the souls of the saints are brought—both at the present time removed from the body, and afterward restored to it anew. Like stars they are concealed in hidden depths.

There all day, as at midday, the fire of the sun burns with a brighter luster, because the brightness of our Creator, which is now obscured by the mists of our mortal state, is made visible more clearly. There the beam of the orb seems to raise itself to higher regions, because Truth from himself enlightens us more completely and thoroughly. There the light of interior contemplation is visible without the intervening shadow of change. There the heat of the supreme Light is felt without any dimness from the body. There the unseen bands of angels glitter like stars in hidden realms, which mortals cannot see now, because they are so deeply bathed in the flame of the true Light.

–St. Gregory the Great, *Moralia in Job*, 9.17

IN GOD'S PRESENCE, CONSIDER . . .

Do I feel the heat of the Holy Spirit burning in me, as it does in all the orders of angels? Or is it chilly where I am now?

CLOSING PRAYER

Lord, teach me to imitate the ardor of your angels, and bestow on me the rich gifts of your all-holy Spirit.

Long for life with the angels

St. Gregory the Great tells us that our time of waiting here is preparing a richer reward for us. When we love God and long for life among the angels, by waiting our love grows even stronger.

"Oh, that I knew where I might find him, that I might come even to his seat!" (Job 23:3).

Those who love still have to wait, so that, because they have loved and waited, they will have stronger title to the reward. So Almighty God is made sweet to us in miracles, but in his own loftiness he remains hidden from our eyes. Thus, by showing a little of himself, by a secret inspiration he sets us on fire with love for him; but by hiding the glory of his majesty he increases the force of our love for him by the heat of our longing desire.

If the holy man had not wanted to see this Being in his majesty, he certainly would not have brought in the words, "that I might come even to his seat." For what is the "seat" of God except those angelic spirits who, as Scripture tells us, are called "Thrones"? So whoever wants to come to the seat of God wants nothing other than to be among the angelic spirits, so that he will not be subject to any more weak moments in time, but now will rise up to lasting glory in the contemplation of eternity.

Nevertheless, these words are also appropriate to the righteous while they are still in this life. When they see anything done against their wish and desire, they turn to the hidden judgments of God to read in them that what seems to happen irregularly on the outside is not arranged irregularly on the inside. When, with the eyes of faith, they see the Creator of all things ruling over the angelic spirits, then they "come to his seat."

–St. Gregory the Great, *Moralia in Job*, 16.33

IN GOD'S PRESENCE, CONSIDER . . .

Does my love increase while I wait for my life among the angels?

CLOSING PRAYER

Send forth your plentiful grace and rich blessing, Lord, and make me worthy of everlasting life among the angelic spirits who make up your throne.

From beast to angel

Animals don't sin, because they follow the laws of nature laid down for them. Angels in Heaven don't sin, because their wills are perfectly in tune with God's. But we, says St. Augustine, are halfway between. If we subdue the part of us that's like the animals, we can rise to the level of the angels.

It is a great question whether there is any rational creature for which there is no pleasure in what is unlawful. If there is such a class of creatures, it does not include man, nor does it include the angelic beings that did not stay in the truth. These rational creatures were made so that they had the *potentiality* of restraining their desires from the unlawful; and in not doing this they sinned.

Great, then, is the creature man, for he is restored by this potentiality, by which, if he had so chosen, he would not have fallen. And great is the Lord, and greatly to be praised, who created man. For he also created inferior natures which *cannot* sin, and superior natures which *will not* sin. Beasts do not sin, for their nature agrees with the eternal law from being subject to it, without being in possession of it. And again, angels do not sin, because their heavenly nature is so in possession of the eternal law that God is the only object of its desire, and they obey his will without any experience of temptation.

But man, whose life on this earth is a trial on account of sin, subdues to himself what he has in common with beasts, and subdues to God what he has in common with angels; till, when righteousness is perfected and immortality attained, he shall be raised from among beasts and ranked with angels.

−St. Augustine, *Reply to Faustus the Manichean*, 22.28

IN GOD'S PRESENCE, CONSIDER . . .

How much does my life have in common with the beasts, and how much with the angels? How can I tip the scales toward the angelic side?

CLOSING PRAYER

God of light, who gives to the faint-hearted who put their trust in you those things into which angels desire to look, sanctify me in soul, body, and spirit, and make me worthy of your gifts.

Serve God as the angels do

How do we treat our own servants? St. Cyril of Alexandria points out that God has a right to be at least as severe on us as we are on the people who serve us. The angels constantly serve God in everything they do: should God expect any less from us?

Come, let us see what blame we incur by our disobedience by looking at what happens among ourselves. We ourselves usually demand obedience mingled with fear from our servants. When they plan rebellion, and throw off the yoke of servitude, we make them humble by bonds and tortures and the scourge.

So when we, who are of earth, and by nature the brethren of those who are bowed beneath the yoke, cannot tolerate them when rebellious, how will God endure it—he whom Principalities, Thrones, and Lordships worship, and in whose presence the high-exalted Seraphim stand, readily rendering their service? For the divine David somewhere says of them in the Psalms,

Bless the Lord, O you his angels,
you mighty ones who do his word,
hearkening to the voice of his word!
Bless the Lord, all his hosts,
his ministers that do his will! (Ps. 103:20-21)

It is dangerous, therefore, and deserves final condemnation, to be unwilling to submit to Christ the Almighty. But those who prize his service shall receive the most excellent blessings.

–St. Cyril of Alexandria, *Commentary on Luke*, Sermon 34

IN GOD'S PRESENCE, CONSIDER . . .

Have I taken up Christ's easy yoke, as the holy angels do so readily? Or is there still part of me that demands to have things my way instead of Christ's?

CLOSING PRAYER

Lord Jesus Christ, I am a poor, unworthy, and sinful servant; but teach me to serve like an angel, and let me bear fruit.

We can be angels

Do you know your own nature? St. John Chrysostom wonders whether you do. If you did, he says, you'd know that you could be an angel—or a beast.

Who, you will say, is ignorant of his own nature?

Many are—perhaps all but a few. If you like, I will show you the proof of it.

Tell me, what is man? If you were asked, could you answer these questions right away: In what part is he different from the animals? In what is he like the inhabitants of Heaven? What can be made of man?

For as in the case of any other material, so in this case: man is the material, but from this material can be made either an angel or a beast. Doesn't that sound strange to you? Yet you have often heard it in the Scriptures. For of certain human beings it was said, "He is the angel of the Lord," and "men should seek instruction from his mouth," and again, "I send my angel to prepare the way before me" (Mal. 3:1)—but then of some, "You brood of vipers!" (Matt. 12:34).

So, then, it all depends on the use.

—St. John Chrysostom, *Homily 32 on Acts*

IN GOD'S PRESENCE, CONSIDER . . .

Am I usually more like an angel or a beast?

CLOSING PRAYER

Holy Guardian Angel, turn my thoughts away from base desires and toward heavenly things, so that I may be, according to my capacity, an angel of the Lord.

Pray to live like an angel

In the Our Father, we ask that God's will be done on Earth as it is in Heaven. What does that mean? We're asking, St. Cyril of Alexandria explains, for the power to live lives like the angels in Heaven, who always do God's will.

"Your will be done on Earth as it is in Heaven."

Let us examine this part of the prayer, for it will be very profitable for the salvation of our souls. Why did he command the saints to say to God the Father in Heaven, "Your will be done on earth as it is in Heaven"?

This petition is worthy of the saints, and full of praise. Asking that the good-will of God may prevail on earth—what else is it but to ask that all humanity may lead praiseworthy and elect lives, and practice and know all virtue? We say that the holy angels live in glory in Heaven this way: for it is written, "Bless the Lord, all his hosts, his ministers that do his will!" (Ps. 103:21). For by clinging to the will of their Lord, and fulfilling that righteousness which transcends human things, they preserve their high place, whereas those who acted otherwise fell from that position.

But to summarize and put together briefly the meaning of the words, we ask that power may be given to those who live on earth to do the will of God, and imitate the conduct of the holy angels in Heaven.

Let us see, therefore, as well as we can, how the powers above and the ranks of the holy angels successfully perform their duty. How do they honor God? Is it by sacrifices of blood? Is it by perfume and frankincense, as indeed the Israel after the flesh did? No, I think it would be completely unbelievable either to think or to say that. Instead, it would be true to say that they perform a spiritual and not a material service, always crowning the Creator of all with lauds and praises, and fulfilling that righteousness which is suitable to holy spirits.

–Cyril of Alexandria, *Commentary on Luke*, Sermon 74

IN GOD'S PRESENCE, CONSIDER . . .

Is my commonwealth in Heaven with the angels now? Or am I still more a citizen of Earth than of Heaven?

CLOSING PRAYER

Lord, give peace to my soul, and deem me worthy to live with the angels in your heavenly kingdom.

Ask to be like an angel

God won't hear your prayer if you ask him to curse someone you hate, says St. Cyril of Alexandria. You should be asking for the spiritual gifts that will make you part of the company of the angels.

When you ask for anyone to die or be exposed to inevitable tortures, because they have annoyed or molested you in any way, God will not grant it. For he wills us to be long-suffering in mind, and not to pay anyone back with evil for evil, but to pray for those who steal from us, to do good to those who injure us, and to be imitators of his kindness.

For this reason Solomon was praised: when offering up prayers to God, he said, "Give your servant a heart to hear, and to judge your people righteously" (1 Kings 3:6-9). And it pleased the Lord that Solomon asked this thing. And what did God, who loves virtue, say to him? "Because you have asked this, and have not asked for yourself long life or riches or the life of your enemies, but have asked for yourself understanding to discern what is right, behold, I now do according to your word. Behold, I give you a wise and discerning mind" (1 Kings 3:11-12).

You, therefore, should ask God to give you abundant spiritual gifts. Ask for strength, so that you may be able to resist every fleshly lust with vigor. Ask God for an uncovetous disposition, long suffering, gentleness, and the mother and nurse of all good—I mean patience. Ask for calmness of temper, continence, a pure heart; and further, ask also for the wisdom that comes from God.

These things he will give readily. These save the soul. These work in it that better beauty, and imprint God's image in it. This is the spiritual wealth, the riches that never need to be abandoned. These prepare for us the lot of the saints, and make us members of the company of the holy angels.

–St. Cyril of Alexandria, *Commentary on Luke*, Sermon 79

IN GOD'S PRESENCE, CONSIDER . . .

Do my desires render me fit to share the company of the angels? Do I always will good things, and never evil, for others?

CLOSING PRAYER

Lord, make me perfect in piety, as the angels are, and lead me quickly to the hope of eternal life, and make me heir of the kingdom of Heaven, by the aid of Christ, the Savior of us all; by whom, and with whom, to God the Father be praise and dominion, with the Holy Spirit, forever and ever.

Love makes us angels

St. John Chrysostom says that love makes an angel out of the one who loves. Real love delivers us from all the evil thoughts that keep us from the serenity we should be enjoying.

Look at love—see how it spreads everywhere and manages everything (1 Cor. 13:5-6). But do not be weary until you have got to know this golden chain completely. For having said that "love does not insist on its own way," he goes on to tell us the good things that come from this.

And what are they?

"It is not irritable or resentful." See how love not only subdues vice, but does not even allow it a foothold at all. He didn't say, "though irritated, it overcomes," but it is not even irritable. He didn't say it does no evil, but it doesn't even think of evil. So far from thinking up evil, it does not even suspect it of the beloved. If love cannot even endure to admit an evil suspicion, how could she do any evil, or how could she be irritated?

"It does not rejoice at wrong"—that is, it does not feel pleasure when someone else suffers. And not only that, but also, which is much greater, "rejoices in the right." She feels pleasure, he says, with those who are well spoken of: as Paul says, "Rejoice with those who rejoice, weep with those who weep" (Rom. 12:15). This is why love does not envy or boast: she actually counts the good things of others as her own.

Do you see how love makes her child an angel step by step? When we are void of anger, and pure from envy, and free from every tyrannical passion, then you can see that we are delivered from human nature from then on, and have arrived in port at the very serenity of the angels.

—St. John Chrysostom, *Homily 23 on 1 Corinthians*

IN GOD'S PRESENCE, CONSIDER . . .

How well do my actual relations with the people around me match what St. Paul says about love? In my family, among my friends, how far am I from the serenity of the angels?

CLOSING PRAYER

Lord, breathe into my soul the sweet fragrance of your love, and lead me toward the serene love your angels know in Heaven.

Virtue makes angels

Human nature is no barrier to living an angelic life, says St. John Chrysostom. The evil angels were expelled from Heaven, but virtuous humans have been taken into Heaven.

But why do I stop at angel? A human being can become God, and a child of God—for we have read, "I say, 'You are gods, sons of the Most High, all of you'" (Ps. 82:6). And what's more, the power to become both God and angel and child of God is put into our own hands! Yes, really—a human being can be the maker of an angel! This startles you, perhaps? But hear Christ: "For in the resurrection they neither marry nor are given in marriage, but are like angels in Heaven" (Matt. 22:30), and "He who is able to receive this, let him receive it" (Matt. 19:12).

In short, it's virtue that makes angels. But virtue is within our power! Therefore we are able to make angels—if not in nature, certainly in will.

After all, without virtue, it's no advantage to be an angel. The devil is a proof of this: he was an angel once. But with virtue, it's no loss to be human by nature—and John is proof of this, who was a man, and Elijah, who went up into Heaven, and all those who are about to depart for Heaven. These human beings had bodies, but that didn't keep them from living in Heaven—but the evil spirits, though they had no bodies, could not remain in Heaven.

So you shouldn't be grieved or angry at your nature as if it were a hindrance to you. It's your will that's a hindrance to you.

—St. John Chrysostom, *Homily 32 on Acts*

IN GOD'S PRESENCE, CONSIDER . . .

Do I sometimes give up in the face of strong temptation and say, "It's just human nature"? Does it help to remember that I have the power to make my own nature more angelic?

CLOSING PRAYER

Guardian Angel, I beg aid from you for the strengthening of my soul, so that in perfect love and true faith I may care for everything the Father has given me.

We can be almost angels—if we want

What if you found an enormous diamond—but you threw it away because you thought it was a doorknob? Wouldn't that be a huge loss to you? In the same way, says St. John Chrysostom, you're missing an enormous treasure if you don't realize what your human nature is capable of.

The devil was incorporeal, but he became a lion—look, it says, "Your adversary the devil prowls around like a roaring lion, seeking someone to devour" (1 Pet. 5:8).

But we were corporeal, and we become angels.

If someone should find some precious metal, and not care about it at all because he's not a craftsman, it would be a great loss to him—or if he should see pearls, or a pearl shell, or any other thing of that sort. In the same way, if we are ignorant of our own nature, we won't care about it at all—but if we know what it is, we'll work hard and reap enormous profits. From this nature a king's robe is made—and a king's palace, and a king's members. We're all kingly.

So let us not misuse our nature and do ourselves harm that way. He has made us a little lower than the angels (Ps. 8:5)—lower, I mean, because of death, but even that little we have now recovered. So there is nothing to keep us from becoming near to the angels if we want. Let's want it! Let's want it, and having given it our best effort, let us give honor to the Father, and the Son, and the Holy Spirit, now and forever, world without end. Amen.

—St. John Chrysostom, *Homily 32 on Acts*

IN GOD'S PRESENCE, CONSIDER . . .

Do my desires tend to focus on money or success? How can I focus them on becoming near to the angels?

CLOSING PRAYER

Glory to you, O Lord—glory to you for your unutterably precious gift of a human nature capable of being made equal to the angels.

Like angels on earth

St. Ambrose tells us that the death and resurrection of Christ actually changed human nature, making us capable of sharing the grace of a new creation. We don't have to wait until we die: through Christ, we can live like angels on earth.

This is why his grace and goodness have been formed upon us in Christ Jesus: so that, though we were dead according to works, we could be redeemed through faith and saved by grace, and receive the gift of this great deliverance. Our very nature, raised in him, so to speak, now shares in the grace of a new creation. We are newly created in Christ. Before, we had fallen away through the corruption of our guilty ancestry, but now we can walk in good works.

Now that the strife that existed in the flesh before has been removed, a universal peace has been made in Heaven. Human beings can be like angels upon earth, and the Gentiles and Jews can be made one, and both the new and old man can be united—the middle wall of partition, which, like a hostile barrier, had once divided them, has broken down. When the nature of our flesh had stirred up anger, discord, and dissension, and the law had bound us with the chains of condemnation, Christ Jesus subdued the wantonness and intemperance of the flesh by mortification, and made void the law of commandment contained in ordinances. In that way he declared that the decrees of the spiritual Law are not to be interpreted according to the letter. He put an end to the slothful rest of the Sabbath and to the superfluous rite of outward circumcision, and opened access for all by one Spirit to the Father. For how can there be any discord, where there is one calling, one body, and one spirit?

—St. Ambrose, *Letter 76*, 8-9

IN GOD'S PRESENCE, CONSIDER . . .

What's the first thing I'd have to change about my life if I really wanted to live like an angel on earth?

CLOSING PRAYER

Lord who created me, brought me to life, and showed me the way to salvation, send your holy angels to me, so that I may live according to your Word.

Rejoice in God's power, not your own

If you want to impress people with your power, says St. Augustine, your priorities are all wrong. You have far more real power if your will is in line with God's. Instead of doing what an angel does, you can be what an angel is.

Those who seek God through those powers that rule over the world, or parts of the world, are removed and flung far away from him—not by distances in space, but by difference of affections. They try to find a path outwardly, and abandon what is inside themselves, which is where God is.

They may have heard some holy heavenly power, or may have thought of it somehow. But they covet its deeds, which human weakness marvels at, and do not imitate the piety by which divine rest is gained. Through pride, they would rather be able to do what an angel *does*, instead of, through devotion, being what an angel *is*.

For no holy being rejoices in his own power, but rejoices in the power of God, who gives him the power appropriate for him to have. The holy being knows that it is more of a sign of power to be united to the Omnipotent by a pious will than to be able, by his own power and will, to do things that make others who cannot do them tremble.

−St. Augustine, *On the Trinity*, 8.7

IN GOD'S PRESENCE, CONSIDER . . .

By letting go of my foolish pride, St. Augustine says, I can be what an angel is—a joyful servant of God. Looking at myself honestly, how much do I worry about impressing other people?

CLOSING PRAYER

Lord, make me worthy to serve you as faithfully as your angels do, so that when I boast, I may boast only in you.

"Thy will be done"

What does it mean when we pray, "Thy will be done, on Earth as it is in Heaven"? It means that we should be as ready to do God's will as the angels are, says St. Augustine.

In the third petition we say, "Thy will be done, on earth as it is in Heaven."

What does this mean? It means, "As the angels serve you in Heaven, let us serve you that way on Earth."

For his holy angels obey him. They do not offend him. They do his commands because they love him. This is what we pray for, then: that we may also do God's commands in love.

We can also understand these words another way. "Thy will be done, on Earth as it is in Heaven." Heaven is the soul; Earth is the body. Then what does it mean to say, "Thy will be done, on Earth as it is in Heaven?" It means, "As we hear your teaching, let our flesh consent to us." If flesh and spirit are fighting, we will not be able to fulfill God's commands.

—St. Augustine, *Sermon 9 on the New Testament*, 5

Am I ready to take God's assignment and do his will as the angels do? What is God asking me to do right now that I'm avoiding doing?

My Guardian Angel, teach me to love, pray, and fight the good fight on Earth, so that I may faithfully reflect your life of service in Heaven.

Peace comes from being regulated by God

God creates everything so that it all works together when it follows his will, says St. Gregory the Great. Whenever his creations resist him, they lose that peace, because it is only possible when things are regulated by God. Satan's punishment comes from going against his own nature.

God, who creates all things marvelously, regulates them himself so that, after they have been created, they agree with themselves. Whenever any resistance is made to the Creator, that agreement in peace is broken up, because things can never be well regulated when they lose the management of regulation from above. Things that would still have been at peace if they were subject to God make confusion by their own act when they are left to themselves, because, when they fight against the Creator, they do not find in themselves that peace that comes from above.

Thus the highest angelic spirit, who might have stood at the height if he had been subject to God, has been banished, and now has to bear the burden of himself. He roams uncomfortable in his own nature. In the same way, the first parent of the human race, because he went against the Creator's command, was immediately exposed to the insolence of the flesh. He was laid low beneath himself; because he would not be subject to his Maker in obedience, he even lost the peace of the body.

Thus it is well said, "who hath resisted him, and hath had peace?" (Job 9:4).

−St. Gregory the Great, *Moralia in Job*, 9.5

IN GOD'S PRESENCE, CONSIDER . . .

Is my own nature, like Satan's, making me uncomfortable in some way that shows me I'm not in tune with God's will?

CLOSING PRAYER

Lord, tune my nature to your will, and teach me to be as humble before your power as the glorious angels in Heaven are.

Watching for the vision

In a verse from the Psalms, St. Augustine sees a metaphor for the Church on earth and the Church to come. Our whole purpose on earth is to prepare us for that angelic life Christ promised us.

"Sing praises to the Lord, who dwells in Zion!" (Ps. 9:11).

This is addressed to those whom the Lord does not forsake as they seek him. He dwells in *Zion*, which means *watching*, and which is the image of the Church that exists now—as Jerusalem is the image of the Church that is to come: that is, the city of the saints already enjoying the angelic life. For *Jerusalem* means *vision of peace*.

Now, *watching* comes before *vision*, as this Church goes before the one promised, the immortal and eternal city. But it comes before in *time*, not in dignity. The more honorable thing is the one we strive toward, not the one we are practicing now. We practice watching now, so that we may get to vision.

But no matter how carefully we watch, unless God *dwells* in the Church that exists now, it could fall into all sorts of errors. This is the church to which it was said, "For God's temple is holy, and that temple you are" (1 Cor. 3:17), and, "that Christ may dwell in your hearts through faith" (Eph. 3:17).

So we are told to sing praises to the Lord, who *dwells in Zion*, so that with one accord we will praise the Lord, who *dwells* in the *Church*. Show forth his wonders among the heathen. It has been done, and it will never cease being done.

−St. Augustine, *Exposition on Psalm 9, 12*

Do I recognize that "the angelic life" is the life of the Church on earth, even now? Do I give myself entirely to this life through my participation in the parish?

CLOSING PRAYER

May the glorious name of the Lord be praised and glorified, in Heaven and on Earth, in all things now and forever.

Poverty is the life of the angels

St. John Chrysostom lived in a time much like our own, when everyone seemed to be trying to get rich quick. But why, he asks, do you want to be rich? Poverty is the secure life. Wealth is constant worry, but poverty is the carefree life of the angels.

But since it is right not only to lament and to blame, but also to correct, let's see why this passion and this evil have become an object of desire to you.

Why, then—why has wealth come to be an object of desire? Because, you say, it puts me in honor and in security. I ask, in what kind of security? It makes me confident, you say, that I won't suffer hunger or cold, or be hurt, or be despised.

Well, then, if I promise you that security, will you refrain from being rich? If this is why riches are an object of desire, then if you can have security without riches, why would you need riches anymore?

And how is it possible, you say, to have that security if you're not rich? Well, I say the opposite: how is it possible if you *are* rich?

To be rich you have to flatter many, both rulers and subjects, and to beg countless numbers of people, and to be a base slave, and to live in fear and trembling, and to regard the eyes of the envious with suspicion, and to fear the tongues of false accusers, and the desires of other covetous types.

But poverty isn't like that. It's completely the opposite. It's a place of refuge and security, a calm harbor, a gymnasium and fitness center to learn self-control, an imitation of the life of angels.

Hear these things, all you who are poor—and especially all you who want to be rich. It's not poverty we should be afraid of, but not being willing to be poor.

—St. John Chrysostom, *Homily 90 on Matthew*, 3

IN GOD'S PRESENCE, CONSIDER . . .

No matter how much money I have, or don't have, am I living a life of spiritual poverty—of self-control and trust in God, like the angels?

CLOSING PRAYER

Guardian Angel, help me to know what you know: that I am rich with spiritual treasures—and I know this more keenly the more I am detached from material treasures.

Leave greed behind to be equal to the angels

There are countless poor people and only a few rich. So why did the apostles, all of them poor, worry about their own salvation when Jesus told them how hard it was for a rich man to get into Heaven? Because, says, St. Augustine, they knew he was really talking about covetousness.

When they were saying, "Who then can be saved?" were they thinking of the few rich people? Had they forgotten how many poor people there are? Couldn't they say to themselves, "So it's hard—even impossible—for a camel to go through the eye of a needle. But won't all the poor people go to Heaven, and only the rich be left out?"

There are not many rich people, but there are countless thousands of poor people. We won't look at their clothes in the kingdom of Heaven, but the radiance of righteousness will be everyone's garment. So there will be poor people equal to the angels of God. Clothed with the stoles of immortality, they will shine like the sun in the kingdom of their Father.

Then why should we worry or fuss about a few rich people?

This isn't what the apostles thought. As soon as the Lord had said, "It is easier for a camel to go through the eye of a needle than for a rich man to enter the kingdom of God," they said to themselves, "Who then can be saved?"

What did they mean by that?

They weren't talking about actual wealth. They were talking about desires. They saw that even the poor who don't have money do have covetousness. And Jesus wasn't talking about the rich man's money, but about covetousness.

Abraham had plenty of gold, silver, livestock, servants. He was a rich man. And Lazarus—a poor man—is carried to Abraham's bosom. The poor man is carried to the rich man's bosom—because they are *both* rich men in God, and both poor men in greed.

–St. Augustine, *Exposition on Psalm 52*, 10

IN GOD'S PRESENCE, CONSIDER . . .

We live in a very materialistic society. In keeping purely spiritual company, we will ourselves become more like the pure spirits.

CLOSING PRAYER

Angel of God, deliver me from covetousness, and direct my gaze always toward Heaven.

The angelic virtue of detachment

Why does God let bad things happen to good people? Dionysius the Areopagite tells us that it's not really unfair at all. In fact, it would be unfair to weaken brave Christians by letting them get attached to earthly things. When they have to struggle on earth, they come nearer to the virtue of the angels.

But someone may say, "It is not the mark of justice to leave pious men without assistance when they are ground down by evil men."

To this we must reply that, if those whom you call pious do indeed love things on earth, which are zealously sought after by the earthly, they have completely fallen from the divine love. And I do not know how they could be called pious, when they unjustly treat the divine things that are truly worthy of love, and instead give what is really undesirable and unlovable first place in their esteem.

But, if they love the realities, they who desire certain things ought to rejoice when they attain the things desired. Are they not then nearer the angelic virtues, when, as far as possible, by aspiring to divine things, they withdraw from the affection for earthly things, courageously striving through their perils on behalf of the beautiful?

It is true, then, to say that this is rather a property of the divine justice: not to pamper and destroy the bravery of the best by the gifts of earthly things, nor, if any one should attempt to do this, to leave them without assistance, but to establish them in the excellent and harsh condition, and to give to them, because they are brave, such things that are appropriate for them.

–Dionysius the Areopagite, *The Divine Names*, 8.8

IN GOD'S PRESENCE, CONSIDER . . .

When I can't have the things I love on this earth, do I let that separate me from God—the way covetousness separated Satan and his angels from Heaven? Or do I try to get closer to God, with the loyal angels, and make him the one real object of my aspiration?

CLOSING PRAYER

Holy Guardian Angel, teach me to live with angelic detachment. Turn my eyes to the true treasures of Heaven, and away from the transitory pleasures of this life.

Fasting makes us angels—but prayer comes first

Fasting, says St. John Chrysostom, is an extraordinarily powerful thing. It makes us mortals into angels, and it fights the demonic powers. But more important even than fasting is praying—and even if you're too weak to fast, you can still pray.

Fasting brings considerable power. It trains us in strictness, and makes a mortal into an angel, and fights against the demons. But it doesn't do these things by itself. Prayer is needed too—and prayer must come first.

Why did Christ go up on the mountain? To teach us that loneliness and solitude are good when we pray to God. This is why you see him going away into the wilderness all the time, often spending the whole night there in prayer. He's teaching us that, when we pray, we should look for the kind of quiet you find at that time in that place. The wilderness is the mother of quiet. It is a calm place, a harbor, that delivers us from all storms.

Blessings come from both fasting and praying. If you're praying the way you should, you don't have many needs; and if you don't have many needs, you can't be covetous; and if you're not covetous, you're more likely to give alms. If you fast, you're light and winged; you pray alertly, and put down your wicked lusts, and reconcile yourself to God, and humble your soul when you're lifted up. This is why even the apostles were almost always fasting.

If you pray and fast, you have double wings. You're lighter than the wind itself. And even if your body is too weak to fast continually, it's still not too weak to pray.

–St. John Chrysostom, *Homily on St. Matthew 41*, 1.57

Do I look at prayer as the angels do—as my sustenance, my limbs, my life? Is there a time and place where I can pray without distractions? Do I make use of it every day?

Lord, grant me a time when I can be silent in the presence of your angels, and meditate on nothing earthly, but only on you.

Angels appear when you winnow the wheat

You're not likely to receive the inner truths of the Lord, says St. Gregory the Great, unless you separate yourself from external things that lead you away.

"And he took a potsherd with which to scrape himself, and sat among the ashes" (Job 2:8).

This is why our Redeemer came—to scrape the scabs off our wounds, so to speak, when he said, "You have heard that it was said, 'You shall not commit adultery.' But I say to you that everyone who looks at a woman lustfully has already committed adultery with her in his heart."

The scab is scraped off when sin is separated not only from the deed, but from the thought as well. This is why Jerubbaal saw the angel when he was winnowing corn from the chaff. On the angel's orders, he immediately dressed a kid and set it on a rock, and poured over it the broth of the meat. Then the angel touched it with a rock, and fire came out of the rock and burned it up (Judg. 6:11-21).

What is beating corn with a rod but separating the grains of virtue from the chaff of vices with a righteous judgment? The angel appears to those who do that—meaning that, the more earnestly you get rid of external things, the more likely the Lord is to communicate inner truths.

–St. Gregory the Great, *Moralia in Job*, 3.59

IN GOD'S PRESENCE, CONSIDER . . .

Even if I'm separated from most obvious sins, how completely do I separate myself from sinful thoughts? Am I winnowing hard enough to see the angel?

CLOSING PRAYER

Guardian Angel, I know that you are with me even when I cannot see you. Give me your aid in resisting temptation, and stand by me as I winnow the chaff from my life.

Living like the angels

St. Macrina, a great Christian teacher, showed her own mother how to live a life of asceticism and meditation—a life that her brother, St. Gregory of Nyssa, describes as being little different from the life of the angels.

When the cares of bringing up a family and the anxieties of their education and settling in life had come to an end, and the property—a frequent cause of worldliness—had been for the most part divided among the children, then, as I said earlier, the life of the virgin became her mother's guide and led her on to this philosophic and spiritual manner of life.

Weaning her from all accustomed luxuries, Macrina drew her on to adopt her own standard of humility. She induced her to live on a footing of equality with the staff of maids, sharing with them in the same food, the same kind of bed, and in all the necessaries of life, without any regard to differences of rank.

Such was the manner of their life, so great the height of their philosophy, and so holy their conduct day and night, that it cannot be described in words. Just as souls freed from the body by death are saved from the cares of this life, so was their life far removed from all earthly follies and arranged with a view of imitating the angelic life. No anger or jealousy, no hatred or pride, was observed in their midst, nor anything else of that sort, since they had cast away all vain desires for honor and glory, all vanity, arrogance, and so on. Continence was their luxury, and obscurity their glory. Poverty, and throwing away useless luxuries like dust from their bodies, was their wealth. Nothing was left but the care of divine things and the unceasing round of prayer.

Living in the body and yet in the same way as of the immaterial beings, they were not bowed down by the weight of the body, but their life was exalted to the skies, and they walked on high in company with the powers of Heaven.

–St. Gregory of Nyssa, *Life of St. Macrina*

IN GOD'S PRESENCE, CONSIDER . . .

Are there material things that keep me from being as close to God as I should be—living as the angels do—things that I could easily do without?

CLOSING PRAYER

Lord, one day you will take again what you have given, transfiguring with immortality and grace our mortal and unsightly remains. Give me an angel of light to conduct me to the place of refreshment, where is the water of rest, in the bosom of the holy Fathers.

Choosing an angel's life

St. Augustine writes to express his joy at hearing that the daughter of an illustrious family has chosen to become a nun. It's a glorious thing to be the mother of an extensive family, he says, but even more glorious to belong completely to Christ.

Who can declare in words, or expound with adequate praises, how incomparably greater is the glory and advantage gained by your family in giving to Christ women consecrated to his service, than in giving to the world men called to the honors of the consulship? For if it be a great and noble thing to leave the mark of an honored lady upon the revolving ages of this world, how much greater and nobler is it to rise above it by unsullied chastity both of heart and of body!

Let this maiden, therefore, illustrious in her pedigree, yet more illustrious in her piety, find greater joy in obtaining, through espousals to her divine Lord, a preeminent glory in Heaven, than she could have had in becoming, through espousal to a human consort, the mother of a line of illustrious men. This daughter of the house of Anicius has acted the more magnanimous part, in choosing rather to bring a blessing on that noble family by forbearing from marriage, than to increase the number of its descendants, preferring to be already like the angels in the purity of her body, rather than to increase by the fruit of her body the number of mortals.

Let the virgins who covet the glory of the Anician family be ambitious rather to emulate its piety; for the glory lies beyond their reach, however eagerly they may desire it, but the piety will be in their possession at once if they seek it with full desire.

—St. Augustine, *Letter 150*

IN GOD'S PRESENCE, CONSIDER . . .

How could I give more support to young women today who choose to live an angel's life?

CLOSING PRAYER

Lord, hear my prayer for all who choose the life of the angels—the life of virginity, celibacy, and service to you.

Virginity is to marriage as angel is to human

God forbid we should say anything against marriage, says St. John of Damascus. After all, Christ himself honored marriage as a guest at the wedding in Cana. But virginity is a higher state—an imitation of the angels.

Virginity is the rule of life among the angels, the property of all incorporeal nature. We say this without speaking ill of marriage—God forbid! For we know that the Lord blessed marriage by His presence (John 2:1), and we know him who said, "Let marriage be held in honor among all, and let the marriage bed be undefiled" (Heb. 13:4).

But we know that virginity is better than marriage, however good. For among the virtues, just as among the vices, there are higher and lower grades. We know that all mortals after the first parents of the race are the offspring of marriage. (The first parents were the work of virginity and not of marriage.) But celibacy is, as we said, an imitation of the angels. For that reason, virginity is as much more honorable than marriage, as the angel is higher than a human being.

But why do I say angel? Christ Himself is the glory of virginity, who was not only begotten of the Father without beginning or emission or connection, but also became man in our image, being made flesh for our sakes of the Virgin without connection, and manifesting in himself the true and perfect virginity.

Therefore, although he did not command us to virginity by law (for as He said, not everyone can receive this saying (Matt. 19:11)), yet in actual fact he taught us that and gave us strength for it. For it is surely clear to everyone that virginity now is flourishing among us.

—St. John of Damascus, Exposition of the Christian Faith, 4.24

IN GOD'S PRESENCE, CONSIDER . . .

In my prayer, am I praying to the guardian angels of the priests and religious who serve me?

CLOSING PRAYER

Father, send your holy angels to protect all those who have consecrated their lives to your service.

Living the resurrected life now

Those who have taken vows of chastity, says St. Ambrose, are living the life of the angels now—the life we will all live after the Resurrection. There is a special brightness reserved for them in Heaven.

But you who have taken the vow already, chasten your bodies more strictly, and do not allow yourselves to loosen the reins of desire even after those things that are permitted. You should not only turn away from an unlawful connection, but despise even a lawful look.

Remember, in whichever sex you are, whether men or women, that you are leading on earth the life of angels: for the angels are neither given in marriage nor marry (Mark 12:25). This is what we will be like when we have risen again. How much better are you, who before death begin to be what all of us will be after the resurrection!

Keep your proper degrees, for God keeps for you your honors. The resurrection of the dead is compared to the stars that are set in Heaven. One star differs from another star in glory, as the Apostle says; so also is the resurrection of the dead. In one way virginity will shine there, in another wedded chastity will shine there, after another holy widowhood will shine there. They will shine in different ways, but all will be there—the brilliance unequal, the Heaven the same.

–St. Ambrose, *Sermon 82 on the New Testament*, 3

IN GOD'S PRESENCE, CONSIDER . . .

Even if I'm not called to a vow of chastity myself, how can I help and encourage the people in my community who are leading on earth the life of angels?

CLOSING PRAYER

Lord, send your angels to guard all your holy deacons, priests, bishops, monks, and nuns throughout the world.

Virginity is heaven on earth

Consecrated virginity, says St. Gregory of Nyssa, is something like Heaven on Earth. Christ promised that we would live as the angels live in Heaven; but whoever gives up marriage for Christ's sake is already, in a way, living the life of the angels.

In fact, the life of virginity seems to be an actual representation of the blessedness in the world to come. In itself it shows many signs of the anticipated blessings reserved for us there.

To help you see how this statement is true, this is why I say it:

First, because a man who has thus died to sin once and for all lives for the future to God. He brings forth no more fruit unto death. He has made an end of this life within him according to the flesh, at least as much as he can. From then on, he awaits the expected blessing of the appearance of the great God, and he keeps himself from putting any distance between himself and this coming of God by an intervening posterity.

Secondly, because even in this present life he enjoys a certain exquisite glory of all the blessed results of our resurrection. For our Lord has announced that the life after our resurrection will be like the life of the angels. Now the peculiarity of the angelic nature is that they are strangers to marriage. So the blessing of this promise has been already received by someone who has not only mingled his own glory with the halo of the saints, but also by the stainlessness of his life has imitated the purity of the incorporeal angels.

If virginity can win us favors like these, what words are fit to express how much we admire so great a grace? Where can we find another gift of the soul that is so great and so precious that it does not suffer by comparison with this perfection?

–St. Gregory of Nyssa, *On Virginity*, 13

IN GOD'S PRESENCE, CONSIDER . . .

Even if I have not been called to consecrated virginity, can I arrange my life so that I live, as the angels do, more for God than for myself?

CLOSING PRAYER

Holy angels, watch over our priests, monks, nuns, and all consecrated virgins everywhere, and keep them strong in their trials.

Keep to the straight and narrow

Human integrity, says St. Cyril of Alexandria, is not the same as the integrity of the angels, who are superior to us by nature. But we still need to do as much as we can within our human capacity to keep to the straight and narrow.

Now I consider it my duty to mention why the door is "narrow" through which we go in to life.

Whoever wants to enter must necessarily possess—first and foremost—an upright and uncorrupted faith. Second is a spotless morality, in which there is no possibility of blame, according to the measure of human righteousness. For so the prophet David also somewhere says, very excellently wording his prayer to God, "Judge me, O Lord, according to my righteousness and according to the integrity that is in me" (Ps. 7:8). For the integrity or righteousness of the holy angels, since it is in proportion to their nature and glory, is entirely distinct from the kind that belongs to the inhabitants of earth. Our integrity is of a lower kind, and inferior in every respect, just as we are inferior to the angels in nature.

Nevertheless, those who wish to live a holy life cannot do so without labor. The pathway, so to speak, that leads to virtue is always rugged and steep, and for most of us too difficult to walk on. Labors spring up before us, and we certainly need fortitude, and patience, and nobility in our behavior—and we especially need a mind that cannot be prevailed on to take part in immoral and degrading pleasures, or to be led by irrational impulses into carnal lust.

Whoever has reached this state of mind and spiritual fortitude will enter easily by the straight door, and run along the narrow way.

—St. Cyril of Alexandria, *Commentary on Luke*, Sermon 99

IN GOD'S PRESENCE, CONSIDER . . .

Could I be in better shape morally if I were more diligent in enlisting the help of my guardian angel?

CLOSING PRAYER

Guardian Angel, help me to be worthy of God's perfect mercy. Make my path straight, and keep me grounded in the fear of the Lord.

Be an angel in adversity

Christ came, says St. Augustine, so that we might live as angels. What does that mean? It means, he says, that we should constantly bless the Lord, the way the angels do—even when we're having difficulties.

"I will bless the Lord at all times; his praise shall continually be in my mouth" (Ps. 33:1).

So speaks Christ; a Christian should speak the same way.

For a Christian is in the body of Christ. The reason Christ was made Man was so that a Christian might become an angel who says, "I will bless the Lord at all times."

When shall I bless the Lord? When He blesses you? When the goods of this world abound? When you have plenty of grain, oil, and wine, of gold and silver, of servants and cattle; when this mortal health remains undamaged and sound; when all your children grow up, nothing is taken away by immature death, happiness wholly reigns in your house, and all things overflow around you; then shall you bless the Lord?

No; but at *all* times.

Bless him when you have plenty; but also bless him when, according to the time, or according to the scourges of our Lord God, these things are troubled, are taken away, are seldom born to you, and when born pass away. For these things happen, and after them come poverty, need, labor, pain, and temptation.

But you have sung, "I will bless the Lord at all times; his praise shall continually be in my mouth." When he gives you good things, bless him; and when he takes them away, bless him. For it is the Lord who gives, it is he who takes away: but he does not take himself away from anyone who blesses him.

−St. Augustine, *Exposition on Psalm 34, 2*

IN GOD'S PRESENCE, CONSIDER . . .

Am I as unstinting as the angels in my praise of God? Do I recognize his wisdom even in the hard times I must face?

CLOSING PRAYER

Lord, let me bless and praise your name together with the bodiless host of angels in the highest Heaven.

Invest in the poor

The sure way to earn a good return, says St. Cyril of Alexandria, is to invest in the poor. Instead of mere money, you earn the praise of angels and the invitation of the Son.

What good is there in prodigal abundance beyond what necessity requires? For as Christ himself said somewhere (Luke 10:42), few things are needful, or rather one, to take care of the wants of the body. So to escape the danger of losing the return on our investment, by expending our wealth in such pursuits as will bear good fruit, he has commanded us to invite the poor, and the maimed, and the blind, and those who are suffering under other bodily maladies, so that by our generosity in doing so, we may earn the hope that comes from God above.

Do you like to be praised when you have friends or relatives feasting with you? I tell you of something far better: angels will praise your bounty, and the rational powers above, and holy men as well. And he who transcends all, and who loves mercy and is kind, will also accept it. Lend to him fearing nothing, and you will receive with interest whatever you gave: "He who is kind to the poor lends to the Lord," it says (Prov. 19:17). He has acknowledged the loan, and promises repayment.

The investment is not unprofitable: in fact, compassion for the poor will make your wealth breathe forth a sweet scent. Purchase the grace that comes from God; buy the Lord of Heaven and Earth for your friend. After all, we often purchase someone's friendship with large sums of gold, and if those of high rank are on our side, we feel great joy in offering them presents even beyond what we can afford, because of the honor that comes to us from them. And yet these things are only transitory, and quickly fade away, and are like the fantasies of dreams.

–St. Cyril of Alexandria, *Commentary on Luke*, Sermon 103

IN GOD'S PRESENCE, CONSIDER . . .

How much of my fortune is invested in the poor? Do I believe that the praise of the angels will be the return on my investment?

CLOSING PRAYER

Lord, bless the widow, the orphan, and the stranger; and let me join your angels in serving and protecting them.

Make the angels rejoice

St. Ambrose, bishop of the empire's administrative capital of Milan, was never shy about advising even the Emperor in his religious duties. Here he reminds the Emperor that his power was given to him by God, not earned. He should use that power to make the angels rejoice.

So since you know, Emperor (for now I'm not only going to talk about you but address myself to you), how severe the Lord's censures can be, you must take care, in proportion as you become more illustrious, to submit so much the more humbly to your Maker. For it is written: When the Lord your God has brought you into a foreign land, and you eat the fruits of others, do not say, "By my own strength and righteousness I obtained these things," but, "The Lord God gave them to me, Christ in his mercy conferred them on me" (a paraphrase of Deut. 9:4).

So love the body of Christ—that is, the Church. Pour water on his feet and kiss them. In that way, you will not only absolve those who have been taken in sin, but in giving to them peace you will bring them into agreement and restore to them rest. Pour ointment on his feet, so that the whole house where Christ sits at supper may be filled with the odor of your ointment, and let all who sit at supper with him rejoice in your fragrance.

What I mean is this: pay such regard even to the lowest, that in their absolution the angels may rejoice—as they do over one sinner that repents—and the Apostles may be glad, and the prophets may exult.

For the eye cannot say to the hand, "I have no need of you," nor the head to the feet, "I have no need of you." Since, therefore, each member is necessary, protect the whole body of the Lord Jesus, so that he, in his divine mercy, may also protect your kingdom.

–St. Ambrose, *Letter 41*, 26

IN GOD'S PRESENCE, CONSIDER . . .

How do I use whatever power God has given me—in my job, or in my family, or in my church? Does the way I use my power, however humble it may be, make the angels rejoice to see it?

CLOSING PRAYER

Holy angels, give me wisdom to understand God's gifts, and the strength to serve him along with you.

Living an angel's life on earth

Recalling a holy monk who was well known for his ascetic life, St. Ambrose says that he led an angel's life on earth—and in doing so became a model for the rest of us.

Now this endurance in holy Eusebius was thriving under the monastic discipline. Because he was used to a stricter rule, he drank in a power of bearing hardships.

I'm positive that, in the higher kinds of Christian devotion, these two things are the most excellent: the clerical function and the monastic rule. The first is trained to be obliging and courteous in its behavior; the second is used to abstinence and endurance; the one lives as on a theater stage, the other in secret; the one is seen, the other hidden. This is what one noble combatant said: "we have become a spectacle to the world, to angels and to men" (1 Cor. 4:9).

He was truly worthy to have angels as his spectators, when he wrestled that he might attain the prize of Christ, when he struggled to lead an angel's life on earth, so that he might overcome the wickedness of spirits in Heaven—for he wrestled with spiritual wickedness. The world was right to be a spectator of him whom it was called on to imitate.

–St. Ambrose, *Letter 63*, 71

IN GOD'S PRESENCE, CONSIDER . . .

How angelic is my life? What material comforts or possessions most get in the way of my living the life of the angels on earth?

CLOSING PRAYER

Lord, let me imitate the angels who have been well pleasing to you since their creation, and graciously preserve me from the temptations of the world.

Live like an angel now to live like an angel later

In his commentary on the Apostles' Creed, Rufinus of Aquileia explains what Christ means when he says the resurrected will be like angels in Heaven. We will live with the angels then, but only if we live like angels here on earth—which we can do with the sanctification of the Holy Spirit.

"For when they rise from the dead, they neither marry nor are given in marriage, but are like angels in Heaven" (Mark 12:25).

This means that the power of the resurrection confers on us an angelic state. Whoever has risen from the earth will not live again on the earth with the brute animals but with angels in Heaven. But that will only happen to the ones whose purer life has fitted them for that state—meaning those who right now keep the flesh of their soul in chastity, and have brought it into subjection to the Holy Spirit, and thus with every stain of sins done away and changed into spiritual glory by the virtue of sanctification, have been counted worthy to have it admitted into the society of angels.

—Rufinus of Aquileia, *Commentary on the Apostles' Creed*, 41

IN GOD'S PRESENCE, CONSIDER . . .

Have I put "the flesh of my soul" under the guidance of the holy angels? How would I do that? Have I made use of the sacraments of the Church—such as penance—that Christ gave us for our sanctification?

CLOSING PRAYER

Lord, sanctify my soul, and body, and spirit; and turn my thoughts to holiness, that with the holy angels I may bring you the sacrifice of praise.

The service of angels

St. Ambrose recommends the life of a much-respected monk as an example to us all. To spend your days in praising God and celebrating the Lord with hymns—this is the way the angels live, he says, and you can do it too.

But now I think we have said enough of the teacher. Let us now follow up the lives of his disciples, who have given themselves to praise the divine Name, and celebrate it with hymns night and day. For this is the service of angels, always to be praising God, and with frequent prayers to appease and implore the Lord. They give themselves to reading, and occupy their minds with continual labors. They keep away from all female society, and they protect each other.

What a life this is! There's nothing in it you need to fear, but much for you to imitate! The pain of fasting is repaid by tranquility of mind, eased by familiarity, made bearable by rest, or beguiled by occupation. Worldly cares don't burden this life, and outward troubles don't absorb it, nor do the distractions of the city cause it any trouble.

—St. Ambrose, *Letter 63*, 82

IN GOD'S PRESENCE, CONSIDER . . .

Worldly responsibilities keep most of us from living a monastic life. But even in the world, where can I find time to praise God along with the angels? Can I do it privately when no one needs me at work, or on the subway, or driving in traffic?

CLOSING PRAYER

Lord, send your angels to protect all who are passing their lives in virginity, and celibacy.

The peace of the angels

St. Augustine's advice to soldiers: Peace is your goal, and everything you do must work toward it. The peace we desire on earth is only a shadow of that peace God gives the angels now and will give us after our trials here.

Think, then, of this first of all, when you are arming for the battle: that even your bodily strength is a gift of God. If you think about this, you will not employ the gift of God against God. For, when faith is pledged, it is to be kept even with the enemy against whom the war is waged. And how much more with the friend for whom the battle is fought!

Peace should be the object of your desire; war should be waged only as a necessity, and waged only that God may by it deliver people from the necessity and preserve them in peace. For peace is not sought in order to stir up war, but war is waged in order that peace may be obtained. Therefore, even in waging war, cherish the spirit of a peacemaker, so that, by conquering those whom you attack, you may lead them back to the advantages of peace; for our Lord says: "Blessed are the peacemakers; for they shall be called the children of God" (Matt. 5:9). But if peace among humans is so sweet because it gives us safety in this world, how much sweeter is that peace with God that gives us the eternal happiness of the angels!

Let necessity, therefore, and not your will, slay the enemy who fights against you. As violence is used towards him who rebels and resists, so mercy is due to the vanquished or the captive, especially in the case in which future troubling of the peace is not to be feared.

—St. Augustine, *Letter 189*

IN GOD'S PRESENCE, CONSIDER . . .

As a citizen, what am I doing to promote the peace the angels know in Heaven among nations, among neighbors, and in the Church?

CLOSING PRAYER

Lord, I beseech you, make me an instrument of your peace, and keep the example of your holy angels in Heaven before my eyes.

A leader praised for toleration

Citing the instructions "to the angel of the church in Ephesus," St. Augustine says that toleration for the sake of unity earns us high praise.

In the Revelation of John (2:1-5) we read, "To the angel of the church in Ephesus write: 'The words of him who holds the seven stars in his right hand, who walks among the seven golden lamp stands. "I know your works, your toil and your patient endurance, and how you cannot bear evil men but have tested those who call themselves apostles but are not, and found them to be false; I know you are enduring patiently and bearing up for my name's sake, and you have not grown weary." ' "

Now, if he wanted us to understand that this was addressed to a heavenly angel, he would not go on to say, "But I have this against you, that you have abandoned the love you had at first. Remember then from what you have fallen, repent and do the works you did at first. If not, I will come to you and remove your lamp stand from its place, unless you repent." This could not be said about the heavenly angels, who keep their love unchanged, since the only beings that have left and fallen from their order are the devil and his angels. The "love you had at first" that it talks about here is the love that was proved when, for the sake of Christ's name, they tolerated the false apostles. He commands them to return to them, and "do the works you did at first."

Now, we are reproached with the crimes of bad people—not what we do, but what other people do, sometimes even when we don't know them. Nevertheless, even if the crimes were actually committed right under our very eyes, if we bore with them for the sake of unity, leaving the tares alone on account of the wheat, whoever receives the Holy Scriptures with an open heart would say that we were not only free from blame, but worthy of considerable praise.

—St. Augustine, *Letter 43*, 22

IN GOD'S PRESENCE, CONSIDER . . .

When things that happen in the Church make me angry, do I become a force more for unity or for division? Like the angels in Heaven, do I keep my love unchanged?

CLOSING PRAYER

Lord, give peace to the multitudes of your people; put away scandals, and bring divisions to an end. Let us be united in one Church on earth as your angels are united in Heaven.

Christ sets the example of toleration

Still meditating on the instructions in Revelation "to the angel of the Church in Ephesus," St. Augustine tells us that Christ himself set the example of toleration by tolerating Judas, his betrayer, in the midst of his disciples.

I know I've left out many examples. If you are willing and able, read the divine records for yourself: you'll find that all the holy servants and friends of God have always had to bear with some among their own people. They shared the sacraments of dispensation with them, and not only were they not defiled when they did that, but they were to be commended for their tolerant spirit—"eager to maintain the unity of the Spirit in the bond of peace," as the Apostle says (Eph. 4:3).

Observe, too, what has happened since the coming of the Lord. We find many more examples of this toleration all over the world, if they could all be written down and verified. But listen to the ones that are on record. The Lord himself bears with Judas, a devil, a thief, his own betrayer; along with the innocent disciples, he allows him to receive what believers know is our ransom. The Apostles bear with false apostles. Among people who are looking out for their own things, and not the things of Jesus Christ, Paul—who seeks the things of Christ, and not his own—lives practicing a very noble toleration.

In short, as I said a little while ago, the person who presides over a church and is called an "angel" is commended because, though he hated those who were evil, he still bore with them for the sake of the Lord's name, even when they were tried and found out.

–St. Augustine, *Letter 43*, 23

IN GOD'S PRESENCE, CONSIDER . . .

How do I, like the "angel of the church in Ephesus," find the proper balance between toleration and giving in to evil?

CLOSING PRAYER

Guardian Angel, keep me from anger when divisions arise in the Church, and show me the way to unite rather than divide God's people.

Train to win the angelic wreath

Writing to Christians facing a sentence of death, Tertullian tells them to think of their hardships as training for victory. You don't win the star athlete's wreath without hard work and sweat, and in the spiritual realm the Holy Spirit is their personal trainer, getting them in shape to win a "wreath of angelic essence."

Even in peace soldiers get themselves used to war by work and challenges, marching in arms, running over the plain, working at the ditch, drilling in formation, and doing all kinds of hard labor. The sweat of the brow is on everything, so that their bodies and minds won't balk when they have to go from shade to sunshine, from sunshine to icy cold, from the robe of peace to the coat of mail, from silence to noise, from quiet to tumult.

In the same way, blessed ones, think of whatever is hard in this lot of yours as a discipline for your powers of mind and body. You're about to pass through a noble struggle, in which the living God acts the part of superintendent, in which the Holy Spirit is your trainer, in which the prize is an eternal wreath of angelic essence, citizenship in the Heavens, glory everlasting. Therefore your Master, Jesus Christ, who has anointed you with his Spirit, and led you forth to the arena, has decided, before the day of conflict, to take you from a condition more pleasant in itself, and has imposed a harder treatment on you, so that you might have greater strength.

After all, athletes are set apart to a stricter discipline to build up their physical powers. They're kept from luxury, from expensive food, from more pleasant drinks. They're pressed, racked, worn out. The harder they work in the preparatory training, the more hope they have of victory. And "they do it to receive a perishable wreath," as the apostle says (1 Cor. 9:25). We have the eternal wreath in our eye. We look on the prison as our training-ground, so that at the goal of final judgment we may come out well disciplined by many a trial—since virtue is built up by hardships, but destroyed by indulgence in luxury.

—Tertullian, *To the Martyrs*, 3

IN GOD'S PRESENCE, CONSIDER . . .

How would my own training benefit from a little more work and a little less luxury? What little luxuries might I give up to be in better shape for the angelic wreath?

CLOSING PRAYER

Lord, let me labor honorably in your Church as the angels do in Heaven, and may I always keep the needs of the poor, the widows, and the orphans before my eyes.

Eyes such as angels see with

Didymus was a famous theologian who had been blind since childhood. The historian Socrates Scholasticus recounts his many accomplishments, and then tells us about a famous piece of advice St. Anthony gave to this illustrious scholar.

About the same period God brought into observation another faithful person, deeming it worthy that through him faith might be shown: this was Didymus, a most admirable and eloquent man, instructed in all the learning of the age in which he flourished. At a very early age, when he had scarcely acquired the first elements of learning, he was attacked by a disease in the eyes that deprived him of sight. But God compensated him for the loss of corporeal vision by giving him a sharper intellect. For what he could not learn by seeing, he was enabled to acquire through the sense of hearing; so that being from his childhood endowed with excellent abilities, he soon far surpassed his youthful companions who possessed the keenest sight.

He made himself master of the principles of grammar and rhetoric with astonishing ease; and went on from there to philosophical studies, dialectics, arithmetic, music, and the various other departments of knowledge to which his attention was directed. He so treasured up in his mind these branches of science, that he was prepared with the utmost readiness to enter into a discussion of these subjects with those who had become familiar with them by reading books.

It is said that after Anthony had conversed for some time with this Didymus, long before the reign of Valens, when he came from the desert to Alexandria on account of the Arians, perceiving the learning and intelligence of the man, he said to him, "Didymus, do not let the loss of your bodily eyes distress you: for you are deprived only of such eyes as are the common possession of gnats and flies. Rather rejoice that you have eyes such as angels see with, by which the Deity himself is discerned, and his light comprehended."

–Socrates Scholasticus, *Ecclesiastical History*, 4.25

IN GOD'S PRESENCE, CONSIDER . . .

Do I make a real effort to use my angelic vision—the intelligence God gave me—for the purposes for which he meant it to be used?

CLOSING PRAYER

Guardian Angel, teach me to use the intelligence I share with you for the right ends, and lead me ever closer to the angelic vision of God.

Contemplation should direct action

Contemplation, says St. Augustine, is the highest part of reason, which is the highest part of the soul, which is the highest part of our nature. In everything we do, then, we should be guided by our contemplation of God.

Each of us, we know, consists of soul and body; but so does a beast. Again, it is plain that in the order of nature the soul is superior to the body. Moreover, in our own souls there is reason, which does not exist in a beast. Therefore, as the soul is superior to the body, so in the soul itself the reason is superior by the law of nature to the other parts which are found also in beasts; and in reason itself, which is partly contemplation and partly action, contemplation is unquestionably the superior part.

The object of contemplation is the image of God, by which we are renewed through faith to sight. Rational action therefore ought to be subject to the control of contemplation, which is exercised through faith while we are absent from the Lord, as it will be hereafter through sight, when we shall be like him—for we shall see him as he is. Then in a spiritual body we shall by his grace be made equal to angels, when we put on the garment of immortality and incorruption, with which this mortal and corruptible body shall be clothed, so that death may be swallowed up in victory, when righteousness is perfected through grace.

For the holy and lofty angels have also their contemplation and action. They require of themselves the performance of the commands of God, whom they contemplate, whose eternal government they freely obey because it is sweet to them.

But our bodies are dead because of sin, till God enlivens our mortal bodies by his Spirit dwelling in us. We live righteously in our feeble measure, according to the eternal law in which the law of nature is preserved, when we live by that sincere faith that works by love.

—St. Augustine, *Reply to Faustus the Manichean*, 22.28

IN GOD'S PRESENCE, CONSIDER . . .

How does contemplation affect what I do in my daily life? Do I let contemplation guide my action the way the holy angels do?

CLOSING PRAYER

Purify me from every stain, Lord, and make me worthy to contemplate your mysteries along with your holy angels in Heaven.

Equal to angels

Answering the resurrection-denying Sadducees who tried to trip Jesus up with a tricky question about marriage in the life to come, Christ says that in that future life we will be equal to the angels (Luke 20:27-40). That tells us, says St. Cyril of Alexandria, what our blessed life of the future will be like.

"The sons of this age," Christ says—those, that is, who lead worldly carnal lives, full of fleshly lust—for the procreation of children "marry and are given in marriage"; but those who have maintained an honorable and elect life, full of all excellence, and have therefore been counted worthy of a glorious and marvelous resurrection, will certainly be raised far above the life we lead in this world; for they will live as saints ought to live who already have been brought near to God.

"Because they are equal to angels and are sons of God." Since all fleshly lust is taken away, and no place at all is left in them for bodily pleasure, they resemble the holy angels, fulfilling a spiritual and not a material service, as is appropriate for holy spirits. At the same time, they are counted worthy of the kind of glory that the angels enjoy.

–St. Cyril of Alexandria, *Commentary on Luke*, Sermon 136

If I've been called to marriage, how is my married life now a preparation for the heavenly life we will share with the angels?

Guardian Angel, teach me to be attentive to the guardians of those with whom I live, that I may give good example, that I may serve at all times, and my speech may abound in kindness.

Equal to angels—but not identical

If we're to be like the angels, who have no bodies, then what becomes of the resurrection of the body? St. Methodius of Olympus explains that we're to be equal to angels, but not identical. Our nature will never be other than human.

Here's another point you should consider, Aglaophon—for you're very much misled here, if you'll forgive me for being blunt when the subject is so important. You said that the Lord declared plainly that those who gain the resurrection will be as the angels (Matt. 22:30). This was your objection: the angels are as happy and glorious as can be because they have no flesh. Since we are to be made equal to the angels, we must be stripped of flesh like them, and be angels.

But, my dear sir, you forgot this: God, who created the universe out of nothing and established its order, made the immortal beings to be not only angels and ministers, but also Principalities, Thrones, and Powers. Angels are one kind of being, and Principalities and Powers are another—immortal beings are not all the same rank, nature, group, and family, but there are differences of kind and group.

The Cherubim do not stop being Cherubim and become Angels. Angels do not take on another form. They can only be what they are, what they were made to be.

Since humanity was made in the original order of things to live in the world and rule over everything in it, when we are immortal we will not be changed from human beings into angels or anything else, just as the angels do not change from angels into something else. When Christ came, he did not announce that human nature, when it is immortal, would be remade or transformed into some other nature, but that it would be made again into what it was before the Fall.

—St. Methodius of Olympus, *Discourse on the Resurrection*, 1.10

IN GOD'S PRESENCE, CONSIDER . . .

Do I live with a fixity of purpose as the angels do? Am I true without corruption to the nature God has given me?

CLOSING PRAYER

Our Father, Thy will be done, on earth as it is among the angels in Heaven.

We restore the ranks of the angels

The fall of the angels left a gap in the heavenly hierarchy, says St. Augustine, and the redemption of humanity will fill that gap.

The redemption of mankind rebuilds the ruins left by the fall of the angels. Of course, the holy angels, who learn from God (for they are blessed with eternal contemplation of God's truth), know how many of the human race are required to fill up the full census of that commonwealth.

This is why the apostle says that all things are restored to unity in Christ, "things in Heaven and things on Earth" (Eph. 1:10). The part in Heaven, in fact, is restored when the number lost from the fall of the angels are replaced from the ranks of humanity. The part on Earth is restored when those human beings who are predestined to eternal life are redeemed from the old state of corruption.

Thus by the single sacrifice, of which the many victims of the law were only shadows, the heavenly part is set at peace with the earthly part, and the earthly reconciled to the heavenly. This is why the same apostle says: "For in him all the fullness of God was pleased to dwell, and through him to reconcile to himself all things, whether on Earth or in Heaven, making peace by the blood of his cross" (Col. 1:19-20).

–St. Augustine, *Enchiridion*, chapter 16

IN GOD'S PRESENCE, CONSIDER . . .

What could I change about my life that would make it more of a preparation for taking my place among the angels in Heaven?

CLOSING PRAYER

Lord, restore your kingdom, and make me worthy to take my place among the angels above.

Know love, know God

If you love your brother, says St. Augustine, you know God—because God is love. Love is what binds us together with the angels. When you are filled with love, you really are filled with God, and you know God more intimately than you can know your closest friend.

No one should say, "I do not know what I love." Love your brother, and you will love that same love. For you know the Love you love with more than you know your brother—so now you can know God more than you know your brother. Clearly you will know him more, because he will be more present. You will know him more, because he is more certain. Embrace the love of God, and by love embrace God.

Love itself is what holds all the good angels and all the servants of God together by the bond of sanctity. It joins us and them together—equally with ourselves, and subordinately to God.

The more we are healed from the swelling of pride, the more we are filled with love. And when you are filled with love, what are you filled with—except God?

—St. Augustine, *On the Trinity*, 8.8

IN GOD'S PRESENCE, CONSIDER . . .

When I think of the people I live with or work with every day, is love the thing I feel most? Or do other feelings come first? Am I bound together with the good angels, or are my gripes and grudges keeping me apart from them?

CLOSING PRAYER

Unite me to the blessed assembly of your angels, Lord, and let me share in your love for all your people.

The knowledge even angels can't teach

God's perfect knowledge is something no human could teach us, says St. Augustine. Angels couldn't teach it to us; they couldn't even teach it to other angels. But we can have it if we knock at God's door.

We see the things you have made because they exist. But they exist because you made them. And we see from outside that they exist, and from inside that they are good; but you saw them where you made them when they were made.

We were moved to do good after our hearts had conceived of your Spirit; but before that, forsaking you, we were moved to do evil. But you, the One, the good God, have never stopped doing good.

We also have certain good works, ours by your good gift, but not eternal; and after them we hope to rest in your great hallowing. But you are the Good, and have no need of good; you are always at rest, because you yourself are your rest.

How could a human being teach another to understand this? Or how could an angel teach an angel? Or how could an angel teach a human being? Let it be asked of you, sought in you, knocked for at your door. Then it will be received, it will be found, it will be opened.

—St. Augustine, *Confessions*, 13.38

IN GOD'S PRESENCE, CONSIDER . . .

How do I seek the knowledge even angels can't teach? Do I read Scripture, listen attentively at Mass, or study God's creation?

CLOSING PRAYER

Holy Guardian Angel, I know that there is knowledge you cannot teach me; but lead me to the door where I can receive it as you do.

We were meant to live like angels

In the Garden of Eden, says St. John of Damascus, Adam and Eve lived like angels—without a care in the world. That's the way we were all meant to live, and that's the way Christ has been trying to teach us to live.

Before they took of the fruit, "the man and his wife were both naked, and were not ashamed" (Gen. 2:25).

For God meant that we should be thus free from passion, and this is indeed the mark of a mind absolutely void of passion. Furthermore, he meant us to be free from care, and to have one work to perform: to sing the praises of the Creator as the angels do, without ceasing or intermission, and to delight in contemplation of him and to cast all our care on Him.

This is what the prophet David proclaimed to us when he said, "Cast your burden on the Lord, and he will sustain you" (Ps. 55:22). And, again, in the Gospels, Christ taught his disciples saying, "Do not be anxious about your life, what you shall eat or what you shall drink, nor about your body, what you shall put on" (Matt. 6:25).

–St. John of Damascus, *Exposition of the Orthodox Faith*, 2.11

IN GOD'S PRESENCE, CONSIDER . . .

When I am single-minded, as the angels are, I will worry less.

CLOSING PRAYER

Holy angels, teach us to care, but not to be anxious.

We were made to glorify God on earth

The angels glorify God in Heaven, says St. Gregory of Nyssa, and human beings were made so that God would be glorified by intelligent beings in the material part of creation.

"So God created man in his own image, in the image of God he created him" (Gen. 1:27). Certain writers before us have explained the reason for creating this animate being this way:

The whole creation is divided into two parts: that which is seen, and that which is not seen, to use the Apostle's words—"not seen" meaning the intelligible and immaterial, "seen" meaning the sensible and material. Since it is divided that way, the angelic and spiritual natures, which are among the things not seen, live in places above the world, and above the heavens, because such a residence corresponds with their constitution—for an intellectual nature is a fine, clear, unencumbered, agile kind of thing, and a heavenly body is fine and light, and perpetually moving, and the earth on the contrary, which stands last in the list of sensible things, can never be an adequate and congenial spot for intellectual beings to sojourn in. For what correspondence can there possibly be between that which is light and buoyant, on the one hand, and that which is heavy and gravitating on the other?

Well, to keep the earth from being completely devoid of the intellectual and the immaterial living in it, man (these writers tell us) was fashioned by the Supreme forethought, and his earthy parts formed over the intellectual and godlike essence of his soul. So this mixing with what has material weight enables the soul to live on this element of earth, which has a certain relation to the substance of the flesh.

The purpose of everything born, then, is that the Power which is above both the heavenly and the earthly universe may be glorified by intelligent beings in all parts of creation.

–St. Gregory of Nyssa, On Infants' Early Death

IN GOD'S PRESENCE, CONSIDER . . .

As an intelligent being, I am akin to the angels. God made me that way. Does my life reflect that truth?

CLOSING PRAYER

Lord, you are always willing to sanctify me. Send me your Holy Spirit, so that I may show forth your glory in my thinking, as the angels do in theirs.

Let everyone see that you're a citizen of heaven

St. John Chrysostom tells us that the best way to draw back those who don't come to church is not by preaching to them, but by showing them the difference the Mass makes in our lives. If they see in our behavior that we've been let into Heaven to sing with the choirs of angels, they'll come running.

I'll never stop begging you, with all earnestness, as I have often done before: Bring your brethren to us! Urge the wanderers! Advise them not just by words, but by deeds!

The teaching that comes through our manners and behavior is more powerful. Even if you don't speak a word, but, when you leave this assembly, show the people left behind what gain you've brought away with you by the way you carry yourself, the way you look, and all the rest of your behavior—that's enough to urge and teach them. We ought to leave this place as we would from a sacred shrine, as if we've come down from Heaven itself, as if we've become calm and philosophical, and do everything and say everything in proper measure.

When a wife sees her husband coming back from this assembly, and a father his son, and a friend his friend, and an enemy his enemy—let them all get an impression of the benefit you've gained from coming here. And they *will* get it, if they can see that you've become milder, more philosophical, and more devout.

Think of the privileges you enjoy—you, who have been initiated into the mysteries! Think with what company you offer up that mystic hymn, with what company you sing out the "Holy, holy, holy"! Teach outsiders that you have joined the chorus of the Seraphim, that you are ranked as a citizen of the commonwealth above, that you have been enrolled in the choir of angels, that you have conversed with the Lord, that you have been in the company of Christ!

If we act that way, we won't have to say anything when we go out to those who are left behind. They'll be able to see their own loss by what we've gained, and they'll come here running to get the same benefits themselves.

—St. John Chrysostom, *"If Your Enemy Hunger, Feed Him,"* 4

IN GOD'S PRESENCE, CONSIDER . . .

What do people see when I come home from Mass? Can they tell I've been singing with the Seraphim?

CLOSING PRAYER

Lord, unite my voice with the voices of your holy angels, and of all the saints who praise you and give constant witness to your glories.

Secret wisdom of God

What an honor for the human race! God reveals his most secret wisdom to the angels at the same time as to us, says St. John Chrysostom.

"But we impart a secret and hidden wisdom of God" (1 Cor. 2:7). Why is it "secret" and "hidden"? For surely Christ says, "what you hear whispered, proclaim upon the housetops" (Matt. 10:27). How then does he call it a secret?

Because neither angel nor archangel, nor any other created power, knew of it before it actually took place. This is why he says, "that through the church the manifold wisdom of God might now be made known to the Principalities and Powers in the heavenly places" (Eph. 3:10). God did this in honor of us, so that they should not hear the secrets without us. Whenever we make friends, we call this the surest proof of friendship: that we tell our secrets to no one in preference to them.

Hear this, you who make a sort of triumphal show of the secrets of the Gospel, and indiscriminately display the pearls and the doctrine to everyone, and cast the holy things unto dogs and swine, and useless reasonings. For the secret needs no decoration. It is simply declared to be what the fact is. It will not be a divine secret, whole in all its parts, if you add anything of your own to it.

–St. John Chrysostom, *Homily 7 on 1 Corinthians*

IN GOD'S PRESENCE, CONSIDER . . .

God shows his love to us and to angels by revealing himself. Am I as receptive as the holy angels when I encounter divine revelation?

CLOSING PRAYER

Lord, open my heart, that I may receive the secret wisdom of the Gospel through the ministry of your angels, and may proclaim it on earth with their help.

Join your heart with the angels

Even when you work at earthly things, says St. Augustine, you're a citizen of Heaven if you have your heart there and not on Earth.

Look and see the two kinds of people. One kind works, and the other they work among. One kind weighs their hearts down, the other joins their hearts with angels. The one trusts in the earthly things that are so common in the world, but the other puts their confidence in heavenly things that have been promised by God, who never lies.

But these two kinds of people are all mixed together. The citizen of Jerusalem, of the kingdom of Heaven, may have some position here on earth. One is a senator, or a judge, or a mayor, or a governor, or even the emperor, directing the earthly republic. But if he's a Christian—if he's a believer—if he is godly—if he despises the things of the world he lives in, and trusts in the things of the world he hasn't reached yet—then he has his heart above.

So we shouldn't despair of the citizens of the kingdom of Heaven when we see them involved in Babylon's business, doing earthly things in the earthly republic. And we shouldn't rush to congratulate everyone we see involved in heavenly business: even the sons of pestilence sometimes sit in the seat of Moses, of whom Jesus said, "practice and observe whatever they tell you, but not what they do; for they preach, but do not practice" (Matt. 23:3).

So long as everything is still mixed together, let us hear our voice, the voice of the citizens from Heaven—for we should aspire to put up with evil men here, rather than to be put up with by good men. Let us join ourselves to that voice, both with our ears and with our tongues, and with our hearts and with our work.

–St. Augustine, *Exposition on Psalm 52*, 2

IN GOD'S PRESENCE, CONSIDER . . .

When I look honestly at my life, does it seem as though my heart is more with the angels, or down on earth? What changes could I make in my life to put my heart in the right place?

CLOSING PRAYER

Lord, I join my heart with the angels in praising you. As long as I keep their light company, I will not be weighed down by earthly troubles.

Work like an angel

If you're lazy now in doing good works, asks St. Clement of Rome, how will you look the Lord in the eye when he comes to give you your reward? Remember how the countless angels stand around him, always ready to serve him.

The good servant receives the bread of his labor with confidence; the lazy and slothful servant cannot look his employer in the face. We must therefore be prompt in doing good; for all things come from the Lord. He forewarns us in these words: "Behold, your salvation comes; behold, his reward is with him, and his recompense before him" (Isa. 62:11).

He exhorts us, therefore, to pay attention to one thing with our whole heart: that we should not be lazy or slothful in any good work.

Let our boasting and our confidence be in him. Let us submit ourselves to his will. Let us consider the whole multitude of his angels, how they stand ever ready to minister to his will. For the Scripture says, "a thousand thousands served him, and ten thousand times ten thousand stood before him" (Dan. 7:10) and cried, "Holy, holy, holy is the Lord of hosts; the whole earth is full of his glory" (Isa. 6:3).

So, conscientiously gathering together in harmony, let us cry to him earnestly, as if we all had one mouth, so that we may share in his great and glorious promises. For it says, "What no eye has seen, nor ear heard, nor the heart of man conceived, what God has prepared for those who love him" (1 Cor. 2:9).

−St. Clement of Rome, *Epistle to the Corinthians*, 34

IN GOD'S PRESENCE, CONSIDER . . .

If God were paying me by the hour, how would I account for the hours I've spent so far today? Have I been as ready to serve as the angels who surround him?

CLOSING PRAYER

Lord, I fall far short of your angels in serving you; but remember your humble and unprofitable servant, not according to my worth, but according to your great mercy and compassion.

Imitating the hymns of angels

The historian Socrates Scholasticus relates the traditional story of how respon-sive singing began in the liturgy. According to the tradition, St. Ignatius had a vision of angels responding to each other in song.

We must now however make some allusion to the origin of this custom in the church of responsive singing.

Ignatius, third bishop of Antioch in Syria from the Apostle Peter, who also had conversations with the Apostles themselves, saw a vision of angels hymning in alternate chants the Holy Trinity. Accordingly he introduced the mode of singing he had observed in the vision into the Antiochian church. From there it was trans-mitted by tradition to all the other churches. Such is the account we have received in relation to these responsive hymns.

−Socrates Scholasticus, *Ecclesiastical History*, 6.6

IN GOD'S PRESENCE, CONSIDER . . .

Even if I'm not much of a singer, do I make a real effort to participate in the liturgy we share with the hosts of Heaven when I'm in church?

CLOSING PRAYER

Lord, let me sing with the Cherubim and Seraphim, and accept this hymn from me, sinner though I am.

The holy temple, below and above

We make up the Church below, says St. Augustine, and the angels make up the Church above. But Christ came down to us and took on human form to make us the equals of the angels.

"I bow down toward your holy temple" (Ps. 138:2).

What holy temple? The temple in which we will dwell, where we will worship.

But certainly, God obviously dwells in the angels. Therefore, when our joy is in spiritual things rather than earthly, and it takes up a song to God to sing before the angels, that very assembly of angels is the temple of God. We bow down toward God's temple.

There is a Church below, and there is also a Church above. The Church below is in all the faithful; the Church above is in all the angels. But the God of angels came down to the Church below, and the angels served him on earth, while he served us. I came, he says, "not to be served but to serve" (Matt. 20:28). And what did he serve us, except what we eat and drink even today?

Since the Lord of angels has served us, then, we should not despair of being equal to the angels. For he who is greater than angels came down to us. The Creator of the angels took on our nature. The Lord of angels died for us. Therefore "I bow down toward your holy temple"—not the temple made with hands, I mean, but the temple that you, Lord, have made for yourself.

—St. Augustine, *Exposition on Ps. 138, 4*

Christ gave us a chance to unite ourselves with the indescribable joys of the angels in Heaven. How much effort do I put into making sure my joy is in spiritual things? Do I consciously examine my desires and pray for help in redirecting them?

CLOSING PRAYER

Fill my mouth with your praise, Lord, and my lips with joy, so that I may sing of your glory with all the hosts of Heaven.

Anticipate the angels' work

At the end of time, says St. Augustine, the angels will separate the wheat from the chaff. Until then, we're all mixed up together. But we can anticipate their work by separating ourselves from everything wicked.

As long as the chaff is being bruised with the wheat, as long as the bad fish swim together with the good in the nets of the Lord, till the time of separation comes, it is your duty rather to endure the mixture of the bad out of consideration for the good, than to violate the principle of brotherly love towards the good from any consideration of the bad. For this mixture is not for eternity, but only for a time; nor is it spiritual, but corporal. And the angels will not make any mistakes when they collect the bad from the midst of the good, and commit them to the burning fiery furnace. For the Lord knows those who are his.

But if we cannot depart in body from those who practice iniquity as long as time lasts, at any rate, let everyone that names the name of Christ depart from iniquity itself. For in the meantime you can separate yourself from the wicked in life, and in morals, and in heart and will, and in the same ways depart from their society; and separation such as this should always be maintained. But wait till the end of time for the separation in the body—wait faithfully, patiently, bravely.

–St. Augustine, *Letters of Petilian the Donatist*, 3.3

IN GOD'S PRESENCE, CONSIDER . . .

How much of my life is chaff and how much is good wheat? What can I do to anticipate the angels' work and start getting rid of the chaff?

CLOSING PRAYER

Though I am as chaff that the storm carries away, Lord, make me worthy to be stored with your wheat when your angels come to bring in the harvest.

The incorruptible riches of the angels

The two greatest commandments, as Jesus taught us, sum up the whole of the Scriptures: love God and love your neighbor. True believers who remember those commandments, says St. Augustine, are promised the incorruptible riches of the angels.

All is contained in these brief sentences: "You shall love the Lord your God with all your heart, and with all your soul, and with all your mind," and "love your neighbor as yourself."

In this love, all our holy fathers, patriarchs, prophets, and apostles pleased God.

In this all true martyrs contended against the devil even to the shedding of blood, and because it never grew cold or failed in them, they became conquerors.

In this all true believers daily make progress, seeking to acquire not an earthly kingdom, but the kingdom of Heaven; not a temporal, but an eternal inheritance; not gold and silver, but the incorruptible riches of the angels; not the good things of this life, which are enjoyed with trembling, and which no one can take with him when he dies, but the vision of God, whose grace and power of giving happiness transcend all beauty of form in bodies not only on Earth but also in Heaven; transcend all spiritual loveliness in human beings, however just and holy; transcend all the glory of the angels and powers of the world above; transcend not only all that language can express, but all that thought can imagine concerning him.

And let us not despair of the fulfillment of such a great promise because it is so very great, but rather believe that we shall receive it because he who has promised it is so very great.

—St. Augustine, *Letter 189*

IN GOD'S PRESENCE, CONSIDER . . .

Am I really progressing daily toward the incorruptible riches of the angels, or do I see myself sliding backwards from time to time?

CLOSING PRAYER

Lord, though I am unworthy, I desire an eternal inheritance with your angels in Heaven. Grant that, in the end, I may be united to your love.

Flying home

St. Augustine says that our real home is the Zion in Heaven, which is the bliss of the angels. Though we live here on earth for the present, we can go back home, if we wish, on wings of love.

Zion was a particular city. It fell, and among its ruins certain saints lived according to the flesh. But the true Zion, the true Jerusalem (Zion is the same as Jerusalem), is "eternal in the Heavens" (2 Cor. 5:1). She is our mother. She is the one who has given birth to us. She is the Church of the saints. She has nourished us—she who is partly a pilgrim, and partly at home in the Heavens.

The part at home in Heaven is the bliss of the angels. The part that wanders in this world is the hope of the righteous. Of the part in Heaven it is said, "Glory to God in the highest"; of the part in this world it is said, "and on earth peace among men with whom he is pleased" (Luke 2:14).

If, though you live in this world, you are sighing for your native land, run by love, not by the feet of your body. Look not for ships, but for wings. Grasp the two wings of love. What are the two wings of love? Love of God, and love of our neighbor.

—St. Augustine, *Exposition on Ps. 149*, 5

IN GOD'S PRESENCE, CONSIDER . . .

How firm is my grip on the two wings of love? Do I seem to be flying home to the bliss of the angels yet? What could I do to grip either wing—love of God or love of neighbor—more firmly?

CLOSING PRAYER

Lord, teach me to love you perfectly, and unite me by the bonds of peace and love with my neighbors, so that at last I may fly home on the wings of love to live in the bliss of your angels forever.

Brought near the holy angels

With the Incarnation, says St. Cyril of Alexandria, the Church below is made one with the Church above. Christ has opened Heaven for us, and we have been brought near the angels.

And the Evangelist says that the Heavens were opened, as if they had been closed a long time. For Christ said, "Truly, truly, I say to you, you will see Heaven opened, and the angels of God ascending and descending upon the Son of man" (John 1:51).

Since the flock above and that below have now been made one, and one chief Shepherd is appointed for all, the Heavens were opened, and man on earth brought near to the holy angels. And the Spirit also again came down as if our race were being begun again—upon Christ first, who received it not so much for his own sake as for ours: for by him and in him are we enriched with all things.

So it is very appropriate to the economy of grace that he endures with us the things that belong to the human state: for where else would we see him emptied, who in his divine nature possesses the fullness? How could he become as poor as we are, if he had not been conformed to our poverty? How could he have emptied himself, if he had refused to endure the measure of human littleness?

—Cyril of Alexandria, *Commentary on Luke*, Sermon 11

IN GOD'S PRESENCE, CONSIDER . . .

If I'm brought near to the angels, is my spirit dressed appropriately for the occasion?

CLOSING PRAYER

Lord, receive me as I draw near to you, and purify my spirit from every kind of baseness and pollution. May I be pure as the angels in your presence.

Hear the music of the endless holiday in Heaven

We hire a band for a wedding or a birthday, St. Augustine says, and everyone who hears it knows that something special is going on. But if we listen and don't let the world distract us, we can hear the music of the angels singing at that endless festival in Heaven.

Here, where we have festivals just for the fun of it, we put bands or singers in front of our houses, or any kind of music that tempts us to indulgence. And what do passers-by say when they hear them? "What's going on here?" And the answer is that it's some festival. It's a birthday being celebrated, or there's a wedding going on. That's what we say so that the songs don't seem inappropriate, but the luxurious indulgence may be excused by the festive occasion.

In the house of God there's a never-ending festival. It's not just an occasion to be celebrated once, and then it's over. The angelic choir makes an eternal holiday, because the presence of God's face is a joy that never fails. This kind of holiday doesn't start at dawn, and it doesn't end at evening. And your heart can hear a certain sweet and melodious melody from that perpetual holiday—as long as the world doesn't drown out the sounds.

—St. Augustine, *Exposition on Psalm 42*, 8

N GOD'S PRESENCE, CONSIDER . . .

Can I find some quiet place every day to listen to the music of Heaven?

LOSING PRAYER

"Blessed are those who dwell in your house, ever singing your praise!" (Ps. 84:4).

Christ alone can give divine power to us

Often the Fathers use the angels as examples of great but limited power, contrasting the abilities of superior but still created beings with the omnipotence of God. Here St. Cyril of Alexandria argues that Christ is fully God because He can do what no angelic being can do: grant us power over demons and sickness.

"The fruit of good deeds is honorable"—that's a true saying. If you wish to lead a life as pure and undefiled as it's possible for a human being to lead, then Christ will adorn you with his gifts, and give you an abundant compensation for all your saintly deeds, and share his glory with you. It's not possible that he could be lying when he says, "As I live, says the Lord, those who honor me, I will honor" (1 Sam. 2:30).

I take the glorious company of the holy apostles as a plain and clear proof of this. We see them greatly honored and crowned with more than human glory by this fresh gift from Christ: "He gave them power and authority over all demons and to cure diseases" (Luke 9:1).

Here again, the Incarnate Word of God goes beyond the limits of humanity, and shines with divine dignity. For it's beyond human power to give anyone he likes authority over unclean spirits, and to enable them to deliver the afflicted from sickness. You may mention the angels or the Archangels, or the Thrones and Dominions, or the Cherubim and Seraphim—which are of even higher rank. But know that none of them can do it. It's true that they have great authority by the powers given to them from above. Language can't describe their power, and nature could never have given it to them. But reason forbids us to suppose that they could give these powers to others.

But Christ does give them, because he is God, out of his own fullness. For he himself is the Lord of glory and powers.

–St. Cyril of Alexandria, *Commentary on Luke,* sermon 47

IN GOD'S PRESENCE, CONSIDER . . .

Do I listen in prayer to the voices of the angels? Do I allow them to lead me toward the power of Christ?

CLOSING PRAYER

Bright Spirit, whom the Lord of Love has sent to me from Heaven to guard me and cherish me, love me and guide me, let me not forget your presence. May I always heed your promptings.

Angels rejoiced at our baptism

All the angels, and the Lord of angels, rejoice at a baptism, says St. John Chrysostom. In that water a sinful human being dies and a new person is born. So if we're dead to the flesh, why do we worry so much about material things?

"When Christ who is our life appears, then you also will appear with him in glory" (Col. 3:4).

So if we shall appear, let us not grieve when we are not honored. If this life is no life, but our real life is hidden, then we should live this life as though we were dead. Then, he says, you will also appear with him in glory—in *glory*, he says, not just that we should appear. The pearl is hidden when it's in the oyster.

So if we're insulted, or whatever we suffer, let us not grieve. This isn't our life; we're foreigners and travelers. "For you have died," he says (Col. 3:3). Who would be stupid enough to buy servants, or build a house, or make expensive clothes for a corpse already dead and buried? No one. Then you shouldn't either. The only thing we need is not to be naked; that's all we should look for.

Our first man is buried—not in the earth, but in water; not destroyed by death, but buried by death's destroyer; not by the law of nature, but by the commandment that's stronger than nature. Whatever nature has done may perhaps be undone, but what has been done by God's command can never be undone.

Nothing is more blessed than this burial. Everyone rejoices at it—angels, humans, and the Lord of angels. There's no need of an expensive suit, or a coffin, or any of those things at this burial.

Would you like to see a symbol of it? I can show you a pool where one was buried and the other raised. It's the Red Sea: the Egyptians sank under it, but the Israelites walked up out of it. In the same act God buries the one and regenerates the other.

–St. John Chrysostom, *Homily 7 on Colossians*

IN GOD'S PRESENCE, CONSIDER . . .

Do I recognize the presence of the angels when I celebrate the sacraments? They were there at my baptism, but they are also with me at every Confession and every time I receive Holy Communion.

CLOSING PRAYER

Lord, we thank you for the graces you have given us in the sacraments. Not the least among these graces is the companionship of the holy angels.

Giving us life for death

St. Augustine portrays Christ as a merchant buying and selling. But the deal he offers us is one we can't refuse. We can trade our death and hard work for his life and endless bliss.

Christ is himself the Bread which came down from Heaven (John 6:51); but Bread that refreshes the failing, and does not fail; Bread that can be tasted, and cannot be wasted.

This Bread is what the manna prefigured. This is why it is said, "He gave them the Bread of Heaven," and "man ate the bread of angels" (Ps. 78:24-25). Who is the Bread of Heaven, but Christ?

But in order that man might eat angels' Bread, the Lord of angels was made man. For if he had not been made man, we would not have his flesh. If we had not his flesh, we would not eat the Bread of the altar.

Let us hasten to the inheritance, since we have already received a great security deposit from it. My brethren, let us long for the life of Christ, seeing we hold as a deposit the death of Christ. How could he not give us his good things, when he has suffered our evil things?

In this our earth, in this evil world, what is there that is plentiful, but to be born, to work, and to die? Examine thoroughly the human condition—convict me if I lie—consider whether all of us are in this world for any other purpose than to be born, to work, and to die. This is the merchandise of our country: these things are plentiful here. To such merchandise did that Merchant descend. Now, every merchant gives and receives—gives what he has, and receives what he does not have. When he procures anything, he gives money, and receives what he buys. So Christ too in this his business gave and received. But what did he receive? He received what is plentiful here: to be born, to work, and to die. And what did he give? To be born again, to rise again, and to reign forever.

—St. Augustine, *Sermon 80 on the New Testament*

IN GOD'S PRESENCE, CONSIDER . . .

Do I willingly offer up the trials of birth, labor, and death, or do I still cling to this earthly existence in spite of the bread of angels that Christ offers me?

CLOSING PRAYER

O Good Merchant, I give you thanks that you have already bought me and paid the price. Feed me with the bread of angels, so that I may rise again and reign forever.

What really happens at Mass

When a priest celebrates the Mass on earth, he takes part in the worship of Heaven. He corresponds visibly to the invisible angels.

Whenever the priest invokes the Holy Spirit and offers the most awesome sacrifice—when he constantly handles the common Lord of all—tell me what rank shall we give him? What great purity and what real piety must we demand of him? For consider what kind of hands ought to minister in these things, and what kind of tongue utter such words. And shouldn't the soul that receives so great a spirit be purer and holier than anything in the world?

At such a time, angels stand by the priest; and the whole sanctuary, and the space round about the altar, is filled with the powers of Heaven, in honor of him who lies on it. For this, indeed, is capable of being proved from the very rites that are being then celebrated.

I myself have heard someone once relate, that a certain aged, venerable man, who often saw revelations, used to tell that, at such a time, he saw suddenly, so far as was possible for him, a multitude of angels, clothed in shining robes, and encircling the altar, and bending down, as one might see soldiers in the presence of their king. For my part I believe it.

—St. John Chrysostom, *On the Priesthood* 6.4

IN GOD'S PRESENCE, CONSIDER . . .

Do I pray for priests, so that they will live up to their holy calling, pure as angels?

CLOSING PRAYER

Holy guardian angels: watch over our priests as they minister to God's people on earth. Give them strength in temptation, wisdom in their words, constancy in their deeds.

The Eucharist is the angels' food

Our Mass in our own parish church, says St. Athanasius, is already part of that great heavenly banquet that we will share with the angels.

This bread, my brethren, is the food of the righteous not just here, but in Heaven as well. It is not only the saints on earth who are nourished by such bread and such blood. We will also eat them in Heaven. The Lord is the food even of the exalted spirits; he spares them all according to his mercy. The Lord has already given us angels' food. And this is what he promises those who continue with him in his trials: "I assign to you, as my Father assigned to me, a kingdom, that you may eat and drink at my table in my kingdom, and sit on thrones judging the twelve tribes of Israel" (Luke 22:28-30).

What a banquet that is! How great the harmony and gladness of those who eat at that heavenly table! They delight themselves, not with food that is thrown away, but with the food that produces everlasting life.

–St. Athanasius, *Festal Epistle 8*

IN GOD'S PRESENCE, CONSIDER . . .

When I approach the Eucharist to receive the food of angels, am I filled with harmony and gladness? Or do I still have lingering resentments against others who might be sharing the banquet with me?

CLOSING PRAYER

Lord, feed me with the food of the angels; let me share it now, and eternally with all the just in Heaven.

We're fed with what angels tremble to see

Do you really know, St. John Chrysostom asks, what an honor it is to be invited to communion with Christ? Angels tremble even to see the body of Christ, but we're invited to make our bodies one with his.

Think of how indignant you are against the traitor, against the ones who crucified Jesus. So look out! Make sure you yourself don't also become guilty of the body and blood of Christ. They slaughtered the all-holy body, but you receive it in a filthy soul after such great benefits. It wasn't enough for him to be made man, to be smitten and slaughtered, but he also commingles himself with us, and not by faith only, but also in actual deed makes us his body.

Then if you have the benefit of this sacrifice, shouldn't you be purer than anything? The hand that is to sever this flesh, the mouth that is filled with spiritual fire, the tongue that is reddened by that most awful blood—shouldn't they be purer than any sunbeam? Think what an honor it is, what sort of table you're sharing! When angels see the Body of Christ, they tremble, and dare not so much as look up at it without awe because of the brightness that comes from it. But we're fed with it, commingled with it, and made one body and one flesh with Christ.

—St. John Chrysostom, *Homily 82 on Matthew*

IN GOD'S PRESENCE, CONSIDER . . .

Do I recognize that God has given me to possess mysteries "into which angels long to look" (1 Peter 1:12)? Am I grateful for this gift?

CLOSING PRAYER

Holy angels, who worship with me in the Mass, lead me to the heights and depths of the mystery of our Lord's real presence.

The Word of God feeds the angels

The angels don't need sermons or readings to tell them God's word, says St. Augustine. They have God's Word, God the Son, with them all the time. And we'll be like that when we're with the angels in Heaven.

"Give us this day our daily bread" comes next in the prayer.

We might be asking the Father for the support we need for the body, "bread" meaning whatever we need; or we might mean that daily bread we're about to receive at the altar—either way, it's good for us to pray that he should give it to us.

What else are we praying for, after all, but that we might not do anything evil that would separate us from that holy bread? And the word of God preached daily is daily bread. Just because it isn't bread for the body, that doesn't mean it's not bread for the soul.

But when this life is gone, we won't look for the bread hunger looks for, and we won't have to receive the sacrament of the altar either. Then we'll be with Christ, whose body we receive now. I won't need to speak these words to you anymore, and you won't have to read the Scriptures anymore, because we'll see the One who is the Word of God himself, by whom all things were made. By him the angels become wise. They don't need longwinded speeches: they just drink in the only Word, and then, filled with him, they burst out in unfailing praise.

–St. Augustine, *Sermon 9 on the New Testament,* 6

IN GOD'S PRESENCE, CONSIDER . . .

Do I spend enough time with the Word of God? Would it help me be more regular in reading Scripture, or listening to the readings and the homily at Mass, if I remembered that I'm gaining, however imperfectly, the knowledge the angels have in Heaven?

CLOSING PRAYER

Father, feed us as you feed your angels, with bread from Heaven.

Fire to eat and Spirit to drink

St. Ephrem the Syrian is deeply aware of the miraculous power of the Eucharist. It's a new miracle, he says: we're being given the very substance of the angels to eat and drink.

When the Lord came down to earth among mortals, he made them a new creation. Just as in the angels, he mingled fire and spirit, so that they might be made of fire and spirit in a hidden way.

The Seraph did not bring the living coal near with his fingers. It only came close to Isaiah's mouth; he did not take hold of it or eat it (Isa. 6:6). But the Lord has given it to us both to hold and to eat.

To the angels, which are spiritual, Abraham brought bodily food, and they ate. But this is a new miracle: now our Lord gives to bodily creatures Fire and the Spirit as food and drink.

Fire came down on sinners in wrath and consumed them. But the Fire of the Merciful One comes down in bread and stays. Instead of the fire that devoured sinners, you eat a Fire in bread and are made alive.

As fire came down on the sacrifice of Elijah and consumed it (1 Kings 18:38), the Fire of mercy has become a living sacrifice to us. Fire ate up the oblations, and we, Lord, have eaten your Fire in your oblation.

—St. Ephrem the Syrian, *Rhythm 10*

IN GOD'S PRESENCE, CONSIDER . . .

When I go to Mass to take the food of angels, do I try to keep myself aware of what a miracle is happening?

CLOSING PRAYER

Heal my fright at the dangers, Lord, and let me take heart in you, so that with your angels surrounding me, I may partake of the Spirit in your bread and the Fire in your cup.

We share in the praise of the Seraphim

Explaining the Christian liturgy to his students, St. Cyril of Jerusalem tells them that the "Sanctus"—the "Holy, Holy, Holy" hymn that we still sing in our liturgy—is our way of sharing in the eternal praise of the Seraphim who surround the throne of God.

After this, we mention heaven, earth, and sea; the sun and the moon; the stars and all creation, rational and irrational, visible and invisible; Angels, Archangels, Virtues, Dominions, Principalities, Powers, Thrones; the Cherubim with many faces. In effect, we repeat the call of David: "O magnify the Lord with me!" (Ps. 34:3). We also mention the Seraphim, whom Isaiah in the Holy Spirit saw standing around the throne of God: with two wings they veiled their faces, with two they veiled their feet, and with two they flew, crying, "Holy, holy, holy is the Lord of hosts" (Isa. 6:3).

We recite this confession of God, which has been handed down to us from the Seraphim, so that we may share with the hosts of the world above in their hymn of praise.

–St. Cyril of Jerusalem, *Catechetical Lecture 23*

IN GOD'S PRESENCE, CONSIDER . . .

How does knowing that I'm joining the heavenly choir in praising God change my perception of the Mass? Does it make me want to be at Mass more often?

CLOSING PRAYER

Before the resplendent throne of your majesty, O Lord, the awe-inspiring seat of the strength of your love, and the altar of salvation that your will has established, in the land of your pasture, with thousands of Cherubim praising you, and ten thousands Seraphim sanctifying you, we draw near, adore, thank, and glorify you always, O Lord of all.

The angels' holiday

St. Athanasius reminds us that the heavenly feast, where we share the Bread of Life with the angels, is not for the impure.

Who will lead us to such a company of angels as this? Who will come with a desire for the heavenly feast and the angels' holiday, and will say like the prophet, "I went with the throng, and led them in procession to the house of God, with glad shouts and songs of thanksgiving, a multitude keeping festival" (Ps. 42:4)?

The saints also encourage us to such a state: they say, "Come, let us go up to the mountain of the Lord, to the house of the God of Jacob" (Isa. 2:3).

But this kind of feast is not for an impure person. It is not for sinners to approach it. It is for the virtuous and diligent.

> Who shall ascend the hill of the Lord?
> And who shall stand in his holy place?
> He who has clean hands and a pure heart,
> who does not lift up his soul to what is false,
> and does not swear deceitfully (Ps. 24:3-4).

And the psalmist adds that, when he goes up, "He will receive blessing from the Lord" (Ps. 24:5).

—St. Athanasius, *Festal Epistle 6*

IN GOD'S PRESENCE, CONSIDER . . .

How careful am I to make sure that I've purified my heart before I celebrate the Eucharistic holiday with the angels?

CLOSING PRAYER

Lord, send your holy angels to guide me in the ways of purity, and present me holy beside your holy altar.

Remember where you are, and mind your manners!

When we're at Mass, St. John Chrysostom reminds us, we're standing right there with the choirs of angels, singing "Holy, holy, holy" along with them. Are you singing that heavenly hymn with the same mouth you just used to insult your neighbor?

Think who you're standing with at the time of the mysteries: with the Cherubim and the Seraphim! The Seraphim are never insulting. No, their mouths have only one duty: to sing the hymn of praise—to glorify God.

How can you sing "Holy, holy, holy" with them if you use your mouth for insults?

Suppose there were a royal vessel, always filled with royal delicacies, and set apart only for that purpose. Now suppose that one of the servants used it for carrying dung. Would he ever again venture to put it away with the other dishes for royal delicacies after it had been filled with dung? Of course not!

That's what it's like when you make fun of people or insult them.

"Our Father"—but wait! That's not all! Listen to the next words: "who art in Heaven."

The moment you say, "Our Father, who art in Heaven," that word raises you up. It gives wings to your mind. It reminds you that you do have a Father in Heaven.

Don't have anything to do with earthly things, then. Don't talk about them. He has set you among that host above! He has numbered you among the heavenly choir. Why drag yourself down? You're standing beside the royal throne—and you insult someone! Aren't you afraid the King will think it's an outrage?

Even among us, we rebuke a servant if he beats or assaults his fellow servant—even if he has a good reason to do it. We think it's an outrage.

And yet you, standing with the Cherubim right beside the King's throne—you insult your brother?

—St. John Chrysostom, *Homily 14 on Ephesians*

IN GOD'S PRESENCE, CONSIDER . . .

Do I look on my body as a sacred vessel, like the chalice and the paten used at Mass?

CLOSING PRAYER

Lord, through the ministry of your angels, be always in my heart and mind and on my lips. Purify me as a vessel of your presence in the world.

Christ became man so we could feast with angels

The angels feed on the vision of the Word, says St. Augustine. We can't see the whole vision yet—only the angels can do that. But Christ became man, taking on weak human flesh, so that we could have that angelic food in a way we could comprehend.

He who was born of a virgin brought you a temporal miracle: he was not born of a father—not of a man for his father, I mean—yet he was born of the flesh. But it shouldn't seem impossible to you that he was born of his mother alone, since he made man before there was a father or a mother.

So he brought you a temporal miracle, so that you may seek and admire him who is eternal. For he who came forth as a bridegroom out of his chamber—that is, out of the womb of the virgin—he brought a temporal miracle, but he himself is eternal. He is coeternal with the Father.

He is the one who "In the beginning was the Word, and the Word was with God, and the Word was God" (John 1:1). He did what it took to cure you, so that you could see what you didn't see before.

What you despise in Christ is not yet the contemplation of someone who is cured, but the medicine of the sick. Don't run to the vision of the whole too quickly. The angels see it; the angels rejoice; the angels feed on it and live. What they feed on never fails, and their food never lessens. In the thrones of glory, in the regions of the heavens, in the places above the heavens, the Word is seen by the angels, and that is their joy and their food, and the Word endures.

But so that we could eat the bread of angels, the Lord of the angels became man. This is our salvation—the medicine of the weak, the food of the healthy.

—St. Augustine, *Sermon 76 on the New Testament*, 5-6

IN GOD'S PRESENCE, CONSIDER . . .

The Word became flesh so that flesh could see what the pure spirits see in Heaven—and share the feast of Heaven even here on earth. This is the wonder of salvation.

CLOSING PRAYER

Lord, who gave us the bread of angels to be our food, send your Holy Spirit to enlighten my mind as I contemplate your holy Word.

Feast like Moses, fast like Daniel

When we approach the Eucharist, says St. Athanasius, we should remember that we're joining the angels in the feast.

Let us not act like people who keep the feast on earth. Let us act as if we knew we were celebrating it with angels. Let us glorify the Lord by temperance, righteousness, and all the other virtues. And let us rejoice in the Lord, not in ourselves, so that we may also inherit with the saints.

Let us keep the feast as Moses did. Let us be wakeful like David, who got up seven times, and in the middle of the night gave thanks for the righteous judgments of God. Let us be early: as he said, "O Lord, in the morning you hear my voice; in the morning I prepare a sacrifice for you, and watch" (Ps. 5:3). Let us fast like Daniel; let us pray without ceasing, as Paul told us to do. Let us all recognize the season of prayer—but especially those who are honorably married, so that when these things witness for us, and we keep the feast by them, we may be able to enter into the joy of our Lord in the kingdom of Heaven.

—St. Athanasius, *Festal Epistle 6*

IN GOD'S PRESENCE, CONSIDER . . .

How do I normally prepare for the Eucharist? How would my preparation be different if I expected to meet angels at the table?

CLOSING PRAYER

Lord, let your angel touch my heart, as the angel touched the lips of Isaiah the prophet.

Give thanks for the food of the angels

God became man, says St. Augustine, so we could eat the food of angels—which is truth, wisdom, and the goodness of God. We should give thanks at least as readily as we do when someone gives us something good to eat.

So I have said, praise the Lord, for the Lord is good; sing to his name, for he is sweet.

He is Mediator, and is sweet for that reason. What is sweeter than angels' food? How can God not be sweet, since man ate angels' food?

Human beings and angels do not live on different foods. The angels' food is truth, wisdom, and the goodness of God, but you can't enjoy it in the same way as the angels. So that man might eat angels' food, the Creator of the angels was made man. If you taste, sing praises; if you have tasted how sweet the Lord is, sing praises; if what you have tasted has a good flavor, praise it.

Are any of us so unthankful to a cook or a food vendor that we don't return thanks by praising what we taste if we're pleased with the food? If we're not silent on such occasions, how can we be silent about God, who has given us everything?

–St. Augustine, *Exposition on Psalm 135*, 4

IN GOD'S PRESENCE, CONSIDER ...

Am I thankful every day to God for the food of angels? For that matter, am I thankful every day for the food I eat, both to God and to the people who made it for me? How can I cultivate a habit of gratitude?

CLOSING PRAYER

O God, who sent forth the heavenly bread, the food of the whole world, our Lord Jesus Christ, to be a Savior, and Redeemer, and Benefactor, bless me, and lead me to join the choirs of angels in grateful praise.

The company of Heaven is with us on Earth.

St. Basil shows us a way to imitate the angels in the midst of our ordinary work.

Pious exercises nourish the soul with divine thoughts. What state can be more blessed than to imitate on earth the choruses of angels? To begin the day with prayer, and honor our Maker with hymns and songs? As the day brightens, to accompany our labor with prayer, and to season our work with hymns as if with salt? Soothing hymns compose the mind to a cheerful and calm state. Quiet, then, as I have said, is the first step in our sanctification; the tongue purified from the gossip of the world; the eyes unexcited by fair color or comely shape; the ear not relaxing the tone or mind by voluptuous songs, nor by that special mischief, the talk of light men and jesters. Thus the mind, saved from dissipation from without, and not through the senses thrown upon the world, falls back upon itself, and thereby ascends to the contemplation of God.

–St. Basil the Great, *Letters* 2.2.

IN GOD'S PRESENCE, CONSIDER . . .

Do I begin my days well, with a prayer of "Morning Offering"? Do I renew that prayer often throughout the day?

CLOSING PRAYER

O Jesus, through the immaculate heart of Mary and in union with the angels, I offer you all my prayers, works, joys and sufferings of this day.

Angelic harp or earthly lyre?

St. Augustine, who was an expert musician, sees a metaphorical meaning in the musical instruments mentioned in the Psalms. When we do what God commands, we're playing the harp with the angels; when we suffer here below for the sake of our faith, we're playing the earthly lyre.

"I will praise you with the lyre, O God, my God" (Ps. 43:4).

What does it mean to praise him with the lyre, or with the harp? For he does not always praise with the lyre or harp.

These two musical instruments each have a particular meaning and it's worth our while to consider what it is. Both are carried in the hands, and played by touching. They stand for certain bodily works of ours. Both are good—if you know how to play the lyre or harp. But the harp has its sounding board—that drum or hollow piece of wood that the strings vibrate against, making the sound—on the *upper* part, whereas the lyre has that same curved sounding board on the *lower* part.

We can make that same distinction between our works on the lyre or on the harp. Both, however, are acceptable to God, and grateful to his ear.

When we do anything according to God's commandments, obeying his commands and listening to him so that we will know what to do—when we are active and not passive—then we're playing the harp. This is what the angels do, for they have nothing to suffer.

But when we have to suffer tribulations or trials or insults on this earth, this is the lyre. We suffer only from the *lower* part of us—that is to say, from the fact that we are mortal, and that we owe some of our trouble to our original cause, and we suffer much from those who are below us. This also is a sweet melody rising from below.

So when we suffer, we play the lyre; when we sing, we play the harp.

–St. Augustine, *Exposition on Psalm 43*, 5

IN GOD'S PRESENCE, CONSIDER . . .

Do I recognize that everything I have is a gift from God intended for use in glorifying him? Do I glorify God with all my gifts, as the angels do?

CLOSING PRAYER

Angel of God, help me to use my gifts for God's glory and offer my sufferings for his glory as well.

Sailing into port

After a long and stormy voyage, says St. Cyril of Alexandria, the soul finds rest in the safe haven above, carried there by the angels of Heaven.

"The poor man died and was carried by the angels to Abraham's bosom. The rich man also died and was buried" (Luke 16:22).

Look at the Savior's words carefully. The poor man, he says, was carried by angels to Abraham's bosom—but of the rich man there is nothing of the sort, but only that he died and was buried.

Those who have hope in God find that their departure from the world is a deliverance from anguish and pain. Ships that sail on the sea stand the shock of savage waves, and struggle with the violence of mighty winds. But afterwards, when they arrive at tranquil havens fit for their rest, they end their tossing about there. In the same way, I think, human souls, when they emerge from the turbulence of earthly things, enter the mansions that are above, like a haven of salvation.

–St. Cyril of Alexandria, *Commentary on Luke*, Sermon 112

IN GOD'S PRESENCE, CONSIDER . . .

How does it change my view of death to think of it as sailing out of the storm, surrounded by angels, rather than sailing into it?

CLOSING PRAYER

Angel of God, be my guide and my help in my voyage, and bring me at last to a safe and tranquil haven.

Guided into eternity

Scripture tells us that we have guides to take our souls when we die, says St. John Chrysostom. Whatever our eternal destination, the heavenly beings come with us to make sure we get there.

It's quite certain that souls when they leave the body do not still linger here, but are led away immediately. Here's how we know: "The poor man died and was carried by the angels" (Luke 16:22).

Not only the souls of the just, but also those of sinners are led away. This also is clear from the case of another rich man. For when his land brought forth abundantly, he said within himself, "I will do this: I will pull down my barns, and build larger ones" (Luke 12:18). Yes, he really did pull down his barns—for secure storehouses are not built with walls of stone; they are "the mouths of the poor." But this man forgot about these: he was busy with his stone walls.

But what did God say to him? "Fool! This night your soul is required of you." And look closely: in one passage it is said that the soul is carried away by angels; in the other, that "it is required"—and in the latter case they lead it away as a prisoner; in the former, they guard and conduct it as a crowned victor.

When a fighter in the arena has received many wounds and is drenched with blood, with his head encircled with a crown, those who stand ready by the spot take him up, and with great applause and praise they carry him home amid shouting and admiration. In the same way the angels on that occasion led Lazarus away. But in the other instance dreadful powers, probably sent for that purpose, required the soul. The soul doesn't depart this life of its own free will; in fact, it can't. If we need guides when we travel from one city to another; much more does the soul need those who can conduct it, when it is separated from the flesh, and is entering upon the future state of existence.

–St. John Chrysostom *Four Discourses, Chiefly on the Parable of the Rich Man and Lazarus*, Discourse 2, chapter 2

IN GOD'S PRESENCE, CONSIDER . . .

Will I be carried home by the angels amid shouting and admiration?

CLOSING PRAYER

Sanctify my soul, Lord, so that I may at last be carried home by your holy angels to dwell forever among the blessed and the just.

Carried to heaven by angels

A martyr wrote down a dream or vision he had while waiting in prison. In it we see how the very early Christians imagined their deaths: angels carry them to a happy meeting with their departed friends.

We had been martyred, and we had gone forth from the flesh, and we were being carried by four angels into the east, though their hands didn't touch us. We were not floating on our backs looking up, but as if we were ascending a gentle slope.

At last, when we were set free, we saw the first boundless light. "Perpetua," I said (she was beside me), "this is what the Lord promised us! We've received the promise!"

And while we were carried by those same four angels, we saw a vast space like a pleasure-garden, with rose bushes and every kind of flower. The trees were as tall as a cypress, and their leaves were falling incessantly.

In that pleasure-garden four other angels appeared, brighter than the previous ones. When they saw us, they gave us honor, and said admiringly to the rest of the angels, "Here they are! Here they are!"

Those four angels who bore us, greatly afraid, put us down. We walked on foot about an eighth of a mile in a broad path. There we found Jocundus and Saturninus and Artaxius, who had been burnt alive in the same persecution; and Quintus, another martyr who had died in prison. We asked them where the rest were. And the angels said to us, "Come first, enter and greet your Lord."

—Martyrdom of Saints Perpetua and Felicity, 4.1

Will the angels point me out to each other and greet me with joy and wonder? Even if I'm not called to be a martyr, is there some responsibility that I'm disappointing the angels by shirking?

My Guardian Angel, help me to face the death that God has appointed to me with courage, with peace, and with perseverance in faith, hope, and love. May the angels lead me into paradise

Carried by angels to Abraham's bosom

In Jesus' story of the rich man and Lazarus (Luke 16:19-31), we hear that angels carried poor Lazarus to "Abraham's bosom" when he died. Why Abraham? Because, says St. Asterius of Amasea, of all the Old Testament figures Abraham was the one most intimately associated with Christ.

And it came to pass that the beggar died and was carried away by the angels into Abraham's bosom.

Angels were his bodyguard, looking upon him gently and mildly, and showing him by the way they treated him the attendance and relief that awaited him. And he was taken and placed in the bosom of the patriarch—a statement that gives ground for doubt to those who like to question minutely the deep things of the Scriptures, for if every just man, when he dies, should be taken to the same place, the bosom would be a great one and expanded to an endless extent, if it were intended to accommodate the whole multitude of the saints. But if this is absolutely impossible, the thought presents itself to us that the material bosom is the symbol of a spiritual truth.

And what does it mean? Abraham, he says, receives those who have lived an upright life. Then tell us, wonderful Luke, why, when there were many just men, even older than Abraham, did you withhold this distinction from his predecessors, passing in silence over Enoch, Noah, and many others who were like these in their way of life?

Abraham was a minister of Christ, and, beyond other men, received what belongs to the revelation of Christ, and the mystery of the Trinity was adequately embodied in the tent of this old man when he entertained the three angels as wayfaring men. In short, after many mystical enigmas, he became the friend of God, the God who, later on, put on flesh and, through the medium of this human veil, openly associated with human beings. This is why Christ says that Abraham's bosom is a sort of fair haven, and sheltered resting-place for the just. For we all have our salvation and expectation of the life to come, in Christ, who, in his human descent, sprang from the flesh of Abraham.

–St. Asterius of Amasea, *Sermon 1: The Rich Man and Lazarus*

IN GOD'S PRESENCE, CONSIDER . . .

When I find something obscure in Scripture, does it make me doubt, or does it make me prayerfully seek, with the angels' assistance, for the deeper meaning?

CLOSING PRAYER

Lord, count me worthy to know the meaning of your Word, which you have delivered through the ministry of your angels to all your people.

To be with the angels

Overcome by grief himself, St. Jerome nevertheless has the difficult task of consoling one of his dear friends for the loss of her young daughter. He cannot deny his human feelings, but he knows that, for the faithful young woman who died, there is only the unfathomable joy of being carried by the angels to meet Christ.

"O that my head were waters, and my eyes a fountain of tears, that I might weep"—not as Jeremiah says, for the slain of my people (Jer. 9:1), or, as Jesus did, for the miserable fate of Jerusalem (Luke 19:41), but for holiness, mercy, innocence, chastity, and all the virtues, for they are all gone now that Blaesilla is dead. I do not grieve for her sake, but for myself I must; my loss is too great to bear with resignation.

But what is this? I wish to check a mother's weeping, and I groan myself. I make no secret of my feelings; this entire letter is written in tears. Even Jesus wept for Lazarus because he loved him (John 11:35-36). But I'm a poor comforter if I'm overcome by my own sighs, and when tears are wrung from my breaking heart along with my words. Dear Paula, my agony is as great as yours. Jesus knows it, whom Blaesilla now follows; the holy angels know it, whose company she now enjoys. I was her father in the spirit, her foster-father in affection.

But why should death be hard to bear, when we must endure it ourselves one day? And why do we grieve for the dead? We are not born to live forever. Abraham, Moses, and Isaiah; Peter, James, and John; Paul, the chosen vessel (Acts 9:15); and even the Son of God himself have all died; and are we troubled when a soul leaves its earthly lodging?

We should indeed mourn for the dead, but only for him whom Gehenna receives, whom Tartarus devours, and for whose punishment the eternal fire burns. But we who, in departing, are accompanied by an escort of angels, and met by Christ Himself, should rather grieve that we have to linger still in this tabernacle of death (2 Cor. 5:4). For while we are at home in the body, we are absent from the Lord (2 Cor. 5:6).

—St. Jerome, *Letter 39,* 1-3

IN GOD'S PRESENCE, CONSIDER . . .

Does my belief in the angels make it easier for me to be peaceful when I think of my own death? Am I confident that they will guide me safely through any suffering and tribulation?

CLOSING PRAYER

Angel of God, uphold me in faith, and win me the fortitude to face my own death, trusting in you until the end.

Angels are waiting for us

In the end, says St. Augustine, we'll rejoin the angels, and all of us together will make one temple of God, one heavenly Jerusalem.

The house of God is also a city. For the house of God is the people of God. The house of God is the temple of God. What does the Apostle say? "For God's temple is holy, and that temple you are" (1 Cor. 3:17).

All the faithful are the house of God—not only those who exist now, but also those who have existed before us, and those who will come after us, to the end of the world. The innumerable hosts of the faithful are gathered into one body, but counted by the Lord. As the apostle says, "The Lord knows those who are his" (2 Tim. 2:19). Those grains of wheat that are still groaning among the chaff will be made into one mass when the floor has been winnowed in the end. The whole number of faithful saints are destined to be changed from the human state so that they become equal to the angels of God. And then they will be joined with the angels, who are no longer pilgrims, but are waiting for us to come back from our pilgrimage.

All of these together will form one house of God, and one city.

–St. Augustine, *Exposition on Ps. 126, 3*

IN GOD'S PRESENCE, CONSIDER . . .

Am I doing my best to live the unity of the Church now, so that I will be joined forever with the angels when I come back from my pilgrimage?

CLOSING PRAYER

King of Peace, grant your Church peace in unity and love, and unite your servants on Earth with the hosts of angels who make up your Church in Heaven.

Angels rejoice at a new arrival

St. Ambrose remembers holy men whose prayers ended wars on earth. When such a man is taken up to Heaven, he says, the angels rejoice to welcome him.

Don't we know that the saints are fighting even when they're on holiday? Wasn't Elisha at rest? Yes, at rest in body, but in spirit he was active, and he fought by his prayers when the noise of horses and the noise of a great host were heard in the camp of the Syrians, so that they thought that the forces of other princes were marching against them, to bring help to the people of Israel. So they were seized with great panic and fled—and four lepers, who had gone out hoping to die, looted their camp.

And didn't the Lord work similar wisdom in Macedonia—or I might almost say greater—by the prayers of Acholius? For it was not by an idle panic or a vague suspicion, but by a raging plague and burning pestilence, that the Goths were troubled and alarmed. In short, they ran away hoping to escape; afterwards they came back and begged for peace to save their lives.

Thus in the great deeds of this eminent man we have seen former ages revived, and have witnessed the works we have read of the prophet doing. Like Elisha he was all his life in the midst of arms and battles, and by his good works he ended wars. And when tranquility was restored to his countrymen, he breathed out his holy soul—a misfortune heavier than war itself. Like Elijah he was carried up to Heaven, not in a chariot of fire, nor by horses of fire (unless, of course, we just didn't see them), nor in any whirlwind in the sky, but by the will and in the calm of our God, and with the jubilation of the holy angels who rejoiced that such a man had come among them.

—St. Ambrose, *Letter 15*, 7-8

IN GOD'S PRESENCE, CONSIDER . . .

Remembering what great things have been done through prayer, how is my prayer life going? Am I the sort of person whom the angels will rejoice to greet?

CLOSING PRAYER

Lord, may your angels bring peace to the earth—peace to nations, neighborhoods, and homes—and bring all our enmities to an end.

Shining like the sun

Rufinus of Aquileia reminds us that, in the resurrection, our bodies will be changed and glorified, just as Christ's was. What was planted as a physical body will be raised as a spiritual body, fit for the companionship of angels.

But since God's saints have these promises, and an infinite number like them, about the resurrection of the righteous, it should not be hard now for us to believe the promises that the prophets have foretold as well—namely, that the righteous will shine as the sun and as the brightness of the firmament in the kingdom of God (Matt. 13:43, Daniel 12:3). Why should it be hard to believe that they will have the brightness of the sun, and be adorned with the splendor of the stars and of this firmament, if the life and conversation of God's angels are being prepared for them in Heaven? We have been told that we will be molded to the glory of Christ's body! When he speaks of that glory, promised by the Savior's mouth, the holy apostle says that "It is sown a physical body, it is raised a spiritual body" (1 Cor. 15:44).

If it is true, as it certainly is true, that God really will bring every one of the righteous and the saints into companionship with the angels, then it is certain that he will also change their bodies into the glory of a spiritual body.

—Rufinus, *Commentary on the Apostles' Creed*, 46

IN GOD'S PRESENCE, CONSIDER . . .

Which things are hardest for me to believe in Christian teaching? Have I asked my guardian angel to help my understanding? Do I submit myself to the Church's teaching until the understanding is granted to me?

CLOSING PRAYER

Guardian and Guide, touch my understanding, and help me to believe what I cannot understand.

Trust in God's justice

God judged even the angels justly, says St. Gregory the Great, so we should have no doubt that he will judge us justly.

When we have doubts about the things that are done concerning us, we should look at others that we know well, and quiet that grumbling of the thought that came up because of our uncertainty.

Look then: scourges bring the elect back to life, but not even scourges keep the wicked from doing evil. So Almighty God's judgments on us are very secret, and not unjust.

But if we stretch our mind's eye up to the things above, we see by those that we have nothing we can justly complain about in what happens to us. For Almighty God, discerning the merits of angels, decreed that some would remain in eternal light without falling; but others, who had fallen by free will from their height, he laid low in the vengeance of eternal damnation.

So we see that God does nothing unjustly, since he justly judged even a nature more refined than ours.

–St. Gregory the Great, *Moralia in Job*, 15.61.7

IN GOD'S PRESENCE, CONSIDER . . .

I know that God will judge me as justly as he judged the angels; but am I doing everything I can to take advantage of the mercy of his forgiveness? For example, when was the last time I confessed?

CLOSING PRAYER

Lord, you judged angels justly, but for mortals you decreed mercy as well as justice. Be mindful of me, Lord, your lowly, sinful, and untrustworthy servant, and in your mercy blot out my sins.

Angels don't ask about your income

When Christ sends the angels to gather his chosen people, says St. Cyril of Jerusalem, it won't matter at all whether you're rich or poor. On earth, Christ was poor himself, so he won't forget the poor among his elect.

That King, so great and glorious, attended by trains of angels, who shares the Father's throne, will not despise his own servants.

His elect will not be confused with his foes: "and he will send out his angels with a loud trumpet call, and they will gather his elect from the four winds" (Matt. 24:31). He despised no one, not even Lot; so how could he despise many righteous? "Come, you blessed of my Father," he will say to them, and then they will ride on chariots of clouds, and be collected by angels.

But someone here may be saying, "I am a poor man," or "What if when that happens I'm sick and in bed?" or "I am only a woman, and I shall be taken at the mill: shall we then be despised?"

Be of good courage. The Judge is no respecter of persons; "He shall not judge by what his eyes see, or decide by what his ears hear" (Isa. 11:3). He does not honor the educated before the simple, or the rich before the needy. Even if you are in the field, the angels will take you; do not think that he will take the landlord and leave you, the farmer. Even if you're a slave, even if you're poor, don't worry at all: he who took the form of a servant does not despise servants.

–St. Cyril of Jerusalem, *Catechetical Lecture 15*, 22-23

In my own relations with the world, do I imitate the Lord's blindness to status and money?

Lord, help me always to remember the poor, the widows and orphans, the foreigners visiting our land, and all who are in need.

Our redemption benefits the angels as well

Because of our sin, says St. Augustine, there was a wall of hostility between us and the angels. So in redeeming us, Christ gave the angels a great benefit as well: he made us their friends again.

We will not know the other part of the Church as it really is—the part made up of the holy angels and the powers of God—until, at the end of the age, we join it to have eternal bliss along with it. We know the other part better because we're in it: the part that is separated from the heavenly fellowship and wanders through the earth. This is the part that the blood of the sinless Mediator has redeemed from sin. This is our battle cry: "If God is for us, who is against us? He who did not spare his own Son but gave him up for us all" (Rom. 8:31-32).

Christ didn't die for the angels. But still, what was done for man by his death for man's redemption and his deliverance from evil was done for the angels as well: because by it the hostility between men and the angels, which was caused by sin, is removed, and friendship is restored.

—St. Augustine, Enchiridion, chapter 16

IN GOD'S PRESENCE, CONSIDER . . .

Amazing as it seems, the angels want to be my friends. Does my way of life put barriers of sin between me and the friendship of the angels?

CLOSING PRAYER

Father, send your Spirit to make my life worthy of the angel-guardians you have given me.

Like angels, but not exactly like

Even in paradise, says St. Methodius, we will have bodies, which distinguishes us from angels. Christ did not say that we would be angels, but like angels.

Thus it was that, having contrived the parable about the woman and the seven brothers, that they might cast doubt upon the resurrection of the flesh, "The same day Sadducees came to him, who say that there is no resurrection" (Matt. 22:23).

If there had been no resurrection of the flesh, but the soul only were saved, Christ would have agreed with their opinion as a right and excellent one. But as it was, he answered and said, "in the resurrection they neither marry nor are given in marriage, but are like angels in Heaven" (Matt. 23:30)—not because they have no flesh, but because they neither marry nor are given in marriage, but are henceforth incorruptible.

And he speaks of our being near the angels in this respect, that, like the angels in Heaven, in paradise we no longer spend our time in marriage-feasts or other festivities, but in seeing God and cultivating life under the direction of Christ. For he did not say "they shall be angels," but "*like* angels," in being, for instance, crowned, as it is written, with glory and honor; differing a little from the angels, but *near* to being angels.

—St. Methodius, *Discourse on the Resurrection*, 1.12

IN GOD'S PRESENCE, CONSIDER . . .

How much of my present life do I spend living the angelic life—seeing God and cultivating life under the direction of Christ?

CLOSING PRAYER

Grant me, Lord, that I may be pleasing to you in my words, works, thoughts, and deeds, so that I may be worthy of a new and true life among your angels in the kingdom of Heaven.

An eternal body for mingling with the angels

We believe in the resurrection of the body. But we won't all rise with the same bodies, says St. Cyril of Jerusalem. What kind of eternal body we get depends on how we lived our lives here on earth.

We'll all be raised with eternal bodies. But not all our bodies will be alike. If you're righteous, you'll receive a heavenly body, so that you'll be able to mingle with the angels. But if you're a sinner, you'll receive an eternal body fitted to endure the pains of sins, so that it may burn eternally in the fire without ever being consumed.

And it is right that God will assign this lot to either group. We do nothing without the body. With the mouth we blaspheme, and with the mouth we pray. With the body we commit fornication, and with the body we preserve our chastity. With the hand we rob, and with the hand we give alms. And so forth through the rest.

So, since the body has been our servant in everything, it will also share what happens to us hereafter.

—St. Cyril of Jerusalem, *Catechetical Lecture 18*, 19

IN GOD'S PRESENCE, CONSIDER . . .

How have I used my body in God's service today? Have I been preparing myself for mingling with the angels?

CLOSING PRAYER

Lord, you alone are holy; purify my body for your service, so that I may receive an eternal body fit for the company of angels.

Will there be food in Heaven?

Christ ate food in his resurrected body, says St. Augustine, and even angels in the Bible have really eaten. They do so not because they need to eat, but because they can; it's a free exercise of their superior power. St. Augustine speculates that the same will be true of our glorified bodies after the resurrection.

Is there any contradiction between the fact that Christ ate food after his resurrection, and the doctrine that in the promised resurrection state there will be no need of food? After all, we read that angels also have eaten food of the same kind and in the same way, not in empty and unreal simulation, but in unquestionable reality.

But they did not eat under the pressure of necessity, but in the free exercise of their power. For water is absorbed in one way by the thirsting earth, in another way by the glowing sunbeams; in the former we see the effect of poverty, in the latter of power.

Now the body of that future resurrection state would be imperfect in its happiness if it could not eat food; but it would also be imperfect if, on the other hand, it were dependent on food.

I might enter on a fuller discussion here about the changes possible in the qualities of bodies, and the dominion that belongs to higher bodies over those of inferior nature; but I have resolved to make my reply short, and I write this for minds intelligent enough that the simple suggestion of the truth is enough for them.

—St. Augustine, *Letter 102*

N GOD'S PRESENCE, CONSIDER . . .

Angels have eaten food, but they can take it or leave it. Do I always keep God at the center of my desire, or do I allow my appetites to lead me away from God?

CLOSING PRAYER

Father, you gave us the food of angels to eat, the food of the whole world, our Lord Jesus Christ: remember in your love all who are fed by this heavenly food.

Treated like an angel

Angels were treated like humans when they visited us, says Tertullian—eating, drinking, even having their feet washed. So it should not strike us as impossible that humans, after the resurrection, will be treated like angels.

Our Lord puts an effective end to this discussion by declaring that they "are like angels in Heaven" (Matt. 22:30). "Like" in that we will not marry, because we will not die; like, too, of course, in that we will not have to yield to any other similar necessity of our bodily state.

The angels, too, were sometimes "like" human beings, in that they ate and drank, and allowed their feet to be washed. They had clothed themselves in human form without losing their own proper nature.

So if angels, when they became human, allowed themselves to be treated as if they were flesh without any change in the substance of their spirit, then why shouldn't humans, in the same way, be treated like spiritual beings? When they have become "like angels," they will no longer be exposed to the usual demands of the flesh in their angelic dress—no more than the angels were exposed to the demands of the spirit when they were encompassed in human form. We will not cease to exist in the flesh because we cease to be assailed by the usual wants of the flesh, just as the angels did not cease to be spiritual beings when their spiritual qualities had been suspended.

—Tertullian, *On the Resurrection of the Flesh,* 62

IN GOD'S PRESENCE, CONSIDER . . .

How much do I allow the demands of the flesh to get in the way of my acting more like an angel?

CLOSING PRAYER

Purify my flesh from all pollution, Lord, and remove every shameful and foolish thought from me, so that I may live the blissful life of your angels in Heaven.

Wait for the angels to sort us out

Speaking of Jesus' parable of the net, Origen explains that the promised sorting-out cannot happen till the end of time. Meanwhile, we should not be surprised to find evil lurking even in the Church.

"Again, the kingdom of Heaven is like a net which was thrown into the sea and gathered fish of every kind; when it was full, men drew it ashore and sat down and sorted the good into vessels but threw away the bad. So it will be at the close of the age. The angels will come out and separate the evil from the righteous, and throw them into the furnace of fire; there men will weep and gnash their teeth" (Matt. 13:47-50). From this it does not follow, as some suppose, that human beings who are saved in Christ are superior even to the holy angels; for how can those who are cast by the holy angels into vessels be compared with those who cast them into vessels, seeing that they have been put under the authority of the angels?

While I say this, I am not ignorant that those who will be saved in Christ surpass some angels—namely, those who have not been entrusted with this office—but not all of them. For we read, "things into which angels long to look" (1 Pet. 1:12), where it does not say "*all* angels." And we know also this: "we are to judge angels" (1 Cor. 6:3), where it does not say "*all* angels."

Now since these things are written about the net and about those in the net, I say that anyone who desires that, before the consummation of the age, and before the coming of the angels to separate the wicked from among the righteous, there should be no evil persons of every kind in the net, seems not to have understood the Scripture, and to desire the impossible. So let us not be surprised if, before the separating of the wicked from among the righteous by the angels who are sent forth for this purpose, we see our gatherings also filled with wicked persons. And would that those who will be cast into the furnace of fire may not be greater in number than the righteous!

—Origen, *Commentary on Matthew*, 10.13

IN GOD'S PRESENCE, CONSIDER . . .

When I hear of scandals in the Church, does it give me more patience if I remember the parable of the net and that pride and wickedness were found even among the angels themselves?

CLOSING PRAYER

Lord, you have founded your holy Catholic Church on the rock of faith, so that the gates of hell may not prevail against it: deliver it from all heresy and scandals, and from the demons who work iniquity, keeping it till the fullness of time.

An image of the heavenly city

Zion—Jerusalem—is an image of the heavenly kingdom, says St. Augustine. The captivity of the earthly Jerusalem in Babylon is an image of our pilgrimage here on earth; our friends the angels await us in the heavenly Jerusalem.

"When the Lord restored the fortunes of Zion, we were like those who dream" (Ps. 126:1).

By this he meant to say that we became joyful. When? "When the Lord restored the fortunes of Zion."

What is Zion? Jerusalem. The same is also the eternal Zion. How is Zion eternal, and how is Zion captive? In angels it is eternal; in human beings it is captive.

Not all citizens of that city are captives: only the ones who are away from there are captives. Man was a citizen of Jerusalem, but, sold to sin, he became a pilgrim. All the human race came from his descendants, and the captivity of Zion filled all lands.

And how is this captivity of Zion a shadow of the eternal Zion? The shadow of that Zion—which was granted in an image or figure to the Jews—was in captivity in Babylonia, and after seventy years the people were restored to their own city.

–St. Augustine, *Exposition on Ps. 126, 3*

If I am a wanderer here on earth, am I wandering toward or away from the eternal city of the angels?

Lead me, Lord, to your glorious Zion of the angels, and preserve your holy, Catholic, and Apostolic Church throughout the world.

Christ will come surrounded by angels

When Christ comes again, St. Cyril of Alexandria reminds us, it won't be in the form of a poor carpenter. He will come in glory, surrounded by the angels. What a blessing it will be then to be called to inherit the kingdom that awaits us!

And further, to set plainly before us the reward of our being willing to labor, he says: "For whoever is ashamed of me and of my words, of him will the Son of man be ashamed when he comes in his glory and the glory of the Father and of the holy angels" (Luke 9:26).

He says that he will descend from Heaven, not in His former lowliness and humiliation, like us, but in the glory of his Father—in godlike and transcendent glory, with the holy angels keeping guard around Him.

So it would be miserable and ruinous to be condemned of cowardice and indolence when the Judge has descended from above, and the angelic ranks stand at his side. But it is great and most blessed, a foretaste of final blessedness, to be able to rejoice in labors already accomplished, and await the recompense of past toils. For such as these shall be praised. Christ himself will tell them: "Come, blessed of my Father, inherit the kingdom prepared for you from the foundation of the world."

—St. Cyril of Alexandria, *Commentary on Luke*, Sermon 50

IN GOD'S PRESENCE, CONSIDER . . .

What labors have I already accomplished that I might present with pride to the angels who come to judge me? What labors could I accomplish tomorrow if my judgment day hasn't come by then?

CLOSING PRAYER

When Christ comes in the glory of his angels, may I be deemed worthy of his rewards.

Acknowledge Christ; the angels will praise you

At the end of time, says St. Cyril of Alexandria, Christ will come in glory, and the saints and martyrs will receive their reward: the acknowledgment of Christ, and the praise of the angels.

"And I tell you, everyone who acknowledges me before men, the Son of Man also will acknowledge before the angels of God; but he who denies me before men will be denied before the angels of God. And every one who speaks a word against the Son of man will be forgiven; but he who blasphemes against the Holy Spirit will not be forgiven" (Luke 12:8-10).

So whoever confesses Christ before men, as God and Lord, will be acknowledged by him before the angels of God.

But where and how? Clearly at that time when he descends from Heaven in the glory of his Father with the holy angels at the end of this world. Then he will crown his true confessor, who possessed an unwavering and genuine faith, and professed it that way. There also the company of the holy martyrs will shine, who endured the conflict even to the point of life and blood, and honored Christ by their patient endurance—for they did not deny the Savior, nor was his glory unknown to them, but they kept their faith to him. These martyrs will be praised by the holy angels; and will themselves glorify Christ the Savior of all, for giving the saints those honors that belong to them particularly.

And so the Psalmist also tells us, "The heavens declare his righteousness, for God himself is judge" (Ps. 50:6).

This is what will happen to those who confess Christ.

—St. Cyril of Alexandria, *Commentary on Luke*, Sermon 88

IN GOD'S PRESENCE, CONSIDER . . .

How do I confess Christ before the people around me? Am I showing them by what I do that I belong to him? Do my words and deeds earn the praise of the holy angels?

CLOSING PRAYER

Lord Jesus Christ, your angels are my witnesses: I acknowledge your blessed Resurrection from the dead, your Ascension into Heaven, and your seat at the right hand of the Father, and I await your Second Coming, in which you will righteously judge the living and the dead, and render to each of us according to our works.

Night and day

The life of the believer is like day compared to the life of the unbeliever, says St.
Augustine. But it's like night compared to the enlightenment of the angels. That
brilliant day is what we have to look forward to at the Resurrection.

"In the day of my trouble I seek the Lord; in the night my hand is
stretched out without wearying" (Ps. 77:2).

We shouldn't think "trouble" means some particular kind of thing. Anyone
who has not yet made the leap doesn't think that's a "trouble," unless some sad
thing has happened in this life. But the one who makes the leap sees this whole life
as his "trouble."

The life of believers is day—night and day, really: day compared to the life
of unbelievers, night compared to the angels. The angels have a day we haven't
experienced yet. We already have a day the unbelievers don't have, but believers
don't yet have the day that angels have. But they will have it, when they are equal
to the angels of God—which is what's been promised to them at the Resurrection
Matt. 22:30).

So in this day or night—night compared to the future day we long for, day
compared to the past night that we've renounced—let us stretch out our hands to
seek God. Don't let works come to a stop. Let us seek God—let there be no idle
longing. If we're on the way, let's use everything we have to reach the end.

—St. Augustine, *Exposition on Psalm 77*, 1

IN GOD'S PRESENCE, CONSIDER . . .

Do I see my earthly life by the spiritual light God has given me—the light of the
holy angels?

CLOSING PRAYER

Holy God, you have given us light through the ministry of your angels. Help us to know
them as messengers, guides, and revealers of your truth.

One Church in Heaven and on Earth

When we recite the Creed, we say that we believe in one, holy, catholic, and apostolic Church. That doesn't just mean the Church on Earth, says St. Augustine: the angels above are also members, and we will all make up one eternal choir for the proper praise of God.

The order of the Creed rightly demands that the Church be made subordinate to the Trinity—in the same way that a house is subordinate to whoever lives in it, the temple is subordinate to God, and the city is subordinate to its founder.

"The Church" here means the whole Church. It's not just the part sojourning here on Earth "from the rising of the sun to its setting" (Mal. 1:11), praising the Name of the Lord, singing "a new song" of deliverance from its ancient bondage. It's also the part in Heaven, which from the moment of creation has always clung to God, and never felt the pain of falling. This part, which is made up of the holy angels, remains in blessedness. It gives its help to the other part still on pilgrimage, as indeed it ought to do. Both parts together will make one eternal choir (already they are one by ties of love), the whole thing founded to worship the one God fittingly.

—St. Augustine, *Enchiridion*, chapter 15

IN GOD'S PRESENCE, CONSIDER . . .

Am I singing in tune with the celestial choir? How can I make my own praise better match theirs?

CLOSING PRAYER

Lord, let me always have the opportunity to give you praise and prayer along with all your angels in Heaven.

The Church above

We are the Church on Earth, says St. Augustine, but the angels are the Church in Heaven. The wonderful and amazing thing is that God, served by all the angels, came down to serve us on Earth.

"For God's temple is holy," says the Apostle, "and that temple you are" (1 Cor. 3:17). But surely it's obvious that God dwells in the angels. Therefore when our joy, being in spiritual things, not in earthly, takes up a song to God, to sing before the angels, that very assembly of angels is the Temple of God, and we worship toward God's Temple.

There is a Church below, and there is also there a Church above. The Church below is all the faithful; the Church above is all the angels. But the God of angels came down to the Church below, and angels served him on Earth (Matt. 4:11) while he served us. For, as he says, "the Son of man came not to be served but to serve" (Matt. 20:28).

The Lord of angels died for humanity.

–St. Augustine, *Exposition on Psalm 138, 3*

IN GOD'S PRESENCE, CONSIDER . . .

Christ came to serve us, though he had all the angels to serve him. What might I give up to serve my neighbors better?

CLOSING PRAYER

Lord, teach me to imitate Christ in His renunciation, and the angels in their service.

The saints judge with the angels

The saints, says St. Augustine, will judge with Christ and the angels—and in fact will be as good as angels. "Heaven" is the word we use for all the people from around the world who have been made perfect in Christ.

Many will judge with the Lord, but others will be judged—not all equally, however, but according to their deserts. He will come with all his angels, and all the nations will be gathered before him. And among the angels will be numbered those who have been made so perfect that, sitting on twelve thrones, they judge the twelve tribes of Israel (Matt. 19:28).

For mortals can be called "angels": you "received me as an angel of God," the Apostle says of himself (Gal. 4:14). It is said of John the Baptist, "Behold, I send my angel before your face, who shall prepare your way before you" (Matt. 11:10; see Mal. 3:1).

So when he comes with angels, he will have the saints with him as well. Isaiah also says plainly that "The Lord enters into judgment with the elders and princes of his people" (Isa. 3:14).

All those elders of the people, who have just been called "angels," those thousands of thousands of perfected people who come from around the world, are called "Heaven."

–St. Augustine, *Exposition on Psalm 50*, 11

IN GOD'S PRESENCE, CONSIDER . . .

How can I be like an angel, a messenger of God, in the lives of friends, coworkers, and family members?

CLOSING PRAYER

Angel of God, my guardian, teach me to be a faithful messenger as you are.

Some outsiders are on our side

There are evil people inside the Church, says St. Augustine, because the devil planted weeds among the wheat, as Christ says in his parable. But if the devil has his followers inside the Church, we must remember that Christ has followers outside the Church.

But yet "through the devil's envy death entered the world, and those who belong to his party experience it" (Wis. 2:24)—not because they are created by God, but because they go astray of themselves, as Cyprian says himself

But seeing that the devil, before he was a devil, was an angel, and good, how can it be that they who are of the devil's side are in the unity of Christ? Beyond all doubt, as the Lord himself says, "an enemy has done this" (Matt. 13:28), who "sowed weeds among the wheat" (Matt. 13:25).

What belongs to the devil within the fold must be convicted. But in the same way what belongs to Christ outside it must be recognized. Can the devil have what is his within the unity of the Church, and yet Christ not have what is his outside?

–St. Augustine, *On Baptism, Against the Donatists*, 4.9

IN GOD'S PRESENCE, CONSIDER . . .

We know that the devil has followers inside the Church. But what keeps the outsiders outside the Church? Is there anything I'm personally doing that tends to push Christ's followers away?

CLOSING PRAYER

I pray to the guardian angels of all people of good will who are outside the Church: be constantly diligent and seize every opportunity to bring them back to a happy reunion.

The angels hold the keys to Satan's prison

Revelation says that Satan will be let loose for a little while—but even then, says St. Gregory the Great, it is only under the power of the good angels, who serve God's will by unchaining him.

"Then I saw an angel coming down from Heaven, holding in his hand the key of the bottomless pit and a great chain. And he seized the dragon, that ancient serpent, who is the Devil and Satan, and bound him for a thousand years, and threw him into the pit" (Rev. 20:1-3).

But still, at the end of the world, they call him back to more open conflicts, and let him loose against us in all his power. Thus, in the same place, it says, "till the thousand years were ended. After that he must be loosed for a little while."

That apostate angel was created to shine preeminent among all the other legions of angels. But he fell so low by trying to elevate himself that he is now prostrated under the rule of the angels who stand upright. At first they have put him in chains, and keep him buried away from our sight, because they serve our welfare; then they will let him loose to use all his power against us, setting him free for our trial.

–St. Gregory the Great, *Moralia in Job*, 4.16

IN GOD'S PRESENCE, CONSIDER . . .

The good angels have power over the devil. Do I often ask for the angels' aid in facing Satan?

CLOSING PRAYER

Saint Michael the Archangel, defend us in battle. Be our protection against the wickedness and snares of the devil; may God rebuke him, we humbly pray. O Prince of the heavenly host, by the power of God, thrust into Hell Satan and all the evil spirits who wander through the world seeking the ruin of souls.

Evil angels await the last judgment

The devil and his angels, says St. Augustine, have been cast out of Heaven, but they inhabit the lower celestial regions. The important thing about this passage is not St. Augustine's speculative cosmography, but the theological point that the demons are still awaiting their eternal judgment.

But because evil angels also were not formed evil by God, but were made evil by sinning, Peter in his epistle says: "For if God did not spare the angels when they sinned, but cast them into hell and committed them to pits of nether gloom to be kept until the judgment" (2 Pet. 2:4).

Here Peter shows that the penalty of the last judgment is still due to them, concerning which the Lord says: "Depart from me into the eternal fire prepared for the devil and his angels" (Matt. 25:41).

They have already received one hell as punishment—that is, an inferior smoky air as a prison, which although it is also called heaven, is not that heaven in which there are stars, but this lower heaven from whose smoke the clouds are pulled together, and where the birds fly. For a cloudy heaven is spoken of, and flying things are called heavenly—as when the Apostle Paul calls those evil angels, against whom as enemies by living piously we contend, "spiritual hosts of wickedness in the heavenly places" (Eph. 6:12).

—St. Augustine, *On the Nature of Good, Against the Manicheans*, 33

IN GOD'S PRESENCE, CONSIDER . . .

The demons became evil by sinning. What effect are my sins having on my good nature?

CLOSING PRAYER

Guardian Angel, help me resist the temptation to sin, and keep the ill effects of sin constantly in my mind.

Even angels will be condemned for unbelief

How important is it to have a right understanding of the Incarnation? So important, says St. Ignatius of Antioch, that even the angels in Heaven would be condemned if they did not believe that Christ's body and blood were real.

Some ignorantly deny the Lord, or rather have been denied by him, because they are the advocates of death rather than of the truth. These people have not been persuaded by the prophets, or by the Law of Moses, or by the gospel even to this day, or by the sufferings we have individually endured. For they think also the same thing regarding us.

What good does anyone do me, if he commends me, but blasphemes my Lord, not confessing that he had a body? Whoever does not acknowledge this, has in fact altogether denied him, and is enveloped in death. I have not, however, thought good to write the names of those people, since they are unbelievers. Indeed, far be it from me to make any mention of them, until they repent and return to Christ's Passion, which is our resurrection.

Do not deceive yourselves. Even the beings in Heaven, and the glorious angels, and rulers both visible and invisible, will be condemned if they do not believe in the blood of Christ.

—St. Ignatius of Antioch, *Smyrnaeans*, 5-6

IN GOD'S PRESENCE, CONSIDER . . .

If even angels will be condemned because they do not believe, what am I doing to persuade the ignorant on earth to repent and return to Christ's Passion?

CLOSING PRAYER

Lord, have mercy on the straying, and send them your angels to help them find their way back to you.

The angels sing praises by the power of the Spirit

The heavenly life of praise and joy the angels live is possible only through the Holy Spirit, says St. Basil. Only with the help of the Spirit can the angels sing their hymns of praise—and the same is true for us.

How can angels sing "Glory to God in the highest" (Luke 2:14) without being empowered by the Spirit? "No one can say 'Jesus is Lord' except by the Holy Spirit," and "no one speaking by the Spirit of God ever says "Jesus be cursed!'" (1 Cor. 12:3)—as the evil and hostile spirits might say, whose fall proves what we said about the invisible powers having free will. They are always balanced between virtue and vice, and therefore need the help of the Spirit.

Even Gabriel, I tell you, foretells events to come (Luke 1:11) only by the foreknowledge of the Spirit, because one of the gifts of the Spirit is prophecy.

And how could Thrones, Dominions, Principalities, and Powers live their blessed life, if they did not see the face of the Father who is in Heaven (Matt. 18:10)? But it is impossible to see the face of the Father without the spirit. At night, if you take the light away from the house, your eyes are blind and their powers no longer work; you cannot see what things are really worth, and in your ignorance you step on gold as though it were iron. Likewise, in the order of the intellectual world, it is impossible for the high life of reason to continue without the Spirit.

–St. Basil the Great, *On the Holy Spirit*, 38

IN GOD'S PRESENCE, CONSIDER . . .

When I pray to God, do I invite the Holy Spirit to help me pray, as the Spirit helps the angels praise him?

CLOSING PRAYER

Father, send your angels to watch over me, that I may be made fit for your service.

MIKE AQUILINA   351

Imagine the beauty of countless angels

Try to imagine the most wonderful spectacle you've ever seen, says St. John Chrysostom. Now think how much more beautiful it will be when you see the saints and angels in Heaven.

If we go out into a field and see the soldiers' tents with their curtains, and the spears, and the helmets, and the bosses of the bucklers gleaming, then we are filled with wonder. But if we also happen to see the king himself running through the field, or perhaps riding with golden armor, we think we've seen everything!

Then what will you think when you see the everlasting tabernacles of the saints pitched in Heaven? For it says that they will "receive you into the eternal habitations" (Luke 16:9). What will you think when you see each one of them beaming with light brighter than the rays of the sun—not from brass and steel, but from that glory on whose gleaming the eyes of mortals cannot look?

And this is just the human saints. But what if I mentioned the thousands of Angels, Archangels, Cherubim, Seraphim, Thrones, Dominions, Principalities, Powers, whose beauty is beyond compare, passing all understanding?

—St. John Chrysostom, *Homily 6 on Hebrews*, 11

IN GOD'S PRESENCE, CONSIDER . . .

If I meditated on the beauties of the angels in Heaven, how might that change the way I live my earthly life?

CLOSING PRAYER

Bright Cherubim, who are given a deeper insight into the mysteries of God, scatter the darkness in my soul, and by virtue of the Holy Blood of Christ, give me that supernatural light by which alone I can understand the truths of salvation.

Remember that you sing in the angelic choir

In the time of St. John Chrysostom, popular entertainment had become notoriously immoral, depending on sex and violence for most of its effect. (Fortunately, that was all 1,600 years ago.) Chrysostom challenges his flock to put an end to the sin on the stage, but by not giving them any business.

Then let's pull down the stage, they say. I wish it were that simple—or, rather, if you were willing, as far as I'm concerned, it would be pulled down and dug up. But since these places are standing, let's prevent them from having any effect. That would be a greater praise than pulling them down.

At least imitate the barbarians, if no one else. They are completely free of such entertainment. Then what excuse do we have—we, the citizens of Heaven, and partners in the choirs of the Seraphim, and in fellowship with the angels? We make ourselves worse than the barbarians in this respect—and that when we have countless better pleasures within our reach.

If you want to delight your soul, go out to the park. Sit by a flowing river, or by a lake. Visit the gardens. Listen to the grasshoppers singing. Stay by the tombs of the martyrs, where there is health of body and benefit of soul, and no pain and no remorse after the pleasure, as there is on the stage.

—St. John Chrysostom, *Homily 37 on Matthew*

IN GOD'S PRESENCE, CONSIDER . . .

How do my choices in entertainment sit with the angels who surround me?

CLOSING PRAYER

Holy angels, lead my mind and heart to the light by virtue of the holy Blood of Christ.

Don't drown out the angel choir

St. John Chrysostom looks around him in church, and all he sees are people talking about business and money. You've made the church no better than a barn, he says. Be quiet, and listen, and you'll hear the choirs of angels.

We say that Christ has done great things, having made angels out of human beings; then, when we are called on to give account, and asked to show a proof from this congregation, our mouths are stopped. I'm afraid that, instead of angels, I might bring out pigs as if this were a pigsty, and horses mad with lust.

I know it pains you to hear this. But I'm not speaking against all of you, but against the guilty—or rather not even *against* them, if they wake up, but *for* them. Right now everything is lost and ruined, and the church has become nothing better than a stable of oxen, and a barn for donkeys and camels, and I go around looking for a sheep and can't find it. Everyone's kicking, like horses and wild asses, and they fill the place here with piles of manure—that's what their conversation is like. If you could see the things spoken at each service, by men, by women, their words would look more unclean than that manure.

So I beg you to change this evil custom, so that the church may smell of ointment. But now, while we store up perfumes for the senses in the church, we take no trouble to scrub out and drive away the uncleanness of the mind. So what's the use? We wouldn't disgrace the church as much by bringing dung into it as we disgrace it by speaking such things one to another—about profits, about merchandise, about petty business deals, about things that are nothing to us, when there ought to be choirs of angels here, and we ought to make the church a Heaven, and to know nothing else but earnest prayers, and quiet listening.

—St. John Chrysostom, *Homily 88 on Matthew*

IN GOD'S PRESENCE, CONSIDER . . .

Does my own behavior at Mass sometimes distract people from what's really going on at the altar?

CLOSING PRAYER

Lord, when you are present in the bread and the cup on your all-holy altar, keep me in mind of the angels and archangels who surround me.

Keep the prayer of the angels in your heart

Even when you're just out shopping, says St. John Chrysostom, you can still be praising God with the heavenly hosts. True praise isn't just the words you speak: it shows itself in how you live.

What is the hymn of the heavenly beings? You, the faithful, know it. What do the Cherubim above say? What do the angels say? "Glory to God in the highest" (Isa. 6:3).

This is why the hymns come after the psalm, because they are even more perfect. "With psalms, with hymns, with spiritual songs," it says, "with grace singing in your hearts to God" (Ps. 100:4, Septuagint reading).

Singing *in your hearts* to God—not just with the mouth, he means, but with obedience. That's what it means to sing to God. Otherwise you're just singing to the air, and your voice dissipates with no result—you're just singing to show off.

Even if you're in the market, you can remember to sing to God, though no one else will hear you. Moses prayed this way, and God heard him. He says, "Why do you cry to me?" even though Moses said nothing. He only cried out in thought, with a contrite heart, and only God heard him. There's no reason you can't pray to God, and keep your mind on Heaven, even when you're just walking around.

–St. John Chrysostom, *Homily 9 on Colossians*

IN GOD'S PRESENCE, CONSIDER . . .

Have I asked for the help of the angels to change my attitude and the way I treat people around me—on the road, in the supermarket, at work?

CLOSING PRAYER

Holy Guardian Angel, help me be attentive to your promptings, so that all my works and all my words may rise as a hymn of praise to God.

Peace which passes angels' understanding

The peace of God passes all understanding—not just human understanding, but angels' as well, says St. Augustine.

Right now, however great our understanding may be, we only see in part, and "through a glass darkly" (1 Cor. 13:12). But when we are equal to the angels of god, we will see face to face, as they do, and we will have peace toward them as great as they have toward us, because we will love them as much as they love us. And so their peace will be known to us. Our own peace will be like theirs, and as great as theirs, and then it will not pass our understanding.

But the peace of God, the peace he cherishes toward us, will undoubtedly pass not only our understanding, but theirs as well. And this must be so. Every intelligent creature that is happy gets its happiness from God; God does not get his happiness from the creature. So in the passage, "the peace of God, which passes all understanding" (Phil. 4:7), it is better to interpret "all" as meaning that there is no exception, not even the understanding of the holy angels. The only exception we can make is God himself—since, of course, his peace does not pass his own understanding.

–St. Augustine, *Enchiridion*, 63

If even angels cannot understand it, certainly I can never completely understand the peace of God. But do I work diligently to sow peace in the Church and in the world?

CLOSING PRAYER

Lord, your peace passes the understanding even of the angels. Grant that your holy rest and peace may dwell in the four corners of the world, but especially in your holy Catholic Church.

Your soul is a picture of the angelic life

Arguing for the divinity of the Holy Spirit, St. Gregory of Nyssa says that you know from your own experience that the Spirit is divine. Your own soul is intellectual and invisible, like the angels, and like the angels you cannot come near to God except by the Holy Spirit's help.

Whoever agrees with us that the things above us are also ordered by the power of the Spirit with the Father and the Son has the support of clear evidence from his own life.

The nature of man is compounded of body and soul, and the angelic nature has for its portion life without a body. So if the Holy Spirit worked only in the case of bodies, and the soul were not capable of receiving the grace that comes from him, then we might perhaps infer from this, if the intellectual and incorporeal nature which is in us were above the power of the Spirit, that the angelic life too was in no need of his grace.

But if the gift of the Holy Spirit is mainly a grace of the soul, and the soul is similar to the life of the angels in its reason and its invisibility—well, then, anyone who knows how to reach a conclusion would agree that every intellectual nature is governed by the ordering of the Holy Spirit.

For since it is said that the "angels always behold the face of my Father who is in heaven" (Matt. 18:10), and it is not possible to behold the person of the Father except by training the sight on it through his image; and the image of the person of the Father is the Only-begotten, and to him again no one can draw near whose mind has not been illumined by the Holy Spirit—what else do we learn from this but that the Holy Spirit is not separated from anything that is done by the Father and the Son?

—St. Gregory of Nyssa, *On the Holy Trinity*

IN GOD'S PRESENCE, CONSIDER . . .

Like me, the angels are spiritual beings. Unlike me, their spirit is unwavering. Do strive with my angel's help, to live with an angelic consistency in the choices I make each day?

CLOSING PRAYER

Guardian Angel, help me to make my soul a reflection of your purity.

Are we there yet?

No matter how far off the Day of Judgment may be, says St. Augustine, your own death is only a few years away at most. You need to prepare for that day, so that, when it comes, you will be among those who will be taken to rest until they are made equal to the angels.

"Yet a little while, and the wicked will be no more; though you look well at his place, he will not be there" (Ps. 37:10).

How long does each person's life last? Add any number of years you please; extend old age to its longest duration. What is it? Is it not just a morning breeze?

But suppose that the Day of Judgment is far off, when the reward of the righteous and of the unrighteous is to come. Even so, your own last day certainly cannot be far off. Make yourself ready for that!

However you depart from this life, that is how you will be restored to the other. At the close of that short life, you will not yet be where the saints will be, to whom it shall be said, "Come, O blessed of my Father, inherit the kingdom prepared for you from the foundation of the world" (Matt. 25:34). And everyone knows that you will not yet be there. But you may already be where that beggar, once covered with sores, was seen at a distance, at rest, by that proud and unfruitful rich man in the midst of his torments. Surely hid in that rest you wait in security for the Day of Judgment, when you are to receive a body again, to be changed so as to be made equal to an angel.

So how long will it be till we get to what we long for, and are saying, "When will it come? Will it be long?" Our children will say the same thing after us, and our children's children, too; and, though each one of these in turn will say this same thing, that little while that is yet to be passes away, as all that is already past has passed away already!

–St. Augustine, *Exposition on Psalm 37*, Part 1, 10

IN GOD'S PRESENCE, CONSIDER . . .

If I died today, would I be judged equal to the angels?

CLOSING PRAYER

Keep me under the protection of your angels, Lord, and count me worthy till my last breath to partake of your holy rites for the sanctification of my soul and body, for the inheritance of the kingdom of Heaven.

We'll see what the angels see

When things go wrong in this life, says St. Augustine, just remember what you're preparing for. You'll see God the way the angels see him.

"And their heritage will abide forever" (Ps. 37:18).

This we hold by faith. Does the Lord too know it by faith? No, the Lord knows those things in such a clear way that we will not be able to speak of it even when we are made equal to the angels. The things that will be clear to us will not be as clear to us as they are now to him who is incapable of change.

But what does Scripture say even about us? "Beloved, we are God's children now; it does not yet appear what we shall be, but we know that when he appears we shall be like him, for we shall see him as he is" (1 John 3:2). So there is surely some blissful vision reserved for us; and if it can be now in some measure conceived through a glass darkly (1 Cor. 13:12), yet we still have no way of expressing in language the ravishing beauty of the bliss that God reserves for those who fear him, which he consummates in those who hope in him.

In all the troubles and trials of this life, our hearts are being disciplined for that goal. Do not be surprised that you are disciplined for it with trouble. You are being disciplined for something glorious. Why does the now-strengthened righteous man say, "I consider that the sufferings of this present time are not worth comparing with the glory that is to be revealed to us" (Rom. 8:18)? What is this promised glory to be, but to be made equal to the angels and to see God?

How great a benefit anyone gives a blind man if he makes his eyes sound, so that he can see the light of this life! What reward then shall we give to that Physician who restores the health of our inward eyes, to enable them to see the eternal Light—namely, himself?

–St. Augustine, *Exposition on Psalm 37*, Part 2, 7

IN GOD'S PRESENCE, CONSIDER . . .

Will it help me endure my troubles if I remember the beauty and joy they're preparing me for?

CLOSING PRAYER

Fill my mouth with your praise, Lord, and my lips with joy, so that I may sing the praise of your glory forever.

Love God for himself

God is rich in everything, says St. Ambrose. Everything belongs to him. But though Earth is beautiful, and Heaven is beautiful, and the angels are beautiful, what God promises us is not these beautiful things, but something infinitely more beautiful: himself.

And yet, Brethren, our God never can be poor. He is rich. He made all things—Heaven and Earth, the sea and the angels. In the heaven, whatever we see, whatever we cannot see—he made it.

But still, we ought not to love these riches, but him who made them. For he has promised you nothing but himself.

Find anything more precious, and he will give you that. Beauteous is the Earth, the Heaven, and the angels; but more beauteous is he who made them.

Thus those who preach God, because they love God; who preach God, for God's sake; feed the sheep, and are no hirelings. Our Lord Jesus Christ required this chastity of the soul when he said to Peter, "Peter, do you love me?" (John 21:17).

What does "Do you love me" mean? It means, "Are you chaste? Is your heart not adulterous? Do you seek in the Church not your own things, but mine? If you are such a one as this and love me, feed my sheep. For you shall be no hireling, but you shall be a shepherd."

—St. Augustine, *Sermon 87 on the New Testament*, 10

IN GOD'S PRESENCE, CONSIDER . . .

Does remembering that God is more beautiful, more wonderful than Earth, Heaven, and even the angels, help me overcome unhealthy desires for material things?

CLOSING PRAYER

Let Gabriel rejoice and be exceeding glad, with the company of all the angels, in you, the Good Shepherd, who on your shoulders carried the maimed sheep, that the number of a hundred might be preserved.

God alone is good by nature

"Why do you call me good?" Jesus asked the ruler of the synagogue. St. Cyril of Alexandria explains what Jesus meant: If you think I'm only a man, then you're giving me a title that belongs to God alone. Even the angels are "good" only by their participation in God.

He flatters Jesus, and attempts to deceive him, pretending to be well-disposed toward him. And what does the Omniscient reply? He says, "Why do you call me good? None is good but God alone" (Luke 18:19).

You see how this ruler proved at once that he was neither wise nor learned, though he was the ruler of a synagogue of the Jews. For if, Jesus says, you did not believe that I am God, and the clothing of the flesh has led you astray, why did you call me by titles suitable to the supreme nature alone, while you still thought that I was a mere man like you, and not superior to the limits of human nature? In the nature that transcends all, in God alone, do we find the attribute of being by nature and unchangeably good: but the angels, and we upon earth, are good by resembling him, or rather by participating in him. He is what he is, and this is his Name, and his everlasting memorial for all generations (Exodus 3:14); but we exist and come into being by being made partakers of him who really exists. Thus he indeed is good, or is the good absolutely, but angels and human beings are good only by being made, as I said, partakers of the good God.

So being good must be set apart as the special property of God alone above all. It is an essential part of his nature, and is his own particular attribute.

But if I do not seem to you to be truly God, Jesus says, then you have ignorantly and foolishly applied to me the properties and virtues of the divine nature, at the very time when you think I am only a man, one who is never endowed with goodness, which is the property of the unchangeable nature, but only gains it by the assent of the divine will.

–St. Cyril of Alexandria, *Commentary on Luke*, Sermon 122

IN GOD'S PRESENCE, CONSIDER . . .

What things do I commonly call "good"? Do I see how they resemble the qualities of the angels by participating in the goodness of God?

CLOSING PRAYER

Father, may my life be more and more like the lives of your angels in Heaven. May I rise above sin and draw closer to your glory.

Angels as oxen

Interpreting Psalm 8, St. Augustine suggests that the "sheep and oxen" put under Christ are human beings and angels—angels being called oxen because of their incessant work in spreading the word of God.

"You have put all things under his feet," he says (Ps. 8:6). And when he writes to the Hebrews he uses this very testimony from this Psalm, when he wants them to understand that all things are put under our Lord Jesus Christ in such a way that nothing is left out (Heb. 2:8).

And yet he does not seem to be adding anything remarkable when he says, "all sheep and oxen, and also the beasts of the field, the birds of the air, and the fish of the sea, whatever passes along the paths of the sea" (Ps. 8:7). For, leaving the heavenly excellencies and powers, and all the hosts of angels, leaving even man himself he seems to have put under him the beasts merely—unless by sheep and oxen we understand holy souls, either yielding the fruit of innocence, or working that the earth may bear fruit, that is, that earthly men may be regenerated into spiritual richness.

By these holy souls then we ought to understand not those of men only, but of all angels too.

But how can we prove that sheep might mean not just human beings but the blessed spirits of the angelical creatures on high? Might we do it from the Lord's saying that he had left ninety-nine sheep in the mountains—that is, in the higher regions—and had come down for one? For if we take the one lost sheep to be the human soul in Adam, the ninety-nine left in the mountains must mean angelic spirits, not human. As far as the oxen are concerned: human beings are called oxen only because, by preaching the gospel of the word of God, they imitate angels—as where it is said, "You shall not muzzle an ox when it treads out the grain" (Deut. 25:4). It is very easy to understand the angels themselves, the messengers of truth, to be oxen, when Evangelists, sharing their title, are called oxen.

—St. Augustine, *Exposition on Psalm 8*, 13

How could I make a better contribution if—like the angels—I imitated the ox, which just keeps treading out the grain?

Lord, grant me the zeal and earnestness to labor as the angels do, according to your will.

Delight in God alone

Continuing his meditation on holy angels and people, St. Augustine says that what we enjoy in someone who is holy is God himself, the only true source of happiness.

But when you have joy of someone in God, it is God rather than that person that you enjoy. You enjoy God who makes you happy, and you rejoice to have come to him in whose presence you place your hope of joy.

This is why Paul says to Philemon, "Yes, brother, I want some benefit from you in the Lord" (Philem. 20). For if he had not added "in the Lord, but had only said, "I want some benefit from you," he would have implied that he fixed his hope of happiness upon him—although even in the immediate context "to have benefit" is used in the sense of "to use with delight." For when the thing that we love is near us, it is a matter of course that it should bring delight with it.

Now, if you pass beyond this delight, and make it a means to that which you are permanently to rest in, you are using it, and it is an abuse of language to say that you enjoy it. But if you cling to it, and rest in it, finding your happiness complete in it, then you may be truly and properly said to enjoy it. And this we must never do except in the case of the Blessed Trinity, who is the Supreme and Unchangeable Good.

–St. Augustine, *On Christian Doctrine*, 1.33

IN GOD'S PRESENCE, CONSIDER . . .

How much do I allow myself to pin my hopes on other people? Do they lead me beyond themselves to God?

CLOSING PRAYER

Father, give me rest all the days of this life, so that all the inhabitants of the earth may know that you are the only true God the Father, who sent our Lord Jesus Christ, your only Son and your Beloved, to teach us purity and holiness.

The praise of the angels

In this long hymn of praise from an ancient liturgy (attributed to Dionysius the Areopagite), we join our praise with the praises of all the beings in Heaven.

The voiceless, by their silence, the vocal, by their voices, words and hymns, perpetually bless you, because you are essentially good and beyond all praise, existing in your essence incomprehensibly. I, your visible and sensible creature, praise you, and also the intellectual creature, placed above sensible perception. Heaven and earth glorify you. Sea and air proclaim you. The sun, in his course, praises you; the moon, in her changes, venerates you.

Troops of Archangels, and hosts of Angels; the Powers, more sublime than the world and mental faculty, send benedictions to your abode. Rays of light, eminent and hidden, send their "Holy" to your glory. Principalities and Dominions praise you, with their "Make a joyful noise." Powers and Dominions venerate you. Powers, Thrones and seats inaccessible exalt you. Splendors of light eternal, mirrors without flaw, holy essences, recipients of wisdom sublime, beyond all, investigators of the will hidden from all, in clearest modulations of inimitable tones, and by voices becoming a rational creature; many eyed Cherubim of most subtle movement, bless you. Seraphim, furnished with six wings intertwined, cry "Holy" to you. Those very ones, who veil their faces with their wings, and cover their feet with wings, and flying on every side, and clapping with their wings (that they may not be devoured by your devouring fire), sing one to another with equal harmony of all, sweet chants, pure from everything material, rendering to you eternal glory, crying with one hymn, worthy of God, and saying, "Holy, holy, holy."

—*Liturgy of St. Dionysius (the Areopagite)*, bishop of the Athenians

IN GOD'S PRESENCE, CONSIDER . . .

How much of my prayer is given to pure praise of the goodness of God? Do I praise without ceasing as the angels do in Heaven?

CLOSING PRAYER

Lord, give me an angelic peace in my life, so that my heart may always be set on the praise of your Holy Name.

Witnesses to angels

We know that Christ and the angels have been really present with us, says St. John Chrysostom. What will happen when we're called to judgment and have to report that all we ever cared about was money?

There really are many people who seem to think they're never going to die. They set about building and planning in extreme old age—but when will they take death into consideration?

It will be no small punishment that we were called to bear witness, but were not able to bear witness to the things we have seen. We've seen angels with our own eyes—and we've seen them more clearly than those who saw them visibly. We shall be witnesses to Christ.

The people we call "martyrs" (which means "witnesses") are not the only witnesses: we're witnesses too. The reason they're called martyrs is because, when called on to renounce the faith, they endure everything to speak the truth. So when our passions call on us to renounce the faith, we shouldn't be defeated! Money tells us, "Say that Christ isn't Christ." Don't listen to it the way you would listen to God, but despise its commands.

—St. John Chrysostom, *Homily 47 on Acts*

IN GOD'S PRESENCE, CONSIDER . . .

Do I listen when money talks? Would it help me avoid temptation to remember the angels who surround me and see everything I do?

CLOSING PRAYER

Guardian Angel, help me keep from covetousness and every worldly affection that is not in accordance with the holy will of God.

About the Author

Mike Aquilina is the author of more than twenty books on Catholic history, doctrine, and devotion. He is also executive vice-president of the St. Paul Center for Biblical Theology (SalvationHistory.com), and has hosted many series on the Eternal Word Television Network. Mike appears often on Catholic radio, and he blogs on the early Church at (FathersOfTheChurch.com). Mike and his wife Terri have been married for a quarter-century or so and have six children.

Mike's other titles include:

The Way of the Fathers
The Mass of the Early Christians
Living the Mysteries (with Scott Hahn)
Praying the Psalms with the Early Christians (with Christopher Bailey)
A Year with the Church Fathers

MIKE AQUILINA

✠ SAINT BENEDICT✝PRESS

Saint Benedict Press, founded in 2006, is the parent company for a variety of imprints including TAN Books, Catholic Courses, Benedict Bibles, Benedict Books, and Labora Books. The company's name pays homage to the guiding influence of the Rule of Saint Benedict and the Benedictine monks of Belmont Abbey, North Carolina, just a short distance from the company's headquarters in Charlotte, NC.

After acquiring TAN Books & Publishers in 2008, Saint Benedict Press transferred its catalogue of Catholic Classics to the TAN Books imprint, known and loved by generations of readers for its traditional Catholic content.

Saint Benedict Press is now a multi-media company. Its mission is to publish and distribute products reflective of the Catholic intellectual tradition and to present these products in an attractive and accessible manner.

For a free catalog from Saint Benedict Press,
visit us online at
saintbenedictpress.com
or call us toll-free at
(800) 437-5876

 TAN·BOOKS

TAN Books was founded in 1967, in response to the rapid decline of faith and morals in society and the Church. Since its founding, TAN Books has been committed to the preservation and promotion of the spiritual, theological and liturgical traditions of the Catholic Church. In 2008, TAN Books was acquired by Saint Benedict Press. Since then, TAN has experienced positive growth and diversification while fulfilling its mission to a new generation of readers.

TAN Books publishes over 500 titles on Thomistic theology, traditional devotions, Church doctrine, history, lives of the saints, educational resources, and booklets.

www.tanbooks.com

Benedict Books publishes carefully selected works reflective of a Catholic worldview that are of particular relevance to today's reader. All titles are faithful to the magisterial teachings of the Church and presented in an attractive and accessible manner.

TAN Books and Benedict Books are *The Publishers You Can Trust With Your Faith!*

www.saintbenedictpress.com

Benedict Bibles is the only publisher of all three major English translations of the Catholic bible —the Douay-Rheims, the Revised Standard Version Catholic Edition, and the New American Bible Revised Edition. Benedict Bibles also provide custom bibles featuring gold embossing, hand-tipped pages, and special inserts for schools, parishes and ministries. Benedict Bibles is The Source for Catholic Bibles!

www.saintbenedictpress.com

 CATHOLIC COURSES

Catholic Courses shares the riches of our Catholic intellectual heritage through audio and video lectures presented by the best minds of the Church. Courses are offered in six categories—History, Philosophy, Scripture, Literature, Saints, and Theology. God made us for the intellectual life and gave us an inborn hunger for truth. Satisfy that hunger with Catholic Courses and *Learn More.*

www.catholiccourses.com

Labora Books gives voice to the next generation of Catholic writers. We publish fiction and nonfiction from new authors as well as special works from established authors addressing well-defined audiences within the Church.

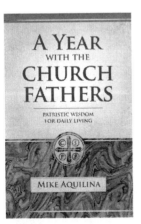

A YEAR WITH THE CHURCH FATHERS

PATRISTIC WISDOM FOR DAILY LIVING

A Year with the Church Fathers is a year-long retreat that in just a few minutes every day will lead you on a cycle of contemplation, prayer, resolution, and spiritual growth. Beautifully embossed cover, sewn binding, with gold edges and ribbon marker, this single volume is guaranteed to bring you closer to God and His truth.

978-1-61890-418-8

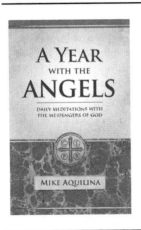

A YEAR WITH THE ANGELS

DAILY MEDITATIONS WITH THE MESSENGERS OF GOD

Mike Aquilina presents a new volume of contemplations and prayers about those most mysterious of all created beings: the Angels. In *A Year with the Angels*, discover the mystery and power of the Angels, through the wisdom and writings of the Church Fathers. Elegant two-tone Premium Ultrasoft cover with gold edges and ribbon.

978-1-61890-417-1

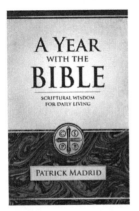

A YEAR WITH THE BIBLE

SCRIPTURAL WISDOM FOR DAILY LIVING

Discover the majesty and power of Scripture in *A Year with the Bible*. This vibrant and spiritual collection is the perfect daily companion, packed with the wisdom of the Scriptures; the Word of God. Beautifully bound and embossed, this daily devotional offers rich passages from the Bible accompanied by thoughtful meditations by Patrick Madrid, world-renown author and scholar.

978-1-61890-416-4

CPSIA information can be obtained at www.ICGtesting.com
Printed in the USA
LVOW060716091012

302013LV00001B/4/P